TWITCHING THE SWAMP

Droppings from the natural world

*To Pamela
with all best wishes
Peter
/5.10.04.*

Peter Marren and David Carstairs

Peter Marren.

SWAMP PUBLISHING
Thatcham

© 2004 Peter Marren (text), David Carstairs (text and pictures) and Jim Gammie (cover and end page illustrations)

First published in 2004 by Swamp Publishing, 122 Derwent Road, Thatcham RG19 3UP, Email: swamp_publishing@hotmail.com.

British Library-in-Publication Data.
A catalogue record for this book is available from the British Library.

ISBN 0-9548267-0-1

Printed in the United Kingdom by Biddles, King's Lynn, Norfolk.

For Pilar, Sue and in memory of David.

"So close — no matter how far,
Couldn't be much more from the heart,
Forever trusting who we are
And nothing else matters."

(James Hetfield and Lars Ulrich)

CONTENTS

Foreword

We all like nature, right? It forms a nice leafy backdrop to our lives and makes charming tweety noises every spring. The trouble is that nature doesn't like us. And who can blame it? For about a million years, man's relationship with nature was concerned mainly with hunting, catching and eating the wildlife. More recently, some of us also enjoyed pinning, pressing or stuffing it. Hardly anyone saw anything wrong with this, and a rattling good time was had by all, except, possibly, the wildlife.

More recently still, the relationship has taken a funny turn. Conscious that harnessing the systems of the planet to our increasingly onerous needs was making the wildlife disappear ever faster, the sort of people who would once have been happily pinning, pressing, scoffing and stuffing now proclaim themselves to be saviours of planet earth. Peter Scott was a good example. Did the new Scott conserve more wild ducks than the old Scott shot? For that matter, have any of us conserved more wildlife than the legions we casually rub out in our ceaseless quest for better services and upmarket lifestyles? Of course not. We might make a big effort to conserve Harry the hedgehog in our garden, leaving a nice pile of leaves for him to snooze the winter away. But what happens when he wakes up? We squash him flat as he staggers blearily onto the drive for his appointment with the speeding Renault. Like a lot of things, conservation is an attitude. It helps us to feel better about ourselves, which is an important thing, and if it ever does help the wildlife, well, hell, that's good too. It's *win, win.*

Me, I quite like wild animals so long as they aren't bothering me, though I can't think of any particular reason why *they* should like *me.* Some I even regard as pets, like Tod the Toad, who used to serenade my door in his regular spot under the light at seven o' clock, on the dot. At least, so I fondly pretended, though no doubt what drew him to my door were the insects drawn to the light in their helpless, unthinking way. And his frankly amateurish singing was intended not for me but some Todette lurking in the ditch nearby. But it can be lonely in the country, and one appreciates the gesture.

Of course it wasn't long before Tod, or at least a toad very like him, was out there on the tarmac, flat as a bookmark, where a lot of my garden friends end up. Bad call, Tod. If it *was* you, that is. Most toads I come across look like Tod, so may be it wasn't him at all, and we can have a happy ending (I mean, *who cares?*).

Where was I? Oh yes, I like wildlife, but I'm not so sure about conservationists. Or at least, not as a corporate mass or as authors of all those thrilling 'action' plans that are designed to save wildlife (from the safety of an office). In the good old pinning-and-stuffing days, I too was a conservationist, or, as we were called then, an amateur naturalist. Today, instead of watching wildlife, I watch conservationists. Some time ago, I rumbled their guilty little secret, a secret so secret they don't even know it themselves. What they don't know is this: that a lot of conservationists are *no good at conservation*. They are good at some (quite different) things. Some conservationists I know get top marks for presentation, propaganda and obtaining money for 'conservation'. They 'grow the business', as the saying goes. What they don't do is to make much difference. Well-run nature reserves are not quite as rare as hen's teeth, but they can be thin on the ground. I've yet to find a small wood managed for wildlife as well as an illiterate wood-turner or charcoal-burner might have done it.

Some might argue that nature reserves are in any case yesterday's solution. Tomorrow's big break is to *interconnect* and *deliver biodiversity*. It's a great word, isn't it, that 'biodiversity'? Handily, it reduces the whole of life, in all its boundless complexity, in its infinite capacity to inspire and surprise, into a dull grey substance that we 'deliver', like pints of milk on the doorstep. A lot of professional conservationists believe in delivering biodiversity for one reason above all: because, along with not being much good at conservation, they *don't know much about wildlife*. At least, that's the conclusion I've come to from thirty years of living in the suburbs of the conservation world. Of course, there are some wonderful exceptions, but individual voices are becoming hard to hear in the heavily corporatised world of modern nature conservation. Everyone seems to be speaking on behalf of someone else.

This collection of short pieces, culled mainly from my column *Twitcher in the Swamp* published in *British Wildlife* magazine, forms a kind of extended comment on the doings of the nature conservation world. As its title hints, though the standpoint is frequently sceptical, it is from the inside. The twitcher, too, is enmired in the swamp. I began the column at the invitation of *British Wildlife's* estimable editor, Andrew Branson – himself a rare and probably endangered example of a conservation *pessimist* (Andrew knows too much about wildlife). Twitcher's page has adorned each bimonthly issue since, usually accompanied by a cartoon by David Carstairs, the brilliant Scotland-based draughtsman and sometime man-about-the-hill. Branson once informed me the column had started 'anecdotal' and gradually became more 'philosophical'. What he meant by that, I think, is that it began with stories and ended with ideas, if only by accident. Words run away with you sometimes. I never had any definite idea of what Twitcher was about, except that the general idea was to mock and subvert anything that looks daft or hypocritical by holding it up to ridicule. Quite often, though, Twitcher ends up enthusiastically endorsing what he came to throw stones at. What has always amazed and delighted me is how often people from within the conservation industry tell me they agree with Twitcher. Perhaps he, too, is starting to speak for someone else.

Who is Twitcher, anyway? He tends to an onlooker, peering at the nature conservation world with cheap binoculars from his bosky retreat. But, as I find on reading these pieces again, he often emerges to take the lead, or at least to set an example. He was the first to warn that the fox-hunting debate was detracting attention from the *victims of the fox*, and set up his own 'league' LACBOB (the League Against Cruel Bullies of Our Bunnies) of ferocious, ever-knitting grannies to stand up for the poor wabbits. Though showing due compassion for squashed ducks, Twitcher's relationship with wild birds is always uneasy. He reveals the true feelings of our feathered friends in the insulting calls he hears on the way to the post box, and the subtle, rarely noticed, ways in which they take their revenge on their human oppressors. His investigations unearth the curious fact that certain kinds of landscape give the 'visitors' an urgent desire to pee, and then afterwards to eat a hamburger. And that although it was illegal to wear a red squirrel, it was perfectly all right to set fire to its tail (this has since been put right). While his feelings towards the Forestry Commission, English Nature, Tony Blair, John Gummer, young people, old people, vegetarians, Jonathan Porritt, the Green Party and anglers are mixed, Twitcher shows commendable open-mindedness when discussing the nature conservation ideas of the Taliban, and reveals a touching concern for hungry harvest mice. Unexpectedly, he admits to being a fan of Geri Halliwell, the flame-haired songstress, and works her into his scheme for rehabilitating badgers. If he is against anything in particular, it is 'dumbing down'. In Twitcher's view, we may be stupid, but there's no need to tell everyone.

A few of the early pieces (*Observe the sheep, The rest is silence, Focus on zebras*) – as well as two letters (1990), believed to have been penned by Carstairs under two of his many *nom-de-plumes* – are taken from *Natural Selection*, the 'unofficial' inhouse magazine of the Nature Conservancy Council, which I edited from 1986 to 1991. 'Old Countryman' by David Carstairs, also began life here, in imitation of a forgotten 'nature notes' column in a nameless newspaper. Carstairs is an old buddy of mine, whose inimitable cartoons have accompanied each 'Twitcher' over nearly 15 years. Several pieces I did for *The Countryman* under the byline 'Looking at nature' have also been included, duly reworked into a more Twitcherish style (*Flushland, Not always welcome, The rocks remain, Bye bye, pool frog*). Some of the pieces have been revised to reveal what Twitcher probably meant to say, but unaccountably didn't. Sometimes bits were cut by Branson on grounds of space, or, more often, of taste. I have carefully put them back in again.

I have also inserted some background where necessary to remind readers of what it was all about. 1990 seems quite a long time ago now. No one, at least in this country, had yet uttered the word 'biodiversity', and we seemed to get along all right without targets, if not action plans. It was my last full year of working for the Nature Conservancy Council. I left in 1991, after the organisation was abolished by Mrs Thatcher's Secretary of State for the Environment, The Right Honourable Nicholas Ridley MP, and turned into 'English Nature'. Though I have written well over a million published words since then, these Twitchers were always the most fun to write. They have, especially, the serious merit of being short. Don't, I beg you, try to read them all at once. The thing to do is buy at least a dozen copies of this anthology, and keep them in different coat pockets to browse whenever the occasion warrants. Conservation meetings might be a good time. Or maybe to restore one's natural amiability after a favourite duck or toad is squashed by a speeding conservationist.

My thanks to David Carstairs for his co-operation in putting the great work together. All the drawings are his, as is everything from the quill pen of Old Countryman and his son, Jim. My lovely friend (and *British Wildlife* cohabitee) Sue Everett valiantly volunteered to publish it, with the triumphant result you see before you. Thanks also to Andrew Branson and the current guy at *The Countryman,* who seemed happy to relinquish any claim they had to the film rights.

Peter Marren, Ramsbury, 2004

1990

On the venerable art of bug-hunting

The following was my first piece as Twitcher in the Swamp, and one of the few that was actually about twitching. At this point I still envisaged it as a 'light-hearted' column about watching wildlife. After a few false starts, I realised it was actually about watching people watching wildlife.

'What's the griff?'

'Well, Steve's checked off a spreddie at Dunge, and Steve's ticked an icky at Gib'.

I should perhaps explain that most top twitchers are called Steve. Dunge is 'twitcherese' for Dungeness, Gib for Gibraltar Point. An icky is an icterine warbler, and worth stopping off for. A spreddie is a spotted redshank, and no big deal. But I interrupt.

'Hell, Steve, I'm in the UK 400. I'm after *megaticks*.'

The UK 400 Club is where all the Steves are, polishing their lifelists while they wait for the telltale throb of the pager. They listen for the call, the landing of some luckless warbler on some far-off rock that will bring the desired megatick. These guys 'tick' 400 different birds a year. They also have month lists, day lists and life lists. A hundred ticks a day is pretty good. Twitchers also have Brit lists, Euro lists and world lists. If your world life-list is under 3,000 ticks, you haven't been trying. 5,000 is big league, 10,000 is the stratosphere. The theoretical limit is about 12,000, after which you run out of birds. As far as I know, no one has yet managed to twitch every bird in the world. There are just too damn many of them.

The bug Mallinson picked up while on holiday in the Antibes was proving the very devil to shift

Though I like birds as much as the other guy, I doubt I'd cross the road to twitch an icky. I chose the byline for this column more for the trippability with which it leaves the tongue than for any innate love of pencilling ticks while up to one's ears in leeches. Actually I'm more of a bug hunter, if you want to know. As befits the smaller size and sedentary nature of our heart's desires, we bug hunters are less mobile than twitchers. Ours is a more genteel world of net-waving, bush-beating, and mild murmurs of pleasure. We don't have pagers, we use a phone booth. And instead of ticking bugs we stick pins into them. But we too have our funny little ways. You've heard of *sugaring*, I suppose, where we paint treacle onto trees, stiles, and, especially, seats, in the hope it will attract moths ('excuse me, dear, I believe you're sitting on a rare moth'). But have you ever been *sallowing*? I have, and it's quite good. It's what you do in the spring to catch moths that feed on catkins. Catkin nectar is, for some reason, extremely alcoholic, and the moths are invariably drunk by closing time at the tree. All you have to do is emerge from the pub, climb the nearest willow and jump up and down until the moths fall out. Naturally you need to make sure you haven't had too many yourself before you do this, or you too could end up down there on the sheet, prone and spreadeagled amid a lot of snoring moths.

'T.H.D.' or *Temporary Habitat Destruction* is a favourite technique of water-beetle enthusiasts, most of whom are called Ron. The Rons are all members of the Balfour-Brown Club, named after the founder, Ron Balfour-Brown, who did a lot of THD. What you do is this: find some swampy ground, then jump up and down in it (I know, there's a lot of jumping up and down in entomology) until the water-beetles float to the surface. It is called 'Temporary' because the surviving beetles have short memories, and the habitat often recovers.

I've never seen *fogging* done, it being mainly a nasty foreign sport. It involves opening the taps of canisters of a 'not necessarily lethal' insecticide, and watching the fumes float up into the green forest canopy. After a bit, the monkeys and things fall silent, and a few minutes later the dazed bugs start plopping down to the ground where you can get a good look at them. It's amazing the things that live up there, just out of reach.

Moth-hunters have a special word, *charlesing*, which is one of the very worst things that can happen to a moth, even worse than fogging.

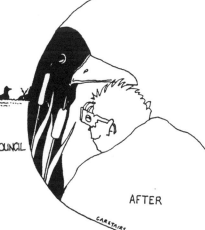

Charlesing is named after the late Baron Charles de Worms, a very keen sugarer and sallower, who in later life became somewhat short-sighted. His attempts to coax a moth to enter a pillbox often ended prematurely when the unfortunate creature got stuck between box and lid with tragic results all round.

Charlesing is an intransitive verb. You cannot 'charles' a moth, you can only commit the act of charles*ing*, and unfortunately that we all do from time to time, in our excitement, and usually to the moth equivalent of a megatick.

* * *

The rest is silence

Having been abolished, and halfway through the gruesome process of being chopped up, the Nature Conservancy Council (NCC) decided to fly the kite for endangered birds everywhere. The species it chose was, well, a kite. The beauty of the idea was that the NCC couldn't lose. Except that it had lost already.

Typical, isn't it. Having been served a summary death sentence by Ridley, and with nothing whatever to prove any more, the Nature Conservancy Council comes up with a really brilliant idea. The basis of any really brilliant idea is the concept of non-loseability. Heads we win, tails you lose, is what brilliant ideas are all about. This is why the NCC's plan to let loose a lot of captive-bred red kites is such a winner. If the birds decide to stay, and sit about the streets of London waiting for scraps, as they did in Shakespeare's day, well and good.

If, on the other hand, they all end up poisoned, like the last scene in Hamlet, so much the better. Their sacrifice will demonstrate better than any number of Government reports the fact that the countryside is no longer a fit place for unsuspecting carnivores to dwell in.

Most of us knew that already of course, but there is something about the sight of a pyramid of dead red kites that stirs the soul. Perhaps if their poisoned corpses create a nuisance on the motorways, we might be able to do something about the traffic problem too.

So, well done NCC, and, by the way, toodle-oo.

Focus on zebras

By 1990, it was suddenly very important for everyone, even the dignified agents of the Crown, to have a fancy logo. The best kind of logo had wavy lines, which in theory radiated a warm, yet efficient and customer-friendly style, but in practice tended to remind people of a dead zebra's bottom. Perhaps, in English Nature's case, this was at least relevant.

I suppose it had to happen. To the genius who thought 'English Nature' was a pretty cool name for a Government agency, the three wriggley lines spelling 'EN' was bound to be a real turn on. Well, hell, let's go with the flow. They really are *good* aren't they, these three wriggley lines. The way

they wriggle, and, er, the way they go along like that. The logo with a difference, shared only with Prudential insurance, Happy-eater snack-shacks, the Natural History Museum, a dozen brands of toothpaste and the Liberal party.

What all these designs seem to have in common is a close interest in zebras. At least we can say that English Nature's logo is more restrained than the Natural History Museum one, which displays in grisly detail the equine beast's bottom. More tastefully, EN's version provides a more discrete view, emphasising the swishing tail, and with the naughty bits airbrushed out. It could of course be argued that zebras are beasts of distant, hot places, and that a more temperate animal should have been chosen to symbolise the glories of the English wildlife. A ventral toad, say, or the last few inches of a newt. Well, too late now, the money is spent (and a tidy sum too, I hear) and we must learn to love zebras. On the day of the launch of English Nature, we must dress up as black and white pantomime horses, our frisky tails wagging with eagerness to plough on with the task ahead.

In the meantime, my man Carstairs shows some of the ways in which the logo can be displayed, with dignity and pride.

* * *

Observe the sheep

The early Nineties were great days for consultants, who sprang up everywhere like dragon's teeth, full of advice and nostrums for bodies that had strangely lost the ability to think for themselves. In its early days, the Government's new nature conservation agency, English Nature (EN), hired consultants by the van load, and one of the fruits was new nature reserve signs that catered exclusively for people who could not read a map, nor had any interest in wildlife.

A new marketing survey carried out for English Nature has concluded that the signs for National Nature Reserves (originally produced by EN's predecessor, the Nature Conservancy Council) were far too informative. To start with, they include a map, and the survey shows that 78% of visitors to the reserves do not know how to read a map.

It is a very insulting thing to be patronised with maps. Some visitors indeed revealed their indigation by beating the sign with their walking sticks, or even rending it with their nails or teeth ('tooth marks were noted at Kingley Vale'). Then there is the text, which is even more offensive, with its frequent use of élitist words like 'ecosystem', 'calcareous' and 'godwit'. One visitor suffered stomach pains while trying to read about peat-bog succession. Another required counselling after learning what bats get up to at night.

Ever eager to obey a consultant, English Nature's public affairs branch, which this week is called the Publicity and Marketing Team ('PMT'), have come up with a more 'user-friendly' sign, high on brand-recognition, low on godwits. Lathkill Dale in the Peak District is the first National Nature Reserve to receive our new improved sign. This consists simply of the word WELCOME, along with a picture of a Dipper, a sheep and a Dead-nettle. These are known as 'key points'.

All very well, you may think, but has this thing been thought through properly? You may need binoculars to watch Dippers, and marketing surveys have shown that only 13% of visitors (of mixed gender, age and hue) possess such an instrument. To note the salient points of a Dead-nettle, on the other hand, you may need a hand-lens, and the same surveys have conclusively proved that 98% of households manage without magnifying glasses, thank you very much. I'm not sure about the sheep. But have they considered the feelings of vegetarians here?

The solution ought to illustrate the two or three plants or animals that 100% of visitors will recognise without technical assistance, preferably without moving from the front seat of their Ford. Every nature reserve must henceforward have a sign depicting a Pigeon, a Sparrow and a Daisy. Once the visitors have ticked these off, they can clear off back to the city, leaving the Dippers and Dead-nettles in peace.

I think marketing is wonderful. It really makes everything *so* much simpler.

* * *

Letters

Among his other accomplishments, Carstairs is a voluminous letter-writer. These two examples arrived out of the blue in response to (a) a request I had made for recent sightings of the Downy Woundwort, otherwise as Stinking Horehound, or Prussian Woundwort, and (b) my book, Woodland Heritage. *I should explain that 'W6' is a kind of woodland covered by the 'National Vegetation Classification' ('NVC'), along with Ws 1-5, and many more. The 'NVC' is the rulebook of people who wander the countryside with clipboards and WeatherWriters, busily ticking boxes and circling latin names.*

Dear Professor Marren

RE: STACHYS GERMANICA

Your recent note in BSBI News regarding records of Stachys germanica prompts me to write.

In 1931 when I was a mere stripling of a spotty youth, my father Gerald would take me for long country rambles. The days were long and carefree, and we would wander the woods and field edges eyeing every nook and cranny.

One day, in late July 1931 I think it was, we were tramping along a hedge bank near Blowthrup in Oxfordshire when I suddenly required to partake of a wee-wee. Unzipping my cavalry twills I let fly on the rich flora that bobbed at my protuberance. Suddenly I noticed below my person a superb plant. Tall, rugose, yet neatly pubescent, it glistened with droplets of urine in the blistering heat of that memorable day. My father (who was pissing on a small ash tree) hastily tucked himself in and rushed to my side. Crouching down amongst the golden swathes of that erstwhile flora, he turned his rugged countenance towards me, and said: 'Geoffrey, this is Prussian Woundwort! You've really done it this time, you little fart'.

Yours sincerely

D. Carstairs of The Streams, St Mawes, Kernow
pp. G.T. Pilswinder (of Shetland)

WeatherWriter

THE WEATHERPROOF CLIPBOARD

NOW IMPROVED!

Used by 1000's of people throughout the world

★ Tougher, more flexible plastic
★ Extra heavy duty press fasteners
★ Improved writing and handling comfort
★ Large range of new "Countryside Colours"

HANGING RING / PAPER CLIP LIFTER

SPRING LOADED FRAME

STOPWATCH STRAP (OPTIONAL)

PEN POCKET (ZIP EXTRA)

TOUGH FLEXIBLE PLASTIC (WATER PROOF SIDEWALLS)

TICKET POUCH

TOUGH, PRESS FASTENERS

CARSTAIRS

STORM STRAPS (FOR EXTRA STRENGTH)

IDENTIFYING NAMEPLATE

TWO VERSIONS AVAILABLE

Size 3 ft x 2 ft x 1 ft 6 ins

12 June 1990

Dear Mr Marren

Recently I received in the post a title: <u>Woodland Heritage</u> by one Peter Marren. I wonder if you are he? The reason I mention it may be of some interest.

Some years ago, my brother Quentin and I were travelling by road from Churt to Bradworthy along the Lower Bottage Road; you probably know it. Anyway, as the journey drew on, we grew increasingly peckish. Unfortunately, there wasn't an ale house to be seen. So we pulled off the highway, just south of Purn, and began tucking into a mixed bag of pork scratchings and water biscuits (full-baked). The hedge was high and tippling with whitethroats and assorted Enberizids. Suddenly, from beyond the thorn, we heard a curious struggling noise, a thrutching unpleasant sound of straining and heaving. After some moments, a small rugose man, with no teeth, burst into view through a gap in the thicket. He was carrying a clipboard and was entirely draped in climbing plants, which included black bryony and honeysuckle. He stumbled nearer towards us, his face swollen appallingly by what looked like some dreadful rash. Suddenly, and the memory still brings tears to my fading eyes, he exploded. Quentin and I awoke to an eerie silence and a foul burnt smell hanging in the air. There was nothing to be seen of the strange fellow who had come out of the hedge. Only the clipboard and a blackened piece of A4 with the cryptic legend: 'THE WORST W6 I HAVE YET SEEN ...'

Quentin and I finished our scratchings and carried on towards Bradworthy.

Yours sincerely

Wilfred Themes (Rev.)

Kangaroo dreaming

As the end of the Nature Conservancy Council loomed, I started looking for another job. What follows is all true. I didn't get the job.

Seeking a new job, like everyone else, I find myself in a dark corridor in the Natural History Museum awaiting an interview. Facing me is a stuffed kangaroo. No one comes to this part of the museum any more, so we are alone, me and this kangaroo. I looked at him. He stared back, glassily.

'Have you been waiting long? ' I turned, but the corridor was empty.

'Only twenty minutes? Big deal. I've been here a hundred years,' he seemed to say. Just then, Clive popped out to see if I wanted anything. Clive was on the Board, and it was important to be agreeable. 'No, I'm fine, thank you,' I chirped. 'Look, I've got this nice kangaroo for company.'

'Ah,' cried Clive, his face lighting up. 'So you're interested in kangaroos?' And before I could protest no, no, I'm not, really I'm not, Clive launched into 101 things it was good for me to know about the delightful jumping creatures. Then he said: 'This kangaroo lived at London Zoo. He never saw Australia, but somehow he knew that was where he wanted to be. Kangaroos born in captivity are always homesick. Not many people know that. Did you know that?' And, it was true, my kangaroo certainly had a miserable look. 'They know what they are missing,' said Clive. 'The only thing that cheers them up is the smell of eucalyptus leaves.'

I was, by this stage, starting to become more interested in kangaroos. We seemed to be sailing into unknown regions here. How can an animal manage to be homesick about something it has never seen or experienced? Did someone tell my kangaroo about Australia? And do the rabbits we foolishly introduced to Australia have similar longings for Salisbury Plain?

Feeling somewhat confused, I took my leave of the kangaroo. I bounded in for the interview, but they seemed to want to talk about something else.

Bat calls

Long ago, before we passed them on to local enthusiasts, I used to answer calls from people harrassed by bats. This poem in Natural Selection *was a memory of them.*

I'm busy doing nothing when the phone begins to ring.
The sun is down, it's getting dark and bats are on the wing.
'They're flying through my window (and baby's in the cot),
They're crapping in the kitchen sink and down the chimney pot,
They're crawling down the rafters, they're squeaking through the wall,
They're floating in the goldfish bowl and hanging in the hall.

Oh help me, help me, NCC, I think I'm going mad:
They're sniffing round my husband, they've bitten my old dad,
The smell is bloody terrible, their eyes are glowing red:
There's only one good bat, and that is one that's lying dead.'

'Now listen dear, no need to fuss, they're friendly balls of fun;
It's just their way of telling you your home is number one.
Their dung is good for roses; their stink prevents the 'flu,
They're very clean (it's in the book, you see, it *must* be true).

When they perch upon your babies, don't scream and flap your coat:
You may not catch the rabies (just cover up your throat).
To stop them biting father, give them something else to eat –
Caviar's a welcome dish, lobster's quite a treat.

I hope you will enjoy your bats, but if they don't behave,
Then I suggest you leave your home and find an empty cave.'

The last few numbers of the former Nature Conservancy Council's staff magazine, Natural Selection, *included short pieces purporting to come from the quill pen of Old Countryman, a native of Strathpeffer in the Highlands. As his editor, David Carstairs, explained, there could be little doubt about the oldster's authenticity and, as they say, knowledge of wind. Some found Old Countryman's style reminded them of certain weekly nature columns in the provincial newspapers. Others said that Old Countryman was actually better than the weekly nature columns in the provincial newspapers, and that they had probably copied him. At any rate, David has selected samples of Old Countryman's rural rambles, which conclude each year's twitching.*

The magic of the Highlands

In nearly twenty years of living and working in the Highlands of Scotland, I have only seen such a similar sight on four occasions. On this occasion, I was sitting watching Stenga, our twelve year old Dachsund, playing at the water's edge below this mountain where ptarmigan were calling their strange call, when I heard a strange call from behind, where the dog was playing, just behind where we were sitting, watching the dog playing. Immediately after hearing this, Stenga and I sat up and, as is often the case with dogs and their amazing sense of direction, we both looked round. There, above us, through the woods and beyond the mountain – well, more beyond the loch and below the mountain, but certainly through the woods – we saw it. It can only have been a few yards away, and Stenga, in her eagerness to see what was going on, ran ahead of where I was sitting with my head turned, and scared it off. Later she came back to where I was, by this time watching a flock of goldeneyes grubbing amongst the birches, and I asked her what it had been, up there beyond the wood below the mountain, yet near the loch. But she said nothing. Bloody dogs, they can be so secretive at times.

1991

Woodland relief

By the 1990s, the conservation cause had become popular enough for advertisers to work it into their campaigns, to show how much they care. *These were two examples. People sometimes ask whether Twitcher's stories are true. They are indeed, but they are presented as Twitcher sees them, through, so to speak, the vapours of the swamp. I have also been asked whether Twitcher is serious. This is a much more difficult area. Is there but one reality? Are sobriety and mockery antithetical concepts? Have you got all day?*

In the course of 'repairing' woods damaged by recent storms, new allies have joined us in the great conservation cause. Bonio, the firm that makes those delicious dog biscuits, has weighed in with its 'plant-a-tree-for-doggy' campaign. Young trees, say Bonio, 'provide ideal locations for outdoor walks with your dog'. I think we all know what they mean by that. If Fido had no tree to cock his leg against, he might well choose some less ideal location. It is nice to learn that trees still have their uses. Though perhaps it's just as well they don't have any feelings. Carry on, Fido. Free vouchers come with 'mini-chop biscuits' and 'yummy cheese crunchies'.

Meanwhile Andrex, the toilet-paper people, are unrolling their own campaign to save our woods. It is called 'Woodland Releaf', which really is extremely amusing. Perhaps they intend to remove those festoons of lavatory paper which are such a regrettable part of today's woodland scene. I hope so. It is hard to see Andrex's products as a worthwhile adornment to our woods, even their environmentally coloured 'spring green' paper for caring bums.

But if Andrex really have the best interests of the woods at heart, they should be encouraging people to make the best use of the natural amenities. If you are caught short during a woodland ramble, dock leaves are the best, but any bunch of sycamore or beech will do *in extremis*. The Romans always used to thrash themselves with stinging nettles afterwards. I'm told it is most invigorating, should you feel like giving it a try.

Real conservation

The Conservative Party also claimed to be friends of nature, citing the wonderful new opportunities for wildlife created by motorways and urban development (see 'A Vision of Moon Daisies'). To lend credence to this unlikely scenario, they invented a Quisling creature called Ollie the Otter. He didn't last long, probably run over by a Eurotruck on the way to his appointment with Mrs Thatcher. And serve him right, many would say.

Trying to improve its wretched environmental image, the Conservative Party has come up with a sprightly little character called Ollie the Otter. Ollie is about to star in an exciting series of adventures, starting with a trip to Downing Street to meet Margaret Thatcher, which sounds a bit like Bilbo Baggins' appointment with the dragon Smaug. According to his spokesman at Central Office, Ollie is a keen supporter of nuclear power. I wouldn't be surprised if he wasn't also in favour of motorways, superstores and factory-farming, though none of these things are any of his business.

The appearance of jolly little Ollie has rather stolen the thunder from a character I was about to introduce, called Clarence the Click-beetle. Less politically committed than Ollie, Clarence speaks for no one but himself. He would like you to know he lives in a mouldy beech stump somewhere in Windsor Forest. He is fully protected by law, but nobody told him and he doesn't care anyway. Clarence has no plans to visit Mrs Thatcher nor even Mr Kinnock, and he couldn't care tuppence about nuclear power. All Clarence wants is to be left alone. His ancestors lived in this rotten old stump, or one very like it, for as long as any beetle can remember, and what

was good enough for them is good enough for him.

Then, in January 1991, a great gale blew over and shattered Clarence's ancestral home. His future looked bleak, for the Clarences of this world can't simply wander off and negotiate a lease on an empty stump. He likes things the way they were. Clarence is a *real* conservative. Fortunately for h-im, in the nick of time came two heroes, Professor John Owen and our man of the woods, Ted Green, who picked up the various bits of Clarence's stump, and stuck them back together again. To finish off, they filled the hollow inside with Clarence's favourite treats: bird muck, rotting funguses and mouldy sawdust. The extent of Clarence's pleasure may be judged by the baby Clarences that were found crawling about the stump shortly afterwards. Well done Prof, well done Ted! Now that's what I call *real* conservation.

STOP PRESS

In 2003 Ted Green was awarded an MBE for his services rendered to old trees.

* * *

A vision of moon daisies

The Department of Transport ran a propaganda campaign claiming that not only were they environmentally-friendly in every possible way, but that the Department's planned new road network was exactly *what the wildlife had wanted all along. Oh, the wildlife wanted more golf, too. And Christmas trees.*

According to the Department of Transport, motorways are not only eco-friendly and savers of valuable oxygen, they are also *the place where wildlife wants to live.* I learned this from their recent advertisement campaign, which is promoting motorway verges as the nature reserves of the future. 'This is a motorway verge,' they say, showing us a picture of a butterfly. 'It is home to some of the rarest wild flowers, butterflies and insects in the UK,' adds the Department of Transport, and they 'are not there by chance'. Indeed not. It seems all these rare species chose to make their homes on motorways knowing that they are part of the Department's 'considered

26

ecological strategy', blending visions of Arcadia with the needs of speeding juggernauts.

If true, this is news to chill the heart of every conservationist. If the rarest 'butterflies and insects' really prefer traffic verges to all the nature reserves we are expensively setting up for them, where would we all be? Out of a job, that's where we'd be. The ungrateful little sods. And so it was with some anxiety that I wrote to the Department asking for more details. Maybe I could bum some much-needed money off them by way of scribbling something suitably proactive about their disgusting highways.

But it's OK. We needn't have worried. The butterflies are indeed 'not there by chance'. They are not there at all. Those 'bright, career-orientated' lads at Transport were just having their usual larks. The 'rarest' species they referred to were just commonplace things like buttercups and moon daisies. They should know all about moon-daisies, since it was the Department who planted them. From a garden centre. Still, it was quite a good joke at the expense of the thick tax-payer, who doesn't know a daisy from a dandelion.

In fact, the only way the Transport guys will ever get rare species on their motorways is to blast a new motorway through a nature reserve. I hope this does not betray a sinister intention behind their amusing prank.

Bug-hunting with 'W-S'

This was about a favourite book of mine when I was about twelve. I loved the author's sceptical tone, his obvious doubt as to whether his young readers were up to the mark.

The trouble with children's nature books nowadays is they are always so damned mimsy and comforting. Everything must be brought down to little Jimmy's level, with the natural world presented as one big happy playground with jumping bunnies, and – ooh, don't touch – a bumblebee busy making us honey for breakfast. No wonder they grow up so stunted and dim. In my young day, we were given nature books that read like the school rules. Written by ferocious authority figures, they ordered you out of bed at five in the morning to clean your boots and prepare yourself for three hours fieldwork in the pouring rain. My first bug-hunting book was like that. It was called *Collecting and Breeding Butterflies and Moths* (you see, they had dull titles too) and it was by B. Worthington-Stuart FRES, a desert explorer and former member of the French Foreign Legion.

Old 'W.S' would have sorted out today's young greenies, with their prattle about the rain forests. His idea of nature study was to get out

BLAIR'S SHOULDER KNOT

there, find where the nature was hiding, drag it back to base and stick it in a cage. Here is his advice on rearing insects:

'If you are too lazy to get up half an hour or even an hour earlier, give your stock and your cages away to somebody who will appreciate them. You are not fit to have them.'

He is equally forthright on the subject of butterfly nets: 'Perfectly satisfactory nets can be made in little more than an hour at trifling cost,' he explains, before going on to describe a contraption of incredible complexity, using a mixture of steel wire, rivets, washers, bolts and tubes. When I was very young my father made me a Worthington-Stuart net. It took a week to assemble, fell to bits at the first swipe, and was the cause of a distressing scene between myself and my baffled parent.

On the other hand, W.S. always showed a touching concern for the dangers you might face when bug hunting. For example, he was certain the countryside swarmed with adders, and insisted you always wore really '*thick*' leather gloves, with a woollen pair underneath them. You can work quite easily in them with a bit of practice'. He had a theory that the wildlife was always trying to get inside your shirt and trousers. His solution? Cycle clips ('at all times'), and also 'I recommend tucking a handkerchief inside one's collar and wearing eyeshields'.

W.S was not without his lighter moments. Bug hunting, he admits, is hard work, 'but it can sometimes be fun too'. Though he had little time for other books on entomology ('tomfoolery ... absolute nonsense'), he was at heart a tolerant man:

'Try their methods by all means and good luck to you! But if, after a

LARGE AND SMALL COPPERS

few evenings spent in unsuccessful moth-hunting, following their directions, you begin to despair of ever securing a capture, try my methods. I think you will be pleasurably surprised at the results.'

STOP PRESS

You will be disappointed to know that *Collecting and Breeding Butterflies and Moths* by B. Worthington-Stuart FRES (rtd.) is out of print.

* * *

Name games

I don't like made-up names. If folk are too dumb to learn scientific names, they should stick to birds and bunny rabbits. I did champion English names for fungi, once, but my heart wasn't in it. Let them learn Latin.

George Orwell once remarked on how the solid, Anglo-Saxon names of British wild animals and fish seem to reflect the eternal peace of the rural scene. 'Roach, Rudd, Barbel, Bream, Chub, Carp, Tench. They're solid kind of names. The people who made them up hadn't heard of machine-guns, they didn't spend their time eating aspirins ...', he wrote in his nostalgic novel, *Coming Up For Air*.

By contrast, just look at some of the feeble attempts at name-coining by today's aspirin-guzzling naturalists: 'ruddy skimmer' – 'long-winged cone-head' – 'semipalmated sandpiper'. If these names conjure up anything it is the nerd-world of computer-geeks, pager-twitchers, list-makers. Some might say the rot started with Linnaeus, but I disagree. Linnaeus was a romantic, with all sorts of funny little hobbies. He insisted on naming favourite moths after womens' undergarments, for instance. But his geeky modern descendants couldn't be expected to show that kind of imagination, even if some of them may share Linnaeus's little peccadillo.

I'm in something of a quandary here, since I plan to write a short article about wild fungi for Andrew Branson's inestimable organ, and most of them are known only by names like *Bjerkandera* or *Krombholziella*, which may or may not be a kind of naughty knickers worn in Uzbekistan. There is, in fact, a move afoot to make up some English names for fungi, but I'm not confident they will catch on. For example, they propose to call one group of toadstools 'crumble-caps', and mean to name each species after its characteristic smell: crumblecap, apple crumblecap, apple-crumble crumblecap (and you think I'm joking, don't you?).

In the end, there was nothing for it but to do was to make up some names myself. The bracket fungus *Ganoderma adspersum* will henceforth be known as Coco-pops. You see, its spores look exactly like Cadbury's drinking chocolate (of which I am very fond), and you might hear a faint popping as they burst forth. If you listen really carefully. As for *Boletus edulis* (of which I am even fonder), I find the name Chubby Tom will do very well. 'Look, here are some Chubby Toms'.But even these seem a bit contrived, compared with Barbel and Tench. How about Cocpop and Tubb? No? Orwell was probably right, those aspirins have obviously done their worst.

STOP PRESS

The move to popularise mycology (the study of fungi) crescendoed in 2002 when the British Mycological Society and assorted conservation organisations paid someone to invent some funky new names for the kidz. With monickers like Lemon Disco, Cinnamon Jellybaby and Winter Twiglet the kiddies will probably think they are sweeties and eat them. Hey, watch me care!

Twitching a Murrelet

This was my best ever bird twitch, and I simply had to share it with you.

Just occasionally one strives to live up to the title of one's column, and so it is with no mean pride, not to say boastfulness, that I announce – loudly and often – that I have *twitched a Murrelet*. An *Ancient* Murrelet, to be precise. For those of lesser status, who will never come close to approaching, let alone surpassing, my tremendous feat, I should explain that an Ancient Murrelet is a kind of sea bird. About the size of a puffin, with white rings round its myopic eyes that look like spectacles, and also some amusing whiskers about the face, emblematic of great age. It is, indeed, the ancient mariner of the avian world, a most wise and distinguished, if daft looking, bird, or at least that's the way it looks in books.

So how do you twitch a murrelet? Well, so far as Britain is concerned, you have to cross the sea to the island of Lundy. (What is the Murrelet, a native of California, doing on Lundy? Don't ask, no one knows.) But getting there is easy, that bit's a doddle. The hard part starts when you learn that the murrelet appears only for an hour or so after dawn, and that it lives on the windiest, rockiest part of the island. This means dragging yourself out of bed at about 4 a.m. and into the waterproof trousers. Setting off, you grope your way across the island through a 60-knot headwind, with a hint of sleet and water trickling down your neck and down both legs of your waterproof trousers; then you tumble down several hundred feet of beetling cliff before realising you've gone too far, and then have to crawl all the way back up again, mugged by yapping gulls. Finally, with a belated realisation that your 'bins' are inadequate for the purpose of singling out a murrelet, you're reduced to begging a glimpse through a snarling fellow twitcher's scope. Then, with luck, you should glimpse a dot out at sea, or possibly a speck on the rocks. That is the Murrelet, and now you can limp back to base, pencil a big, happy tick in your best bird book and retire to bed content. If not, it's the same again tomorrow. And the day after that.

As a result, there is now a new word to grace our mother tongue. The word is 'murreletted'. On a wet day on Lundy, the local bar is thronged with murreletted twitchers, hunched over their pints of Puffin Ale and squinting into the gathering gloom, as they contemplate yet another nocturnal tramp. But you can use the word for any occasion when you're feeling sufficiently cold, wet and cheesed off.

* * *

Worms for sale

It is bad enough giving new species silly names, but getting industry to pay for them was a stroke of genius. I hear that if you pay them enough, the Astronomical Union will name an asteroid after you.

Every time a new New Naturalist book appears, which, these days, isn't very often, one thinks bitterly of the great book that never was nor ever will be. This would have been the New Naturalist on Pond Life by Sir Alister Hardy, the noted authority on plankton, balloons and angels. Hardy put off the task for more than thirty years in order to write about angels, and now, alas, he is an angel himself. He is remembered today by the various objects named after him. These he used to list as 'a boat in Hong

Kong, an octopus, a squid, an Antarctic island and' – here he always lowered his voice – 'two worms'.

How times have changed. The lowly unregarded scientist of today would be in raptures at the thought of even one eponymous worm. However, the Systematics Association, responsible for such things, is strapped for cash at the moment. It has occurred to the Association that it might be a good idea to sell a newly discovered species to the highest bidder, and name it in their honour. I suppose it is not much worse than adopting a swan at Slimbridge. Already some new wasps have been named after a bunch of New York 'debt traders'. And spokesmen for several major British companies say they are keen to pay up, provided that the right sort of cuddly yet enterprising creature with enormous forward vision can be found. 'We're thinking of adopting some sort of bear that images our company's enormous strength yet shows versatility in its drive to end up on top,' chortled some boring creep.

The obvious flaw in the Systematic Association's plan to rake in cash-for-creatures is that all the more obviously marketable species on the planet have names already. What is left are a range of parasites and free-loaders, various worms and sponge-like forms, jellies with no backbones and featureless blobs living on the ocean floor and filtering excrement for a living. I suppose these must be worth something. If there are no takers, perhaps the Systematics Organisation should show a little imagination and pass them round.

Old Countryman: Beyond there but near here

Stenga and I first heard them about a week ago. Today, a week later, give or take seven days ago, me, my simple son Reg, and the dog heard them again. Only, we saw them this time. At least they could have been the same, but they were still far away, and I wasn't sure, being so high.

Suddenly, Reg shouted that he could see them coming through the woods, which were dense and impossible. I rebuked him for his patent stupidity, and with a stout thwack about his head with a rude, open cudgel, sent him on his way.

Stenga and I arrived at the house later to find Reg had been sent to bed with a glass of milk and a packet of pork scratchings.

By the way, we never did see them. To be honest, I'm not sure they'd been there in the first place.

Old Countryman
Docham
Strathpeffer

1992

A 'news special' in The Sun had worried about the effect of 'the worst drought since 1745' on Britain's little known wild beavers. That no one had actually seen any was doubtless because The Sun's bunker-like office in Wapping has few windows.

Here be beavers

As the heatwave goes on, *The Sun* runs a story about wildlife dying of thirst or fighting it out over the last puddle. Otters, frogs and toads 'are badly hit', it reveals, 'as streams and rivers turn to trickles'. Worst hit of all, according to *The Sun's* nature experts, is the beaver. I can certainly confirm that part of it. Neither I nor any of my colleagues at *British Wildlife* have seen sight nor sound of any beavers this year. Frankly, things don't look good for the beaver.

Fortunately the Atomic Energy Authority has better news. There are dozens of beavers up there in Shetland, apparently, no doubt all busy building dams, though with what I'm not sure since there aren't any trees. This startling disclosure was made by one of their top scientists at a public inquiry. His evidence had originally referred to badgers. But that was a misprint, explained the top scientist. He must have meant beavers. Everyone knows there are no badgers in Shetland, he added with a chuckle.

News from two such highly respected authorities must cast fresh light on the stories of the medieval travel-writer and tall-tale teller, Gerald of Wales. According to Gerald, there were beavers in the River Teifi. Lots of them. Well, he hadn't actually seen them himself, but everyone knew about them. They were regarded as a furry kind of fish, and so it was OK to eat them on Fridays. Everybody knew that.

The fact that Gerald was equally sure there were wyverns, basilisks and dragons lurking in the hills of Wales has tended to undermine his credibility to sceptical modern minds. Still you never know. Perhaps the best thing would be to send *The Sun*'s nature expert and the man from the Atomic Energy Authority over there to clear this matter up.

* * *

Of previous interest

Sites of Special Scientific Interest are designated by English Nature and its Celtic colleagues for reasons of their outstanding importance in the natural world. For each SSSI there is a list of prohibited activities. But it is hard to cover all eventualities, as they found when the National Trust blew up an SSSI with dynamite.

I'm thinking about running an occasional feature on important natural areas which have been destroyed in unusual or amusing ways. For this month's Site of Previous Scientific Interest, I have chosen Marsden Point in County Durham, a breathtaking cliff of limestone owned by the National Trust. Deciding that these fossil-bearing rocks were a public danger, and might prove inconvenient for the enormous crowds it hopes to attract, the Trust got nine-year-old Sam Mullen, who lives at Sedgefield Court, Killingworth, to blow them all to bits.

'It was great,' recalled Sam. 'I just pressed the button and the rocks blew up and flew right through the air.' English Nature, responsible for preserving Marsden Point's special interest, namely these particular rocks, were less impressed: 'How would they like it if we blew up one of their bloody stately homes?'. But there is nothing they can do about it, because English Nature forgot to list being blown up with dynamite as a 'potentially damaging operation', requiring advance notice.

They forgot to list bull-fighting as well, but more about that next time.

* * *

Not a peat bog

English Nature was charged with saving peat bogs, Fisons with turning them into bags of fertiliser. In a compromise deal, EN managed to save bits of the bogs in return for allowing Fisons to grind up the rest. This was widely regarded as a sell-out. It all boiled over several years on, when English Nature sought to oblige the fertiliser folk still further by descheduling parts of the SSSI at Thorne Moor. The minister suggested EN think again, and, always obliging, it did.

Nature reserve managers have long toyed with the idea of charging an entrance fee, or increasing their income by selling 'wild-style' trinkets at the gate. Apart from helping to pay for the warden's Range Rover, an income from the land would be of great assistance to planners when weighing the benefits of a nature reserve against, say, another golf course or a land-fill site.

But until now I have never heard it suggested that a nature reserve should pay its way *in advance*. Yet this seems to be the basis of the notorious agreement between English Nature and Fisons, the garden-friendly people who cut up peat bogs into convenient bag-sized portions. Some 5,200 acres of 'worked peat' at Thorne Moors and elsewhere are to be transferred to English Nature, but only on condition that Fisons can continue to turn the peat into fertiliser until there is none left. English Nature thinks this is a pretty good deal. Look, it says, when Fisons (or whoever) have finished with it, we can call it a *National Nature Reserve*. That's good, isn't it?

Some will regard this as indeed the perfect compromise between industry and conservation. The only snag - and many will see it as a piffling detail – is that Thorne Moors would no longer be a peat bog. Exactly what it *would* be is hard to say. A lake, possibly. Or the world's largest expanse of mud. We must wait and see. It would certainly be a rather unusual nature reserve, lacking certain details we have grown used to, such as wildlife.

The important thing to remember is that the area concerned is only 5,200 acres, no more than a third of the total area of lowland bog found in the United Kingdom. One hardly knows what the vol. bods. are making such a fuss about. English Nature's newly appointed Council, which certainly seems to have its head screwed on right, was reportedly able to devote no more than five minutes of its valuable time to the matter, though it did manage to find time to give the deal a 'warm welcome'. It is heartwarming to see English Nature carrying on the late, forgotten NCC's tradition of welcoming anything and everything, especially if it gets them out of a tight corner.

STOP PRESS

Thorne, Goole and Crowle Moors, together with Hatfield Moors, form the largest complex of lowland raised bog in Britain covering an area of over three thousand hectares (9,000 acres). Following a long campaign over commercial peat extraction, in March 2002 it was announced that peat extraction there is to cease. The agreement, brokered between English Nature and Scotts Ltd, the company who owns nearly all of the peat permissions on the three sites, involves compensating the company for lost earnings: £17.3 million over three years. There will be a phased withdrawal from a third site at Hatfield, South Yorkshire, with extraction stopping there altogether by autumn 2004.

* * *

Odds and ends

Twitcher occasionally gave advice on how to manage nature reserves. These were some of his tips.

Top tips for nature reserve wardens. No 1: Looking after downland

This is very, very easy. If the down is full of sheep, advise the farmer to take them off. If there aren't any sheep, advise the farmer to put some on.

Beards in the grass

I wonder who was responsible for the following message, which you always find pegged up somewhere when you find a decent bit of herbage:

**PLEASE HELP US TO
LOOK AFTER THIS
RESERVE AND ENJOY
YOUR VISIT**

It looks like a deal: *we* help *you* to enjoy your visit so long as *you* help *us* to look after the reserve. Perhaps we are only allowed into the 'visitor centre' after we've completed four hours' hard labour on the reserve. I don't know. But I should advise visitors to be wary about any bearded enthusiasts in the undergrowth found urging you to 'enjoy' yourself. Have a nice day.

Sheep remembered

The old visitor centre at Old Winchester Hill used to have a little garden in which you could see all the wild flowers found on the reserve. Each flower had its own label, but since the plants were seasonal, the label was often the only thing you could see. Among the remarks overheard by the warden was this one:

Little girl: 'What are these, mummy?'

Mummy: 'Why it's a little graveyard for animals, dear. This is where they bury their sheep when they die.'

Little girl: 'Ooh – and look, mummy, they've even got their names.'

Mummy (reads): 'Rockrose, Hard-head, Basil, Celandine. Isn't that lovely. They do love their animals here, don't they?'

The thing about the Rabbit is that it is always a problem. There are either too many rabbits, or too few, but never exactly enough. If you have no rabbits, you must buy a lot of sheep to eat the grass exactly the way the rabbits would have done. If you do have rabbits, you must get rid of them as soon as possible. Once they are all gone, you should invest in some sheep.

The other thing about rabbits is that they tend to get messily eaten by stoats and foxes. This should be discouraged, as it upsets the visitors.

Wrong sort of tree

One of many pressure groups which Twitcher supported was CAT-P (Conservationists Against Tree-planting), which campaigned against stupid tree-planting. One look at the farm-woodlands, community woods and millennium forests cluttering up the landscape will show you how successful we were.

My learned colleague, John Bratton, whose temptingly titled book, *Red Data Books: 3. Invertebrates Other Than Insects*, came out this week, has an exciting idea to save the wildlife. He wants us to wear a badge showing a cat peeing on a sapling. This will mark us out as initiates of CAT-P, or Conservationists Against Tree-Planting. CAT-P is here to take the Pith out of Plantations, explains John.

I suppose there must be people left who still believe that tree-planting is good for wildlife. Some birders seem happy to imagine that a few of these planted saplings will one day grow into trees and become a perch for some wretched Blue Tit. But then, some birders know nothing at all, apart from bird stuff. The truth is that most planted trees die within a few years, and that these much-vaunted 'community forests' are as ugly as hell and as dull as ditchwater. Every schoolboy knows there is more fun to be got out of slag heaps, muddy ponds and quarries than dense ranks of unclimbable trees. We are being conned.

It is not clear what we initiates of CAT-P have to do apart from flaunting our little badges. Perhaps, when we see one of these planters busy about his work, sticking EU-approved sycamores into cowslip meadows, or Hungarian oaks into a lime wood, or Christmas trees into a young lad's playground, we are meant to mock his ridiculous beard, or pull faces and waggle our fingers. I do not know. John, our leader, has yet to issue instructions on this point.

I imagine that, even as I write, John is searching *Red Data Books: 3. Invertebrates Other Than Insects* for some poisonous beast to bite holes in

Exasperated by million-tree campaigns? Can you no longer see the woods for the Tuley Tubes?

Support

CONSERVATIONISTS AGAINST TREE-PLANTING

The organisation woodlands can really trust. Badges 40p from: John Bratton, Bratton Mansion, Bratton, Brattonshire.

CAT-P: taking the pith out of plantations.

these disgusting pink 'Tuley Tubes' and pee all over the cowering sapling inside. What CAT-P demands are proper natural trees, which grow where they please and mature into the kind of spindle-shanked, nook-shotten curiosities we are used to in this country. But most of all, we want open spaces between the trees, with a decent view and room to wander without seeing half-grown spruce trees everywhere. Join CAT-P, says John, and say Vamoose to Spruce. I'm thinking of having a word with John.

* * *

Give them a bone

The Hawk and Owl Trust now have a 40-page booklet on building boxes, baskets and platforms for owls. The rot started 150 years ago when Squire Waterton built a special house for 'his' Barn Owls. I think it's all about possession. If the birds are on our land, they are in some sense our property. And if they are ours, why not help them out and build them a nest? Some day, they'll work out a way of making them pay rent.

Twitching through a particularly plashy swamp this week, I notice what look remarkably like doggy baskets secured to the branches of some tall birches. 'Is this a sort of experiment?' I ask the nice warden man, whose name was Tom Bowling (haven't they written a song about him?). 'They are doggy baskets.' Are there dogs stuck up the trees? 'Those doggy baskets are for owls.'

More precisely they are for the long-eared owl, a stupid-looking bird that makes a noise like a rusty gate. It seems that the long-eared owl is so busy waggling its long ears and staring with its mad eyes that it has no time to build a nest of its own. This kind of feckless behaviour, so typical of our times, should by rights get this idiotic bird struck off the red-list. But, of course, the conservation world likes nothing better than messing about with a useless animal that does nothing for itself. The only question is what kind of home to build for it.

I don't suppose the baskets were just a lucky guess. The RSPB, the Terence Conran of designer nest-boxes, will have given much thought to this matter of shelter homes for idle owls, noting such requirements as adequate ear room and hooting space. They probably began by experimenting with cardboard boxes, before building up to tea chests and plastic dustbins. When the owls sneerily rejected these humble offerings, the RSPB would have really got to work. Painted chalet-style lodges with the word 'OWLIE' printed over the door. Hawsered rubber dinghies with en suite habitat accessories. Socking great owl hutches with reception facilities and a complimentary dead mouse. It must have been quite a relief when it turned out that dog baskets would do, though maybe with an old blanket and a couple of rubber bones to amuse the owlets.

Special offer

Twitcher was watching the new-born 'Scottish Natural Heritage' rather carefully at this time. He suspected its much-vaunted service to the 'Scottish people' might come before service to the Scottish wildlife, and he was right.

For those of us waiting impatiently to find out what this exciting new body, 'Scottish Natural Heritage' ('SNH') is like, we now have the first clue. It takes the form of a colour leaflet with details of 'SNH's' 'prospectus for change'. I should perhaps explain that Scottish Natural Heritage, responsible for Scotland's countryside and wildlife, was set up in 1992 to replace the former Nature Conservancy Council (NCC) following a coup by the Scottish Office, aided and abetted by the traitor Ridley and his stooges in the Scottish land-owning establishment. SNH combines the former roles of the Countryside Commission for Scotland and the discredited NCC, which no one north of the Border ever mentions. At its head is Magnus Magnusson, the noted quizmaster and advertiser of cheeses, mail-order items and office products.

Let's have a look at this glossy new 'prospectus', probably available free with every kilogram drum of Scotch Cheddar or LP of bothy ballads. ('Enjoy it, while you sing-along and eat cheese, says Magnus.') Well, it's clear that the approach of 'SNH' is quite different from the dead, weed-covered Nature Conservancy Council, which is, quite properly, not even mentioned. For a start, the new lot are not so bothered about conserving wildlife. What they care about is, in their words, 'achieving a balance for all'. Everybody in Scotland deserves a balance, it thinks, possibly in order to weigh their cheeses. But what makes them think the Scots want a balance? Personally I would have thought balance is a matter for trapeze artistes or jugglers, a trick requiring considerable physical skill. It is hard to imagine the tubby Magnusson surviving long on a tightrope, a cheese in one hand, a set of encyclopaedias in the other. I admire his nerve,

but I hope he knows what he is doing.

The leaflet ends by addressing us directly. '*So,*' it concludes, '*What's* **your** *role in caring for Scotland's natural heritage?*' (*sic*). Yup, they are really up there with the snappy grammar, these reborn Scotties. To remind us of who they mean, there is a picture of six typical people out for a walk in the glen, namely an angler, a climber, a shepherd, a man in a hard hat, a man with a gun and a skier looking for some snow - a quest that seems hopeless, for the scene is obviously in summer. At their feet, nervously drinking tea, is a family enjoying a picnic among the flies and midges. 'Our success depends on working with YOU.'

So, when it gets down to brass tacks, it seems it is the mission of 'SNH' to help us find snow in summer and to shoot anyone found picnicking outdoors without a large slice of delicious Scottish cheese. These are sensible policies which I have no doubt will create a cleaner, safer country for the benefit of all. The cheese is very reasonably priced at £3 the pound, and comes with a complimentary ticket to the nature reserve of your choice.

GREAT KNOT : NEW TO BRITAIN

47

The Fieldfare

I saw it first last Tuesday as Kitty and I walked the strath above the house. The first one was by itself, though within minutes it was joined by many others. At first there were hundreds of them, these grey, noisy thrushes of the thrush tribe, but then Kitty barked and I nearly stumbled into the fence of this national nature reserve which I manage. Later, we came down through the woods where siskins bobbed, as they do in the larches, and the dog looked as if it was cold and wet. I remembered then that this had been another memorable day in the Highlands, and I looked forward to being out again somewhere, and the casserole in the oven waiting for us to get home after our day out in the Highlands to remember. I thought then that I would certainly remember this day after all. After all, the dog and I seemed to agree, this had been a day to remember.

Strathpeffer
November 1954

48

1993

Tender is the night

In 1993, I moved to Ramsbury, close to a disused water meadow gone wild and turning into a swamp. That year the willow thickets were loud with nightingales, and one of them sang all night a few yards from my bedroom window. The funny thing is, you can't help listening. First you are rapt – ooh, aren't I lucky? Then you get a bit bored. Then you get mad. Then it's: 'Shut the **** up, you ****ing ****!'

My heart aches, and a drowsy numbness pains my senses. It's that bloody nightingale again. Since I moved to my new swamp in the Kennet valley, it has sung all day, followed by all night and then all day again, just outside my bedroom window. At first so sweet was my joy it was almost pain. I actually kept the window open while the endangered dryad sang of summer over and over again. It is oddly difficult to sleep with a nightingale in your ear. You feel you ought to be writing a poem or something. After a couple of sleepless nights you feel differently. I clapped the window to with a bang, but still the cheeping found its way in, down the chimney and under the door. Peep, peep, peep. It's amazing how quickly a dream of summer nights becomes an irritating racket. The third night, I opened the window again and threw a slipper at it. Now there is an echo. It has found a mate. I can't stand it.

This monotonous trilling and peeping might explain the medieval reaction to nightingales, which was very different from that of the lyric poets. There wasn't any double glazing in those days, so idiotic nightingale noises drifted in through every shutter and keyhole, driving everybody mad. This must explain why the nightingale is the fall guy in the poem *The Owl and the Nightingale*, a big hit in the reign of King John. Eventually, like the rest of us, the owl loses its temper with its chirpy companion and tells it to sod off:

'.. You're filthy dark and small
Like a sort of sooty ball.
You have no loveliness nor strength,
Your songs lack harmony and length.'

It might have added that nightingales are also sulky, bad-tempered, and completely sex-crazy, a bit like James Dean, though some women like that sort of thing, or so I've been told.

Still, for what it's worth, here is my own ode to the nightingale. There is merit, I feel, in its brevity.

> Light-winged dryad of the trees,
> Summer singer of throated ease,
> Immortal bird of shadows deep,
> BELT UP, damn you, I want to sleep.

* * *

Straining the vegetables

My favourite agricultural machine is the flail. I love the idea of simply beating a hedge into shape. Pretty much the same idea applied to all farming in the 1970s and 1980s. You simply beat the land into doing what you wanted, like an old-fashioned Latin master with a recalcitrant class of fourth-formers.

Knowing that, until now, the Ministry of Agriculture (MAFF) hasn't cared a hedgehog's dying sniff for nature conservation, one begins to wonder whether its brilliant plan to bankrupt farmers, called Set-aside, is not at heart a secret scheme to wipe out any remaining farmland wildlife. The record so far in the great Set-aside Massacre of 1993 is held by the Yorkshire farmer who, in the course of ploughing a 14-acre field in May, managed to destroy (1) two Snipe nests, (2) three Lapwing chicks, (3) two Grey Partridge nests and a brooding hen, (4) one adult Pheasant and seven poults, (5) one Skylark nest, (6) three Meadow Pipit nests, (7) one Willow Warbler nest. Altogether it was quite an impressive bag, and I would be surprised if he doesn't win a Green Farming award for outstanding biodiversity.

There would seem to be some dispute as to who is responsible for the massacre. Our own MAFF officials claim that they were just obeying orders: 'We are trying to be imaginative about these schemes. The stumbling block is not here but at the Commission in Brussels.'

Robin Page, the farming journalist, disagrees. He says the EEC had never insisted that Set-aside land should be ploughed bang in the middle of the nesting season. He pins the blame on the cretins at MAFF, trying to be imaginative.

It seems to me that, whoever ordered the massacre, only two explanations for it are possible. The first is that these people couldn't care less if skylarks are squashed flat, because skylarks are not worth anything. The second is that they hadn't realised that most wild birds nest in the spring. It is hard to decide which explanation is the right one, though the first is certainly more flattering. At the root of the matter must surely be these agri-business courses they run at the agricultural colleges, which all go-ahead young farmers attend. I even attended one myself once. I remember one keen young lecturer introducing us to the joys of 'response curves', 'efficiency diagrams' and 'pushing crops to the limit' (a good phrase this – imagine those sweating vegetables). There was not much reference to skylarks, or even the seasons. The sort of advice the farmers were given was along the lines of: 'Ah yes, a clear case of deflationary growth yield here. I think I can recommend something to help you incline your graph a little more steeply' – with the help of the latest poison, or an even more powerful machine.

Perhaps it is just as well that there was not always complete amity between these ardent young men and the farmers. In the opinion of the response-curve expert, some farmers were simply not pushing their vegetables hard enough. 'We give them all this experimental equipment when they ought to be pushing a brush.'

When I pointed this out to a farmer, his rejoinder was colourful, and to the effect that those college kids wouldn't recognise good soil if they fell into a hole in the ground. I thought it would be tactful at this point to leave them alone to discuss things further. The farmer owned a great deal of really quite vicious-looking machinery.

Shoot them all

Toads and Ruddy Ducks receive a regular airing in Twitcher's column. Like Carstairs, he finds the ongoing romance of the New World Ruddy and the Old World White-headed Duck irresistible. Their persecution by the unromantic RSPB raises their tragedy to the level of Romeo and Juliet.

Years ago I spent several days birdwatching at the Coto Donana in Spain, then still a wilderness of *campos* and *marismas* not yet ruined by pollution and tourist rubbish. One of the birds we were after was the White-headed Duck, a funny looking waterbird with a blue beak and an upright tail as perky as a beagle's. Yet despite having Europe's finest marshland at the tips of its webbed feet, the useless White-head refused to come out and be twitched, and remained skulking somewhere in the *hacienda*. Some species just don't *try*, do they?

Some years on, I thought I had finally tracked it down, in a gravel pit in the West Midlands, of all places. But this was not a *carte blanche* White-head but the next best thing, the Ruddy Duck. Unlike White-heads, Ruddy Ducks don't cower in the reeds but barge about flaunting their blue beaks as though they own the place. Which they don't, it being nothing but a laddish immigrant from America, via Peter Scott's wildfowl collection at Slimbridge. Now the RSPB, the bird-loving protection body, wants to have them all shot.

The reason (and let's not tell the West Midlands Bird Club, whose logo proclaims the Ruddy Duck as their favourite bird) is that our ruddy Ruddy Ducks have been going to the Coto Donana for their holidays, where, needless to say, they behave like a pack of soccer supporters. Yes, there was quacking in the *marismas* last summer, when the Ruddy Duck bucks discovered the White-head wallflowers cringing in the reeds. Now genetics are taking their gruesome course, and Spanish bird-lovers have spotted a lot of suspicious looking baby ducks with pink heads and displaying unruly behaviour.

The RSPB are quite right to demand vengeance. Soccer supporters are a deeply unpleasant aspect of British life, and it would do our image abroad no end of good to shoot a few of them. But the real villain behind the outrage must be the United States, which shelters enormous numbers of these Ruddy Ducks, and even provides them with expensive wildfowl sanctuaries. Fortunately, I see our chaps in counter-intelligence have not been idle. We learn that America is suffering from a mysterious invasion of a large kind of British house spider, harmless enough over here, but which hurls itself biting and scratching at any American it encounters. We also hear that our native Death Cap, said to be the world's most poisonous toadstool, is spreading rapidly in New World woods, shouldering aside the delicious native ceps and chantarelles. The great British counter-invasion seems well under way.

What else can be done to avenge the poor, dishonoured White-heads? Personally I have hopes of the Natterjack Toad. Now and again you catch a strange gleam in that beast's normally torpid eyes, suggestive of an extreme malevolence, of a teeming, simmering paranoia. Over here we have long been accustomed to keeping them down, confining them to remote and uninhabited nature reserves. But there is no telling what the toad might do, given unlimited new opportunities to roam and multiply. We all know a Yank or two across the water. Perhaps it is time we started thinking about this year's Christmas presents.

* * *

Scrap the lot

Twitcher's bright idea for changing the names of everything into numbers in case they offend anybody was ahead of its time. I have never met any of these people who are so ready to be comprehensively offended, but they obviously wield tremendous influence.

Many twitchers spend their lives in blissful ignorance of something called the British Ornithological Union. We could be forgiven for assuming it is one of those leftovers from the olden days, with a current membership of three, like, say, the Peterborough Appreciation Society, or the Black Rat Fan Club. In fact it is an immensely self-important little body that takes upon itself the sole authority to replace bird names if it decides they are in any way politically incorrect. For example, the BOU (pronounced 'boo') has decreed that the robin is henceforth to be known as the Eurasian Robin. Anyone writing about mere robins will have their manuscript returned in pieces, and may well be visited by a BOU representative accompanied by a policeman.

If birders are getting themselves into trouble, I dread to think what the BOU will do when it decides to take a look at our wild flowers. In America, where they are normally a step or two ahead even of the BOU, there is a campaign to stamp out all offensive botanical names. Melvin

Hunter, editor of *The Scientist*, has produced 'a black list' (are you sure you should be calling it that, Melvin?) of incorrect plants, which include Jew's Ear, Pansy and Sweet William, a grossly offensive name, especially to pretty boys called William. 'These names cast an ugly shadow across society,' shouts 'Melve'. 'It's a *very serious social issue.*'

Well, we can't exactly afford to throw the first stone, can we? Consider our homegrown 'Bastard Balm', a clearly unacceptable dig at lone-parent families. Or 'Hairy Violet', a blatant insult to bald pansies, or 'Maiden Pink', which disparages unmarried ladies who vote Liberal. For my part, I'm terrified of causing offence by writing about a protected species called the Starfruit, an unpleasantly élitist name, suggesting that other fruits are not stars. Would 'Asterisk-fruit' be an improvement, I wonder, or perhaps 'Equal-opportunity Fruit'? No, I know! – Let's call it Correct Fruit, or better still, Eurasian Correctfruit, in case it occurs in Eurasia, wherever that is.

On further reflection, I think it might be wiser to scrap English names altogether, and just give them all numbers. Young people seem so much more at home with numbers than with words. Don't you agree?

* * *

New uses for rhinoceroses

The last couple of lines in the following touching piece were cut by the editor, I'm not sure why. Let's write and ask him.

Distressing scenes from the African plains ruined my enjoyment of a television programme about rhinoceroses. Hoping to witness placid scenes of mud-bathing or horn-flaunting, or whatever rhinos get up to, what did I find? A zealous young vet chasing the poor beast with a chain-saw. In one grisly sequence, 'Dr Michael' is seen slicing off the rhino's proud nasal appendage. In the next he is poised over the poor beast's wrinkled bottom waving an enormous syringe. The well-meaning vet explains that it is all being done in the rhino's best interests. If they cut off the most valuable bits, maybe the poachers will leave them alone.

I don't know. Surely the whole *point* (as it were) of a rhinoceros is its mighty horn. Sawing it off will obviously turn the defenestrated pachyderm into a laughing stock in the animal world. Perhaps Dr Michael will decide to help the hedgehog next by shaving off its spines, or the fox by chopping off its brush (I doubt any self-respecting huntsman would want to follow a *tail-less* fox).

But even if they can no longer steal its horn, Dr Michael's well-meant experiments in animal topiary may only encourage the poachers to steal other, perhaps more vital parts. The rhino's trotters, for example. Removing the animal's legs would seem therefore to be a sensible precaution. The rhinos could then be dragged into well-guarded compounds, piled up like frozen turkeys, and fed with lentil soup through a straw, saving a lot of bother for all concerned.

But a long-term solution is still needed. As Dr Michael explains, 'it's nice to have wild animals, but they're a luxury in many ways'. The only way the rhino will be spared is if some use can be found for it. I'm sure the vet will think of something. If we can't ride on their backs, or borrow various bits of them, perhaps the wind energy of their mighty posterior blasts could be harnessed to provide power for, say, a small safari hotel or an outback gas station. When I was very small, I heard a rhinoceros fart. It is something I've never been able to forget.

The Andalusian hemipode has been known to eat
human beings when annoyed

Consolation for foresters

Twitcher was almost alone in calling for the privatisation of the Forestry Commission as simple revenge for all the damage it had done. A lot of conservationists would probably be happy if the state owned everything, really. It's a nursery thing.

What has got into my fellow conservationists, rushing to the barricades to support the Forestry Commission in its hour of need? The Commission's future, we learn, is 'under review'. These are terrifying words for any state employee. Perhaps the Treasury has at last broken through the Commission's outer defence ring of pet ministers and tame politicians and discovered what a shambles lurks beneath its empty bragging about employment in rural areas and producing oxygen for the planet. In fact the FC has wrecked half the ancient woods in Britain at no economic benefit whatever, and then sold off the ruins at a profit to cash-strapped wildlife trusts (who get their money from you and me). If I was in power I'd make the nasty, arrogant brutes apologise for all their vandalism and lies, and then kick them out without a pension, still less a gong. And then sue them.

What my fellow conservationists are really afraid of is private ownership. At heart most of them are believers in Mummy State, and want to 'keep ahold of nurse for fear of finding something worse'. But could the Forestry Commission's spruce forests really be made even worse, even more gloomy and monotonous, than they are already?

Perhaps it is possible to feel regretful at watching yet another national institution on its way to the pulp-mill. But then you think of all the ignorant and annoying things the FC got up to during its days of power: sucking up to the timber companies that are ruining the Highlands, ordering us to kill grey squirrels, and their odious little homilies about the role of the 'community forests' in protecting us from global warming. No, let it be privatised.

Perhaps the Forestry Commission should turn in its hour of need to the Centre for Harmony in Gloucester, run by a retired headmaster called Rod Nicholson. Mr Nicholson teaches us that hugging trees is a wonderful way of releasing inner tensions. When you find a tree that appeals to you, you must wrap your limbs around the trunk and clutch it to your bosom, he says. This allows 'the tree energy to work with you to dissolve the resistances in your body so that your physical energies flow harmoniously and healingly through your whole beingness', according to Mr Nicholson.

The FC's Director, the amusing Australian 'Cobber' Cutler, and his obedient, simpering underlings, should each seek out a suitable Sitka spruce tree to cling to, trying to ignore the sharp spines and showers of droppings and evil-smelling needles that may cascade down on top of them as the harmony flows healingly through their whole beingness. Not only should this console them in their distress, but it may even manage to save one or two of their beloved spruce trees when the men with the chain-saws arrive.

A Fish

The bird disappeared, and reappeared again once more. This time I thought I could see its prey was a fish. Stenga looked up, and I was looking down wondering what it could be, this fish, when my query was answered.

From the other side of the firth a man came walking over the glistening mud, as the tide had fallen a lot since we had been there longer than I had at first thought we would be. I asked him what the fish was. He looked at the dog. Stenga looked back at the man and me. 'Roll-mop herring,' he said. The man, not the dog.

1994

Last rites

In America they have a field guide on squashed wildlife, illustrated entirely by silhouettes. It used to be tough being a duck in Ramsbury. Since then we've put up signs: 'For duck's sake, slow down', 'Give them a duck's chance'. *They still get squashed.*

Spring is awakening in my swamp. The spent fireworks and cans of Christmas lager have been hidden by the burgeoning herbage, and instead we find ducks, ducks in all sorts of shapes and attitudes, lots of ducks, and all of them squashed flat.

As my mallards disperse from their winter quarters on the river, they usually take a day or two to orientate themselves and discover that the road through the swamp is no place to sit around playing ducks and drakes. Not that they are ever given that long by the convoy of commuters flashing past each morning. Vroom-quack-splat! – and there goes another of my little friends. One day there were six of them out there, distributed in various broken attitudes over a hundred yards of tarmac.

The trick to prising old friends off the road is to wait until the sun has dried them out a bit. Then, with a couple of kicks they come loose, allowing you to pick up the remains by one akimboed leg and frisbee them into the hedge. The corpses usually stay in one place for their last flight. *Transit gloria*, Bandy-legs. A far, far better thing, Wiggle-bottom.

... And then one day in July, Coleman's work on Amphisbaenids was brought to a sudden end

Helping Gummer

Whoever coined such terms as 'Sites of Special Scientific Interest' (SSSI), 'Areas of Outstanding Natural Beauty' (AONB), 'Environmentally Sensitive Areas' (ESAs) and 'Non-Governmental Organisations' (NGOs) might have been mustard at planning, but he had a cloth ear for English. Back in 1994, I still had a state-ist view of things, since corrected.

Mr John Selwyn Gummer, this month's Environment Secretary, has been sent a list of suggested replacement names for the notoriously bureaucratic term, 'Site of Special Scientific Interest'. The recommended one, the winner of a competition got up by Friends of the Earth and *The Daily Telegraph*, is *National Heritage Area*. Hm. A bit dull. A much better one was *Special Areas for Environment, Wildlife and You* (catchphrase: 'Is there a SAFEWAY near YOU?').

The trouble is that SSSIs have nothing to do with YOU (or me). Most of them are private land, without access rights, and subject to management agreements that are strictly secret, despite costing YOU (and me) at least £20 million a year. In fact, SSSI is not such a bad acronym. Between the threatening hiss of an angry landowner and the sigh of an English Nature 'Customer Service Team' as it hands over another bag of cash, it captures in an almost onomatopoeic way the sound of the transaction. 'More cash, quick! Hisssss.' 'Here we are, Sir. Have a nice day (sssigh).'

My own suggestion, which is based both on the financial aspect and the landowner's perception of his public responsibilities, is Site Of Daily Offerings or SOD OFF (catchphrase: 'SOD OFF my property'). Apart from being catchy and memorable, this phrase should also appeal to anyone who has disinterestedly watched the conservation process in practice.

Over to you, Gummer.

STOP PRESS

Ten years on: public access to SSSIs had improved, and even larger bags of cash were being handed over for their maintenance. They are still called SSSIs.

The way we were

That year I wrote the obligatory book for a TV series called Postcards from the Country. *It featured a lot of interviews with elderly rural folk who thought the whole place had gone to the dogs.*

The lady from the BBC cracked open one of my books and was silent for a minute or two. 'You know, Peter,' she said at last, 'I think we are going to need something a *fraction* lighter than this.' The conviction with which she said this made me wonder, not for the first time, whether I was being altogether wise to accept John Birt's golden penny and write a book for the BBC. Meanwhile, Frank the designer seemed to be having a little trouble with another of my books. 'Woodja, woodja, woo,' he murmured after a bit, with a sort of fixed smile.

'You see, Peter,' continued Felicity, for that was her name – 'I *can* call you Peter, can't I? – the viewer won't want anything *too* educational at half-past-eight. What they expect is something to wash over them while they recover from Eastenders. That is why we run programmes about the countryside – they're very soothing to watch so long as there isn't much talking. The viewer wants to see lots of horse-drawn ploughs, trawlers with sails and rugged crofters in their knitted jerseys, while the band plays Greensleeves, or, in the case of the crofters, 'The Muckin' o' Geordie's Byre'.

Felicity ticked off successful examples of the genre on her fingers. 'There's Michael Wood, of course. The girls love his tight jeans and boyish grin, and they buy his books to give to their mums. Then there's Michael Palin. The mums all *adore* him, and buy his books to give to their daughters. He's got lovely legs, too,' sighed Felicity, irrelevantly.

I'm not certain what she was getting at here, especially as Felicity had just confused my book, *The New Naturalists*, with nudist bathing parties in Norfolk. Anyway, the upshot of our meeting is that I must go away and write them a sample chapter on the rural delights of the past, with some puffins and maybe a pair of tight herdsman's trousers thrown in. I'm really looking forward to this job. The book is to be called *Sepia Memories* or *Smocks n' Frocks*, or some such rubbish.

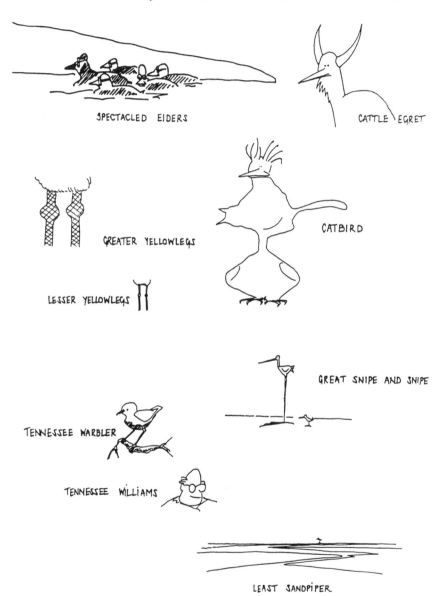

SPECTACLED EIDERS

CATTLE EGRET

GREATER YELLOWLEGS

CATBIRD

LESSER YELLOWLEGS

GREAT SNIPE AND SNIPE

TENNESSEE WARBLER

TENNESSEE WILLIAMS

LEAST SANDPIPER

Happy Christmas (except the English)

More about Scottish Natural Heritage. Its bogus zeal for all things Celtic seems to have been part of a clumsy effort to woo public opinion north of the Border.

'Scottish Natural Heritage, you have chosen the Gaelic language for your Christmas card this year. You have sixty seconds to say why. Starting. Now.'

Perhaps 'SNH's' sudden interest in the Gaelic language has nothing to do with Magnus Magnusson, the noted cheese salesman and SNH 'chairperson'. It may, for ought I know, be a bee in the bonny bonnet of Roger, Magnusson's deputy, who graduated in Liverpool. I do not know how many Christmas cards Roger (whose name translated into Gaelic is Wodger) has printed. There are perhaps a few hundred Gaelic speakers left in the furthermost recesses of the Outer Hebrides, but they all speak English perfectly well. The card shows a pretty picture of a squirrel. This is no use either. There are no squirrels in the Outer Hebrides for the good reason that there aren't any trees.

I expect SNH, or Dualchas Nadair na h-Alba as it prefers to be known, is trying its best to look correct. 'We work with the Scottish people to care for our natural heritage,' is its sexy slogan. Notice, by the way, the clever way in which the words 'Scottish', 'natural' and 'heritage' are subtly woven in. In Gaelic the slogan runs thus: '*Nollaig agus na bliadhna uire oirbh bho*'. Spoken in the brisk, lilting tones of an ancient language, these words must surely remind anyone of the conversations of Bill and Ben the Flowerpot Men, the amusing children's serial.

My older readers will need no reminding that Bill and Ben spent their time messing about with Little Weed, now an endangered species. This must surely be the message Dualchas Nadair na h-Alba is hinting at, in its roundabout way, and a touching one it is. We must all learn to nurture our little weeds, and also squirrels, should there be any. Congratulations, Mag and Wodge, the Heritage Men. Next time, I hope they do one in Icelandic, too.

* * *

Flushland

'Protecting' a nature reserve or beauty spot often involves building a car park, access roads and facilities, of which the most vital is an enormous toilet block. There's no escaping it, some people take one look at nature and rush for the loo.

As a jobbing conservationist I get some pretty terrible assignments sometimes, but I think the bottom of the pit was when I was asked to prepare a gazetteer of 'nature sites' for a computer mapping company. What I hadn't realised was that by nature sites what they really want is nature *sights*. 'We want to highlight places that have a special appeal,' read my instructions, '... places that stimulate and delight, and don't simply pacify people.' What seems to stimulate and delight people most are car-parks, wheelchair access and elaborate toilet facilities. It is well known that grand scenery and spectacular wildlife bring on an urgent desire to pee. After that, they will obviously want to eat some hamburgers.

'Are you sure it isn't heritage centres or public gardens you are after,' I ventured, in my innocence. 'No,' they explained patiently, 'we want *nature*

sites.' 'Well you can't buy hamburgers on St Kilda you know,' I laughed weakly. 'Tell me about the *Facilities* there. Can you drive-in? Is there a ranger service? Don't forget the fax and e-mail number.'

It must say something about the British that I could find only about 20 'nature sites' that measured up to these exacting criteria. But by hook or, more likely, by crook, I was determined to include St Kilda. As a World Heritage Site it is going to get some Facilities sooner or later. Anticipating this development, I devised a complete St Kilda Experience package or Puff-In, with a huge Kildaburger Kabin and 'Gannets', the chippie with a difference. Presiding over it all will be Flushland, the Last Toilet in Europe, 'The Loo with a View'. Get your slogan T-shirt now: 'I peed in the bogs o' St Kilda' or 'St Kilda: last pit stop before America'.

Car stickers are free.

* * *

A shotgun wedding

Gummer, the diminutive but well-loved environment secretary, has exciting news. With Prime Minister John Major looking on, he announces a period of consultation preceding a possible review of the pros and cons of drafting a green paper on the theoretical merger of English Nature and the Countryside Commission, the exciting heritage bodies. 'It might be a massive step forward,' he squeaks.

English Nature has been reorganised two or three times already in its short life, and you would think it would welcome a break from half-baked government reviews. But no, its chief executive professes himself 'greatly excited' by the news. In this he differs from one of his senior directors who was quoted as being only 'quite excited'. And, it seems, this want of excitement grows as we descend the chain. 'I was slightly excited yesterday,' – 'I took an aspirin on Tuesday' – until you reach the boot boys and scientific specialists at the bottom, who seem to have quite different excitements. By contrast, the Countryside Commission does not seem excited at all.

I hope I do not detect a sexual element in all this. There has always been something essentially feminine about the Countryside Commission. I refer not to the curvaceous figures and jaunty little bottoms of its delightful staff so much as the Commission's bustling way of doing things, somewhere between a W.I. bring-and-buy sale and Mrs Goodbody, the parish do-gooder. English Nature, on the other hand, has inherited the masculine disposition of the forgotten Nature Conservancy Council, with its pulpit style and periods of monkish seclusion. Frankly, I'm not sure they are made for one another.

STOP PRESS

As we go to press in 2004, both the former Countryside Commission (now called the Countryside Agency) and English Nature remain individually intact. But not for long. A new 'joined up' rural agency for countryside and wildlife is to be formed. This will also include farm advisers attached to the Government's massive 'Department of Food, Environment, Wildlife, Farming and All Things Rural' department that came into existence when the MAFFIA (aka Ministry of Agriculture, etc) became *persona non-grata* with HM Government.

* * *

Calamity averted

I am happy to report that the jovial Robert Key is still MP for Salisbury and very much alive, although he is now Sir Key rather than plain Mr.

It seems that I have traduced Mr Robert Key, the amiable, conifer-loving MP for Salisbury. I had heard that this man was backing a road scheme called the Brown Alternative which would have turned one of the best remaining chalk downs in Wiltshire into a smoking post-nuclear desert. Hearing of this, as I say, I may, in my righteous anger, have said something along the lines of: 'Will no one rid me of this turbulent former minister of state for transport, construction and traffic lights (now minister for football)? '.

Now a reader tells me Mr Key is innocent. Instead of the dreaded Brown Alternative, he had merely advocated widening the existing road a bit. And, apparently, he wasn't there anyway. He had already moved on to his important football job. I hope the four armed knights who were seen boarding a bus to Salisbury shortly after my hasty exclamation (which, I

HEALTH AND SAFETY ADVICE TO FIELD WORKERS: 1

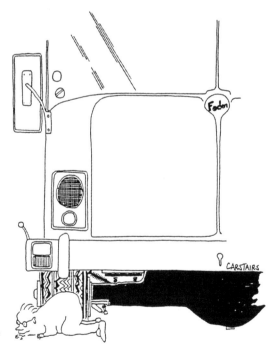

STAFF MUST ENSURE THAT THEY CAN BE SEEN EASILY WHEN LOOKING FOR WILDLIFE ON ROADS AND MOTORWAYS

insist, was made on the spur of the moment) were diverted by that town's excellent shopping facilities and architectural attractions. I hope, too, that Mr Key was nowhere near the Cathedral that day.

This sort of little mistake could be avoided if ministers managed to stay in their seats for more than a few hours. At the moment they are bouncing in and out of office like bungee jumpers. In the weeks that must elapse before my words are printed on this page, we may have greeted and then waved farewell to three or four more ministers, each of them an enthusiast for different brown, pink or green alternatives.

The solution must be to call them all Mr Key. It is hard enough to tell the difference between one smarmy young politician and another nowadays. They all look and act like estate agents who have just sold a dud house over the odds. Few know or care what their names are, nor want to listen to the piffle they spout. In the event that we are ever given a transport minister with views independent of the road lobby, we could always change the name, perhaps to Master Wise or Miss Delectable.

* * *

Not always welcome

Bossiness is a common failing of public bodies. Imparting information, unfortunately, isn't.

I must have known Freeman's Marsh, one of the common lands of Hungerford, for over twenty years. It hasn't changed much, except for the usual ebb and flow of the wild. Sometimes it floods and sometimes it doesn't. You may see a Kingfisher here or you may see it over there. The great thing is that you can just wander about as you please, as every artisan and peasant of the Town and Manor has been able to do since the days of John of Gaunt, whoever he was.

Unfortunately some people just can't leave well alone. Great coloured signboards have now sprung up on the Marsh to 'welcome' you. The word WELCOME is in big arty letters to make you feel even more warm and loved. But in the heritage world, 'welcome' doesn't mean quite what you think it means. It is code for I OWN THIS, YOU BEHAVE YOURSELF. Sure enough, below the arty letters is a sinister warning to STAY WITHIN THE SSSI. Stray beyond the SSSI, and it seems you are not WELCOME anymore. Maybe you would be chased by mad bulls. Perhaps you would fall off the edge of the world into a void. I don't know. We are not told.

To avoid such dangers, I hope there will soon be more signs along the boundary to tell you when you are no longer WELCOME. Under the stiff black letters NOT WELCOME, which, I suggest, should drip with red drops, there should be pictures of the unwelcome things that might happen to you if you strayed from the safety of the SSSI. Cow pats, wasps, flocks of dangerous looking geese, lurking jungles of stinging nettles. Fortunately urban 'visitors' are easily frightened by wilderness. The unpleasant drawing I prepared of a homicidal kingfisher may not be needed.

Quiet day on the Hanglands

Years ago, when I was still warden on a nature reserve near the Fens, I was ringing birds a lot. One day, whilst walking through the mature coppice, I heard a strange call. Suddenly a fox ran out in front of where I was and jumped into the air at a passing Levant Sparrowhawk. The falcon fell to the ground, crushing a stand of Autumn Ladies-tresses as it fell. I bent down and in its beak was a Pallas Leaf Warbler. Meanwhile, the local gamekeeper appeared and shot the fox.

Needless to say, I caught no birds that day which had turned out to be disappointing to say the least. I've often found that with Thursdays.

Old Countryman
Strathpeffer

1995

Not loved

I pinched this idea from an article in The Ecologist *I hoped no one had read.*

Perhaps one of the reasons why the European Union is not loved as much as it might be in Britain is that it has no floral emblem to rally around. England has its rose, Scotland its thistle, France her fleur-de-lys. As far as I know the EU hasn't so much as a daisy. Where can we find a plant to symbolise the Union in all its wonderfully diverse legislative aspects, from inspecting bananas to ... well, inspecting completely different bananas. Could there be a suitable specimen for such a body?

I think there is one. Float forward the humble duckweed. Note the sterling qualities of this estimable plant. Not only does it occur all across Europe, but there is nothing about it that any reasonable person could possibly object to. What is more, it echoes EU practice in all sorts of way. Duckweed drifts aimlessly, at the whim of random drifts and currents, but multiplies with terrifying speed, depriving other life of air and light. It is more or less sterile, producing few flowers and no fruit. Internally it is of a spongy nature, with large air pockets between the cells, and little in the way of communicating ducts.

Better still, a duckweed is utterly standardised. Though there are billions of them, they are all exactly the same, like EU-approved bananas, for example.

Some Euro-bore might complain that the duckweed isn't grand enough. In that case, we have a candidate in reserve, the Brussels sprout, characterised as 'a vegetable with layer upon layer of spirally arranged leaves facing inwards, protecting the tiny central growing point'.

Not allowed

More about the law. It is widely believed that it's a crime to pick wild flowers or touch a wild animal. The true legal situation is, of course, more complicated. Twitcher explains ...

Did you know that if you shine a torch at a hedgehog you are breaking the law? According to Dr Pat Morris, the dormouse expert, there are uncountable laws concerning our wild mammals, many of them as stupid as they are unknown. Far from wishing, to amend them, the Government isn't even aware they exist, to judge by its own booklet on the subject, which leaves out whole rafts of gobbledegook on badgers, seals and shrews. Hence, at the moment you can skin a hedgehog alive but not disturb it. You can set alight to a red squirrel's tail but not wear its fur. You must not touch a newt but you can empty a concrete mixer into its pond.

I suppose we must welcome any attempt to sort it all out, and stop ill-bred children from sticking lighted bangers into toads, or whatever they do nowadays. Yet the result would almost certainly be an ever bigger mess. In the vanished days when children were allowed to play in the countryside, we might have done the occasional unkind thing to tadpoles or nestlings that we are ashamed of now. All the same, it might have been a necessary part of childhood, for there's no getting away from it, children are cruel little beasts. I, for example, once clouted a stag beetle with a cricket bat as it blundered past. But I have been rather fond of stag beetles ever since, and I suspect that that clout sealed our future relationship.

Those who claim to have never harmed a living thing turn into fish-like people with leek-and-water diet fads and no real interest in the countryside or its wildlife. These are the people that have forbidden us to shine torches at hedgehogs.

* * *

A tasteless prank

The law is curiously ambivalent about invasive animals like Signal Crayfish and Grey Squirrels. On the one hand you need a license to catch them. On the other, once caught, it is illegal to put them back. What do you do when you have a squirrel by the tail? Let the FC explain.

Today we learn that the Forestry Commission has refused to allow the planting of beech trees at a site where beautiful beech trees have been grown for hundreds of years, on the grounds that it is 'not native' to that part of England. I suppose this is part of a public relations offensive aimed at showing that the FC has turned over a new leaf. But from the body that has covered England from head to foot with alien conifers, this really is a bit rich.

In another dramatic move, the Commission urges the public to slaughter any Grey Squirrels that might fall into our hands. A Ron Melville has been put in charge of the Control Group to crack down on squirrels. Should we happen to catch one, 'you must kill it', instructs Mr Melville, 'because it is a non-native species and cannot be returned to the wild'.

If the Commission is really serious about getting rid of non-native species, it should have its hands full with Sitka Spruce for the next century or two, including the 200,000 hectares of ancient woodland that it tried to destroy and re-plant with conifers between 1945 and 1980. But I wonder whether they are being wise to pick on squirrels. Many people are rather fond of squirrels, and couldn't care tuppence whether they are non-native or not. Moreover, squirrels have a particularly nasty bite. Squirrel researchers can usually be recognised by the interesting pattern of scars on their faces and hands. I hope the Commission is not going to make itself a laughing stock, or get sued by those bitten by squirrels, or end up being even more unpopular than it is already. That would be a terrible shame.

I would advise anyone who wants to take up this new sport of squirrel-bashing to practice first on something smaller and more helpless, like an earthworm. In her book, *Squirrels*, the late Monica Shorten (who had been severely bitten) supplies some ingenious recipes for squirrel pie and squirrel curry. The tail goes into the stock.

Several months on, the Forestry Commission's crackdown on grey squirrels seems to have ended in fiasco. As I warned they would, the squirrels have turned on their oppressors with a vengeance. According to the *British Medical Journal*, squirrel bites are now more frequent than those of cats, rats, ferrets or gerbils. They have not yet caught up with dogs and pet rabbits, but if this goes on it is only a matter of time. Last year no fewer than 25 people in Edinburgh alone were taken, bleeding from savage squirrel bites, to 'major casualty units'. By urging members of the public to slaughter squirrels, the Forestry Commission has much to answer for. It was a thoughtless and sadistic prank, and they should be thoroughly ashamed of themselves. Frankly, I think it is time this body was put out of its misery.

Contrary to the claims of animal rights campaigners, most animals are quite capable of looking after themselves. I have myself been attacked by an angry ladybird and several kinds of fish. Recently someone was carried to the clinic after being bitten on the finger by a prawn. As I often warn, the countryside is full of terrifying dangers. Visitors from the city should always remember to put on squirrel-proof clothing and smother themselves with prawn repellent before setting out. And never on any account leave their vehicle.

* * *

Youth speaks out

I visited the protesters' camp at the Newbury bypass one cold January day, handing out whisky and shortbread to the shivering protesters, who seemed to be mostly nice, idealistic boys and girls from prosperous middle class homes. One group was shunned by all the rest: 'Don't give anything to them'. 'Why not?' 'Because they're meat-eaters.'

Emerging from writing a big book about the past is like waking up from a Rip van Winkle-style snooze. Suddenly all about you are young persons 'speaking in tongues' about things one has never heard of before, in their delightful language of grunts and sniggers. Clearly I have some catching

ɛ *Ear defenders*
In use they are slightly awkward to fit into the ear, but once in they certainly stay there.

They are obviously much lighter than ear muffs.

Gloves
Disposable, clear, plastic gloves have been tried out

Medical wipes
These are small hand wipes so several are needed to clean dirty hands.

"I will certainly use all three items for stalking in the future".

CARSTAIRS

up to do after finishing my long book, *The New Naturalists*, so brilliantly reviewed by the decreasingly hirsute, but young-in-heart David Pearman. Of course *my* New Naturalists are only new in the sense that the New Forest is new. Everything has to be new once, but I'm afraid my title may seem a touch ironical to the youngsters. What are the new new naturalists getting up to, one wonders. With thoughts of writing a sequel, I decide to watch a television documentary about the protesters up there in the trees at Newbury.

Their spokesman, a dreadlocked yoof wearing a sort of bone necklace, explains: 'We're here because we love nature, and all that shit'.

And lo! Suddenly the idea was born. *Nature and All That Shit. A Young Person's Guide to Saving the Planet*. I can see this masterpiece becoming a compulsory text for the GCSE environmental studies syllabus, with its useful tips on tree-climbing skills and tunnel-digging possibilities. The sequel, *More Droppings from the World of Nature*, may be better suited to advanced level students.

* * *

Save the bunnies

Twitcher formed the pressure group LACBOB to save bunnies from wicked foxes, and served it as Lord High President for Life. LACBOB was a subtle attempt to introduce ecological notions, like food-chains, into the hunting 'debate'. Was anyone listening? I say, hello, out there. Hello?

When you think about it, bunny rabbits get a pretty raw deal out of life. We humans hunt them down using snares, gas, shot and biological weapons. Almost any animal with an all-meat diet enjoys turning them into chutney, even stoats and weasels half their size. And according to Douglas Adams, author of *Watership Down*, the bunny-broker's Bible, even rabbits hate rabbits. Big ones kick the butts of middling ones, which beat the hell out of little ones, which probably limp away to mug a field mouse. What is it with all this hatred and violence? Living in the country, you can hardly bring in the milk without witnessing more dead bunnies. Is this the caring 1990s, or what?

The new Bill to protect wild mammals will only make things worse for the poor, persecuted bunny rabbit. This is because the promoters of the Bill, and their fawning, deluded public, are not interested in the sufferings of our furry, jumping friends. They care only about the fox, which they think is a sort of doggy. The fact that the fox is the most cruel and implacable of all the enemies of the bunny is of no concern to them. All that this wretched new law to ban hunting will achieve is to add to the already vast number of vulpine bunny-muggers marauding about in town and country, with their wicked red eyes and dripping slavering fangs.

It is time for we Chums of the Bunny to take direct action. We have banded together to form a League Against Cruel Bullies of Our Bunnies, or LACBOB, as it is known (Slogans: Rabs are Fabs! Get That Rabbit Habit!). As the only body with the real interests of herbivorous mammals at heart, LACBOB demands that hunting be made compulsory for any able-bodied rustic between 35 and 60. (We tend not to trust anyone under the tender age of 35, fearing they have all been brainwashed by their tepid decaffeinated teachers.) My own small contribution to the debate is to campaign for the release of wolves and other dangerous animals which are known to enjoy catching and eating foxes (among other things). These big, fierce animals will of course benefit from the new law, and anyone found threatening my wolves, bears, wolverines etc will end up on a corrective course and lectured to by gap-toothed, lisping animal-lovers. Surplus parts of dead foxes will be distributed to left-wing town halls by LACBOB agents. It is time these sadistic bunny-haters got a dose of their own medicine.

* * *

The last laugh

The idea of the space shuttle being grounded by malignant woodpeckers made a perfect story for Twitcher. People often tell me stories that 'would be perfect for Twitcher', but they don't understand. It's the little things that get the juices flowing.

The next flight of the space shuttle, *Discovery* has been cancelled. During a routine inspection, curious holes were found in the insulating material

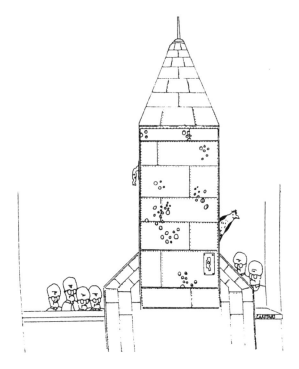

surrounding the fuel tank. Had the rocket been launched it might well have blown to bits. Was this the work of terrorists? Had some technician ordered 'Swiss-style' open-holed insulation instead of the plain sort? (well, these things happen). No, the cause of this sabotage lay nearby, roosting in the trees surrounding the base. Step forward a kind of woodpecker called the Yellow-shafted Flicker. Filling in their holes will cost the American taxpayer $100,000, on top of all the inconvenience.

But what is to stop the Yellow-shafted Flicker from drilling new holes? This is the task of a special anti-bird force, the US Bird Investigation Review and Determent team, or BIRD, as it is known. BIRD has come up with several ingenious suggestions. Their first idea was to 'strategically place' model owls, with an inbuilt 'high-pitched siren' capability, around the rocket. When this failed to fool the woodpeckers, BIRD experts were reported to be considering painting the fuel tank blue – it being well known that woodpeckers dislike the colour blue – or spraying it with cabbage-flavoured water (for woodpeckers dislike boiled cabbage even more than the colour blue) – or even employing a shaman to summon unhelpful spirits. Why not just shoot the birds and be done with them? Because, for some reason, the launch pad is in the middle of a nature reserve. Nature reserves really count for something in America.

But what are the woodpeckers doing on the rocket in the first place? The obvious reason is that they were mounting a protest at being called Yellow-shafted Flickers. Insulting innocent birds with names like babblers, drongos, boubous and what have you is a distressing part of the foreign avian scene. Now, it seems, not content with making a laughing stock out of their own avifauna, these smirking revisionists are intent on assaulting our own good, solid Saxon bird names. But perhaps, as the woodpeckers' behaviour suggests, they are making a grave mistake. I'd hate to see the state of their fruit gardens once the Eurasian Ethnic Turdus (formerly Blackbird) gets wind of its new name.

* * *

Techno-twitching

Richard Mabey gave me this one. Ever since, I have eyed bird twitchers closely for signs of new technology. I'd like to see a super-pager that would bounce them up and down like a pogo stick.

Despite the byline at the top of this page, I seldom meet real twitchers. At this time of year my swamp is overrun with birds of all sorts, all screeching their heads off, and that is quite enough ornithological excitement for me. Perhaps this explains why I don't even understand why they are called twitchers. Is it a corruption of *tickers*, or do they really 'twitch' when they spot a dowitcher in a ditch, or a murrelet among the mulberries? I assumed that they sort of froze and uttered a low caw-ing noise, like a demented rook. I have a feeling that this might be one of those subjects I don't want to know anything about.

Whether or not these people actually 'twitch', they certainly 'bleep'. This is the call note of their electronic pager, held at the hip like a six-gun. The bleeping indicates that another rarity has turned up at some godforsaken spot hundreds of miles away. The problem with this device is that its urgent bleeping may be lost amid the caws and yelps and general hubbub in any large gathering of twitchers.

Fortunately, technology has galloped to the rescue once again. The thoroughly modern twitcher has now discarded his bleeper in favour of a new instrument, from, I think, Japan, which has no need to bleep. Instead, it vibrates. It is a vibrating pager. Even in the noisiest circumstances, one imagines that its insistent juddering and throbbing down there in the anorak would be hard to ignore. If, therefore, you did find yourself among a crowd of twitchers, all buzzing away like an enormous swarm of bees, you will know their little secret.

This development has appalling implications for me. It may soon be time to change the title of this column. What about *Fidget in the Mire?* No column in the history of the world has ever been called Vibrator in the Swamp.

* * *

Missing naturalists

Amateur naturalists have completely disappeared. Or almost. This Twitcher drew a wonderful response from A.W. Jones of Sussex with whom I had corresponded about plant records: 'How dare you... I am the last surviving one. I have a delapidated khaki rucksack, wear subfuse clothing, have been mistaken for a tramp, rattle with tins etc, have two magnifying glasses, and a pen attached to my person with string, and carry a net. And a notebook (spare in rucksack). After I helped you with Ajuga chamaepitys, too'. Such things make it all worthwhile.

David Attenborough is back, presenting another TV blockbuster, this time about botany. But how much does the great man really know about plants? David admits that he cannot in fact tell one grass from another. But that does not matter because, as he so modestly puts it, 'there are 10,000 amateur naturalists in this country who know ten times more than I do'.

If only it were true. Thirty years ago, perhaps, one still met this endangered species, the amateur naturalist, from time to time. They were often solitary wanderers, but occasionally were to be found in pairs or small groups. Their plumage was invariably drab, but draped with *impedimenta*, such as the obligatory army-surplus knapsack containing jam jars, enamel dishes and magnifying instruments. Their manner was quiet, their speech comely but hesitant. The males wore a trilby hat and a pipe, and their tweeds smelled of tobacco or cheese. Females were rarely seen, but they could occasionally be detected by their rich baritone voice and bulky garments, with matching heavy spectacles. They belonged to a nicer, better, age. Now most of them are gone.

There are perhaps 10,000 *professional* naturalists in this country, if one counts all the time managers, buzz-word analysts, and bubblegum manufacturers so necessary to the workings of the modern nature conservation industry. But Attenborough must have been away a very long time if he imagines that these are the sort of people that trip through the pastures, reeling off Latin names as they go.

Accurate figures are hard to come by in this field. I used to work at the head office of the Nature Conservancy Council, which was then the largest employer of professional ecologists, employing more than 100 people who were technically qualified in biological science. But when the push came to the shove, and plants needed identifying, they intimated that this was not the job of a modern conservationist, who is always far too busy with 'management'. Try the expert, they would say, down in the basement, between the boiler room and the car pool. She would appreciate the company. She doesn't get many callers. At a guess, I'd say that about one percent of professional conservationists could tell a Bent from a Brome (see note) without cheating.

Well it is not enough, it is not enough. Attenborough must have seen all there is to see in Africa and the Antipodes by now. He has neglected the Home Country for too long. It is time he presented a new series, *Wildlife Quest*, devoted to finding out what has happened to the Missing Ten Thousand.

Editor's note: Bents and Bromes are types of grass.

* * *

Eastern Promise

The idea of Mad Mullahs driving couch-potato 'environmentalists' into the fields and woods to make them study botany tickled me. He reminded me of how I got started.

Say what you like about Taliban, the Muslim zealots, but they have sound views on many matters of interest to the British naturalist. They disapprove of television for example, and take a dim view of camcorders. Having once spent a holiday with someone who carried a camcorder everywhere,

I can assert with conviction that on this matter of camcorders, Taliban are most definitely right. They begin by chopping off the camcorder's long lens. Then they start looking a little close to home. They also offer sensible suggestions for public recreation. When asked what there was left to do in Afghanistan, now that television, football and singing have been banned, the Taliban man pointed out that these are not necessary. 'Have you not got the flowers, and the trees?' I think his point was that there is a spiritual dimension to the natural world that is wholly lacking in bingo, television, etc., and that its contemplation will lead to true happiness and contentment.

I'm not sure I can follow this man all the way with some of his other ideas. Most women do not look at their best inside a sort of shapeless sack with eye slits, nor do I approve of beatings for being found smoking or reading girlie magazines. Though many of us have been through a form of Taliban regime at school, where almost anything that was not compulsory resulted in beatings, I honestly doubt whether this is really a wise and humane course in the long run.

The important point is that we open our minds to these refreshing ideas from the east. Westerners have for far too long taken a passive attitude to natural history, watching wildlife perform on the telly while they fill their faces with pizzas and crisps. When I come to power I shall decorate the street lamps with their tellies, confiscate their revolting TV dinners, and send my Mullahs to drive them into the fields and woods with swishing canes. Then we shall get down to a little botany.

Those special mountains

When I was still very small, my father would take me to one side and point out of the window. 'Look well and mark my words, for yonder mountains are special, ' he would opine incomprehensibly. Especially as we lived in a council flat in Oldham.

The years passed, and I became a successful nature warden and countryside diarist. I moved away from the grime and the window and found myself living in a lonely croft house, overlooking the wild country I had come to live in and love. Here I was to live and love for over twenty years until one day I was out on the mountains. I was coming over a rocky ridge with my dog Stenga, when I saw him. A small, twisted man dressed in rags and hobbling along with the aid of a surveyor's ranging pole. I drew closer and listened to his thin speech.

'Look well and mark my words, ' he said thinly in the rising wind (I apologised but onions play havoc with my guts). 'Take care my boy, but I must be going. ' He stumbled off down the mountain. 'Wait, ' I shouted weakly, 'where are you going? '

'Oldham, ' came the reply.

Strathpeffer 1896

84

1996

Passerine paranoia

Whenever I am stuck for an idea for Twitcher, I walk down the lane to the letterbox. Often you see something that gives you the spark, the squished remains of an animal you once knew, or a group of kiddies poking something with a stick. The following happens quite regularly, I swear it.

Normally they start around New Year's Day, but this year we had a fortnight's grace. Today, though, as I drag my feet down the frozen lane to post my letters, the great tits decide to break their long silence. They watch me narrowly as I trudge by. It's pretty clear they have been spying on me for some time. 'Pee-ter, Pee-ter, cheat-er, cheat-er' is the mocking chorus as I post my income tax. I could do without this. 'Watch-it' adds one of them, as I offer a look of wounded innocence. 'Two-a-pee, two-a-pee' carols a third, as I stick my fingers in my ears. You have heard, I'm sure, of a charm of goldfinches, a murmuration of starlings. I propose a *commentary* of great tits. There they sit, so full of themselves, on their overhead perches, like a row of critics, making their uncalled-for remarks. Don't they have anything better to do? Do they do it to you, too?

The great tits remind us that the time is approaching when posting a letter in this village takes you past salvos of ornithological abuse. There will be the usual insincere offers of friendship from the chaffinch: 'Pleese to *meech*-you, hee hee hee, to *meech* you'. Nice. There will be the same sarcastic taunts from the song thrush – 'dear dear dear, cheer-up, cheer-up, kiss-me-quick, kiss-me-quick'.

Another lot of them crouch there and insult you from deep cover. 'Tit, *tit*,' mutters the wren as you stroll past. 'Twit,' adds a goldfinch.

Quickening your pace, you can't help overhearing some unpleasant speculation going on from the bushes. 'Did-he-do-it, did-he-do-it?' That sounds like my enemy the song thrush again. 'If he..., if he,' supposes a coal tit (for we get those as well). If he, what? 'Pee-wee?' suggests a finch. 'Si, si, si, si, si,' agree a moronic chorus of long-tailed tits. The greenfinch just sneers. '*Snee-ee-er.*' Thanks very much. Isn't it time you lot were off to your nature reserve?

The appalling mockery follows you all the way back to the house. 'Sissy,' 'Cheap.' 'Tick.' 'Pink.' 'Quack.' 'Ha ha ha.' I'm no expert, but I think that last one's a woodpecker.

According to the *Daily Telegraph*, most RSPB members live in towns and cities where birds are few, and traffic drowns their noises. Here in Wiltshire, where it is quieter, we prefer flowers. Mind you, correct me if I'm wrong, but is that orchid sticking its tongue out at me?

* * *

A sprat to catch a mackerel

The idea of introducing beavers to Scotland has been pushed to and fro for ten years now, and they still haven't got very far with it. The animal is obviously a stalking horse, a rodent ex machina. *Bring Back The Wolf.*

For the moment I have decided to sit on the fence and listen to the arguments regarding the introduction of wild beavers to Scotland. On the one hand, beavers will cause massive flooding and send a wave of writs and claims gushing in to the Scottish Office. On the other hand, they will damage a lot of trees and annoy the foresters. It is finely balanced, I admit.

Of course, everyone knows the argument isn't really about the beaver at all. The beaver is small beer, a sort of stalking rodent. It is coming to prepare the way for a much more interesting bygone beast, the wolf. The wolf is definitely a good thing. These attractive and intelligent animals are the answer to most of the pressing problems of the Scottish Highlands, from the excess of deer and surplus sheep to the over-abundance of ramblers in loud cagoules. As Bill McKibben, author of *The End of Nature*, reminds us, it is a salutary thing to roam the wild knowing that you are now part of the food-chain. It makes you feel really *eco*. The eco-friendliest possible act of any green's life would be to provide a sustaining meal for a hungry wild animal.

It is in this context that we must welcome the beaver, and any other furry, foreign animals that 'Scottish Natural Heritage', in its wisdom, wishes to bring to Scotland in its desire to *serve the Scottish people*. I think we will manage to outmanoeuvre the woodentops on the Scottish Tourist Board, with the help of our little dam-building friend.

* * *

Gardening hints

More legal notes on what you can and can't do in the privacy of your own garden. Mostly can't.

I am busy with another dreary little job: writing a booklet on how to make a wildlife garden. In fact no one needs a booklet to turn their garden into a jungle. All they have to do is to do nothing. But this is the one thing that gardeners are constitutionally incapable of doing. So I have to tell them which flowers to plant to please the butterflies, and where to hang a

Professor Lortman's re-construction of the Padan orchid from Sarawak, using a hitherto unknown floral formula.

nestbox, and so on, and jolly tedious it is. Fortunately we booklet writers get our own back in the obligatory final page about The Law.

I decide to frighten the life out of these would-be wildlife gardeners. Under the headline, *Wildlife, The Law and YOU*, I describe the terrible penalties that lie in wait for anyone foolish enough to shout at a bat or interfere improperly with a crested newt. I remind them that taking a single seed from a 'listed' wild flower will, as night follows day, surely result in a fine of up to £1,000, as well as a criminal record. They won't know which ones are listed and which ones aren't, and ignorance is no defence in law. It is helpful to add that an average orchid holds about a zillion seeds. £1,000 times a zillion will almost amount to capital punishment, I should think.

Weeding the flower beds is a grey area. You might get away with uprooting a wild plant, so long as you are the landowner and can produce the deeds of property. But if any 'Schedule 1' birds are nesting nearby, it may not be possible to enter your garden at all, which would be a pity if an infestation of bats drives you out of the house.

I propose to round it all off with a ferocious Kitchener-like figure brandishing a pair of handcuffs and pointing angrily at the reader. But my client (who strongly approves of the rest) worries that this might prevent anyone from reading the booklet. 'Readers are glad when their neighbours are punished for pulling faces at a lizard,' she explains, 'but they don't like to feel threatened themselves.' And so, regretfully, the full force of the message has had to be diluted. All the same, it might be a good idea to keep an eye on these wildlife gardeners, trying to tempt wild animals to enter the appalling dangers of a housing estate. If they look up, just shake the handcuffs.

* * *

Skool to the reskew

My memories of school tend to revolve around the cold, the challenging food and the cane, all of which seem quite funny at a safe distance. Here, Twitcher found an environmentally-friendly use for our unique school porridge, which would almost certainly have worked.

Is it possible to get all sentimental about a snail the size of a breadcrumb? Very much so, according to Tony Juniper, the haggard-faced green campaigner. His 'Teletext phone survey' has indicated that 'over 80 percent of those contacted' wanted all work on the Newbury bypass to stop until this snail, called Desmoulin's Snail, can be rescued. But even if his 80 percent (which might be four people) are right, it begs the question of how, exactly, you find and then rescue a dim little thing the size of a breadcrumb.

English Nature's man in Newbury sees no problem. Locating the breadcrumbs and moving them somewhere else is 'an option that we have to give serious attention to', he says. This seems to be English Nature's line at the moment. Find out what lives in the path of a bypass, whether it is a newt, a badger or even a microscopic snail masquerading as a breadcrumb, and then 'rescue' them all. Of course there isn't much to be gained in reality when some fluffy-hatted greenie stuffs his bucket with the wrong sort of snails and empties them into his garden pond straight into the gullets of his goldfish. But it looks good and caring, and that is the main thing nowadays.

If only they had asked me, I could have indicated a better way. In Hawaii, endangered snails have been saved by regular doses of porridge. Large intakes of porridge oats have enabled the snails to build up their strength to the point where they can give 'bigger, carnivorous' snails a well-deserved biffing, rather like Popeye did after he had eaten a can of spinach.

A solution that would make everyone happy is to build the bypass out of hardened porridge. Some might object that porridge is scarcely a substance that could sustain the weight of a speeding truck, let alone an entire division of road protesters. That's all they know. For the usual consideration, I will reveal the formula of the porridge we ate for breakfast every day at my school. This lava-like material, which soon solidified to the consistency of concrete, sustained us all during all those long, cold years of privation and brutality. Many admirers attribute my marvellously endowed physique to the cold baths we endured then. And frequent, barbarous beatings doubtless contributed to that serenity of disposition that so many have remarked upon, in hushed, reverential tones.

* * *

Going downmarket

I used to write English Nature's predecessor's publicity efforts, and this piece was probably pure jealousy.

Bill Adams's new book, *Future Nature*, informs us that the wildlife agencies have become much more sophisticated in their public relations since the demise of the NCC, five years ago. In the place of dull, scientific reports we find colourful newsletters and jokey magazines positively falling over themselves to be cheerful and 'customer-friendly'.

English Nature's bimonthly news magazine makes the point with its larky editing. Heading a piece about basking sharks we find LIFE AT THE SHARK END, which is extremely amusing. A boggy place called Whixall Moss becomes A NEW RESERVE TO AD-MIRE (geddit?). EN's contribution to the late *Sea Empress* disaster is praised as a SLICK

RESPONSE TO OIL THREAT, while its proactive marine protection policy is summed up in DEVOTION TO THE OCEAN.

But what really tickled Twitcher's cockles was an article about the threatened demise of the native freshwater crayfish, headed: EXTINCT POSSIBILITY. This was actually a very sad story about something that need not have happened if we weren't ruled by idiots. While it may be creditable to find jollity in an unfortunate situation, as Mark Tapley always did in *Martin Chuzzlewit*, one is slightly surprised to find the joke coming from the crayfish's supposed protectors.

EXTINCT POSSIBILITY may or may not be quite a funny line, but it does suggest the agency may not care all that much about this distinct possibility of extinction for a rare wild animal. By coincidence I myself once wrote a piece about the disease, spread by an imported American crayfish (a bigger and beefier brute), which all but wiped out our native crayfish while the conservationists were looking the other way. This was for the old NCC's news magazine *Topical Issues*, or 'Tropical Tissues' as it was derisively known. Far from seeking a cheap laugh, the original draft castigated MAFF for failing to take any action to halt the disaster, and also the crayfish industry for causing all the trouble in the first place. Needless to say, this version was soon slapped down by my seniors, and the original headline of CRAYFISH! WE NAME THE GUILTY MEN was watered down to something like 'Diminishing Populations Cause Concern'.

I must admit that EXTINCT POSSIBILITY is a better line than either. Perhaps Ridley was right to abolish the NCC after all. When I think of the fun I might have had ...

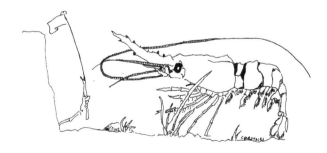

91

CRUNCHY CRAYFISH CASHES ITS CHIPS
CRIKEY! CRAYFISH FEELS THE PINCH
MOBSTER LOBSTER TRASHES WIMP SHRIMP!

Still, it is a comfort to learn that not all is doom and gloom in these challenging times.

* * *

From the mouth of babes

If today's slackjawed 'kids' show any interest in the outdoors, it is only in an effort to look cool and on-message. The bright and cheerful children of Ramsbury are a delightful exception.

As everyone who matters starts to look rather old and moth-eaten, it is time to pay more attention to what youngsters are thinking and saying. When I was small I often found I had an interesting toad or caterpillar to show to the grown-ups, but they usually just wandered off. 'Don't go away,' I would shout after them. 'Look, I have this interesting caterpillar, or possibly a toad.' Young people should be encouraged more. And so I turn to my copy of the *Young Telegraph*, which is devoted this week to what young persons are saying about The Environment.

Goodness, they are serious, this lot. With the headmasterly figure of Jonathan Porritt looking on in approval, his brow furrowed with professional concern, the Tory tots have their say. There seems to be some rivalry among them as to who is the eco-friendliest of them all. James (10) of Bedford, for example, takes a dim view of zoos, considering them to be no part of a sensitive, caring age, and wrong in principle. 'Animals should be allowed to return to their natural habitats, because they might be lonely,' he says.

His classmates Tina and Gemma allow certain exceptions: zoos ought to care for old or sick animals 'which are unable to protect themselves'. Gemma would also lock up dangerous animals on the grounds that they might otherwise protect themselves a bit too robustly.

When it comes to greening the planet, Helen, a cutey of 9, thinks we need to pull our socks up. 'We must stop cutting down trees, ban cars and be aware that animals are becoming extinct because of us,' she warns us. Sara, also 9, agrees about banning cars. Tom (10) worries about the ozone layer, and calls for a more considerate attitude to the rain forests.

Plenty of food for thought there. One thought that occurs to me is that Helen and Sara and Tom might be watching too much television. In practice, little Helen might not like having to walk to school, and Tom will find zoos more convenient than rain forests for seeing animals, and he'll waste a lot less ozone getting there.

Instead of filling their heads with all this right-on rubbish, their wretched, parroting (or should I say Porriting?) teachers should be encouraging their classes to take a little more interest in what lies under their noses. Helen, Sara and Tom would find more wonder and excitement in a drop of pondwater than in any amount of telly-pap about pandas and dolphins. There will be plenty of time to brood about ozone later on, once the careless bright colours of childhood have faded to the grim grey twilight of parenthood. My advice to Helen, Sara and Tom is to leave their TVs and drive to the zoo to see some real animals, while they still have them.

* * *

Poor beetle that we tread upon

People tell me they didn't get this piece about my favourite politician, John Gummer. I don't care. It's what I wanted to say, and I said it. Sorry, Gummer.

Perhaps it is in the nature of the journalist that, faced with the launch of the latest 500-page blockbuster on Biodiversity, he prefers to write about the life of dung beetles. The beetle in question, which threatens to eclipse the scores of action plans and targets outlined in '*Biodiversity Action*', is called *Aphodius niger*. Apparently, it spends its time wallowing about in cow pats around the squelchy margin of a pond in the New Forest. The government is seeking a 'champion' for it on the grounds that *Aphodius niger* is 'endangered', or so they say.

One suspects, though, that the beetle's real job is less to 'meet the challenge of Rio', as the phrase is, than to provide a cue for one of Gummer's little homilies. Certainly the launch had a stage-managed air. We were told that a junior minister had 'jibbed' at the inclusion of the dung beetle, thereby allowing his boss, John Selwyn Gummer, to admonish the jibbing minister with a raised palm and the following lustral words: 'The dung beetle is a part of God's creation, whose loss would diminish us all'. He added, in pragmatic – if slightly mysterious – vein, that one day 'he might come in useful'.

Gummer is noted for lightening these solemn occasions with a little joke – I reported one of them some months back, about a motorist, a spruce tree and a laurel wreath. On this occasion, the *Daily Telegraph* responded loyally with a cheerful leader, comparing the qualities of our environmental minister with the said beetle. 'He may be faintly ridiculous, but the dung beetle has undeniable charm ... The solids, you might say, magically fail to adhere to his glossy carapace.'

This pleasant thought may shed new light on the celebrated occasion a year or two ago, when the Norwegian environment man called Gummer a 'krappvogel' or 'dummerbugg'. Our chaps jumped to the conclusion that the owlish environment secretary had been insulted, and no doubt threatened to send a gunboat up their fiord. We can see now that, by comparing Gummer with a dung beetle, the Norwegian was in fact drawing attention to the charming, unstained carapace of our mirthful minister. When you reflect that rolling balls of dung to and fro is more or less what politicians do all the time, you can see that all the man was saying, in his inscrutable Norwegian way, is that John Gummer is a very good politician.

I hope *Aphodius niger* finds a worthy champion at the Palace of Westminster before very long.

* * *

Let them eat turnip

This is another one that really happened. Of course, they all really happened, but some happened more literally than others. My man Carstairs said he often saw one-legged men chasing butterflies while peddling a mountain bike. Once we went for a stroll together, and then I saw one too. Can you explain it? I can't explain it.

There was hand wringing at the butcher's last time I went there to buy some of Ramsbury's famous hand-crafted snorkers (winner of the coveted sausage of the year award, circa 1985). No one, he complained, was buying his beef anymore. Lovely beef it was, too, look at that marbling. You only get that on really *butch*-looking bullocks, he said, not your typical mamby-pamby, hormonally-challenged moos. Maybe, but nobody was buying it. The customers, you see, have been watching a documentary about mad cow disease, and the terrible things that happen if you eat a mad cow.

Now he has another problem. They are all off pork, too. Fresh from the horror of mad cows, the customers decided to watch a Hollywood film about a lovable talking pig called Babe. Well, I mean, you would have to be a hard-hearted bastard to be hoovering up the pork scratchings while *that* was on wouldn't you? 'Who is doing this to me,' moaned my butcher.

I felt it might be tactless to remind him that lamb is in many ways the worst of the lot. It was sheep that caused all the trouble in the first place, when their infected brains were fed to the shortly-to-be-mad cows...

I was on the point of suggesting there might still be a place for another greengrocer in the village, when suddenly the penny dropped. Why not make a film about a lovable but slightly-mad talking turnip? This would surely get these impressionable people queueing up for their snorkers again, while babbling away about plant crime and vegetable vice. If not, well the silly buggers will have to starve, won't they?

* * *

Twitcher's top tips for Christmas

The only thing I had against Jonathan Porritt was the relentless earnestness of his writings. It must be exhausting, being married to a Liberal.

1. Short of money? Take a trip along the country roads and scrape up the squashed wildlife! A badger doormat will make the ideal Christmas present for Mum and Dad. The neighbours will be equally delighted at your thoughtful stoat n' weasel bookmarks – just leave the tail sticking out to mark the place. Animals run over by lighter vehicles make amusing 'muppet-style' glove puppets for the kids.

2. Fox-hunters! Fed up with constant abuse? Try hunting fallen leaves. Properly mounted they make attractive trophies, especially if you cheer them up with a lick of paint. Nor are there any Leaf Rights protesters to stop you. Well, not yet anyway.

3. Journalists! Fed up with human beings? Try keeping earwigs. Though fairly monogamous, democratic creatures on the whole, they are very impressionable. My special journalist's earwig kit comes complete with bribes (worms, mostly), nip-n'-tell loose-livin' earwigs, and the odd wasp (to arrange what journalists call a sting). Hours of frenzied reporting guaranteed.

4. Hungry? A plain but reasonably nutritious cake can be made out of unwanted English Nature reports, rival wildlife magazines, the collected works of Jonathan Porritt, etc. Kick them all into a bucket, douse in light ale for a couple of months, add nuts, raisins and candied peel, and then half-bake for a while. When you come to eat it, you may find yourself constantly spitting out words like 'sustainability' and 'biodiversity', but look on it as a recycling exercise. You are returning to the environment raw materials that should never have been taken from it in the first place.

Tidal wave

We saw him first on the merse but he probably thought he could see us. Anyway there was no telling until we spoke, and we didn't because he was too far off and Stenga and I were in no mood to tarry.

The following day, on the flowing tide I went with Stenga walking slowly in the half light of dawn, and the tide coming in all the while. The dog played with the wrack. Then we saw him. He was waving from the now wet mud of the merse. Stenga and I were pleased to see that at last the man was friendly and was waving in the wind and tide. We waved back. Everyone seemed so happy, waving, and the water and the tide and wind. Stenga and I walked on thinking of Gladys and her boiling chicken heads for supper tonight.

We looked back for a final, friendly wave. But he was gone. I don't know, some people.

The Merse
February 1962

1997

Tempted by WWF's offers of gold, I wrote a critique of English Nature for them. It gave the WWF some welcome publicity, but I wish I hadn't done it. Life is too short to waste it complaining about people no one has heard of.

Imaginary landscapes

I don't know about you, but I normally have a problem with February. It's a spiteful crab of a month, full of sullen refusals and unkept promises. It wears you down, then spits in your eye. However, this year was an exception. One grim grey winter's day I picked up my pen, and when I laid it down again the sun was smiling in a blue sky, larks sang and yellow butterflies were chasing one another down the dappled hedgebanks. I didn't notice February at all. What was it like?

If you feel the same way as I do about Februarys, you might like to know how this miracle came about. As it happened, I found myself writing a report about 'English Nature', the wildlife agency, and its sibling agencies in Scotland and Wales, at the behest of the top man from the World Wildlife Fund. But what was this to me? 'You were one of them once,' they said. 'Go on, kick their butts for us. You know you want to. Look at all this lovely money,' they added sensuously flicking a wad of fivers. 'But,' I protested, 'who in their right mind would want to mull over the soiled underwear of a dim government body hardly anyone has ever heard of?' 'Oh, we would,' they chorussed. 'We think they've sold out. They don't talk to us. They call us 'customers'. They don't do science. They don't prosecute anybody. They're scaredy-cats. They're bums.' Oh, all right then.

Honestly though, I don't know what all the fuss is about. You only have to open the first page of English Nature's latest annual report to see how busy they are. We are told, in no uncertain terms, that 'EN' has:

'Heightened the challenges, deepened the common cause and broadened horizons through the progressive implementation of measures deriving from EC and global initiatives.'

Phew! Inspiring stuff, I think you'll agree, and there is plenty more where that came from. In the mind's eye you can just see those tall challenges standing like grain silos on a broad horizon, interspersed with goalposts, each of them perched on raised awareness levels. It looks a bit like a computer game, and I wonder whether 'English Nature' has considered the exciting marketing possibilities of an interactive annual report. You could have some badger or newt dodging the targets and jumping over the challenges on the way to its strategic goal, or 'burrow', as they are ordinarily known. With only minor changes to EN's annual report – such as some occasional mention of badgers or newts – it could be made into a really useful instruction booklet.

Frankly, I think the vol. bods. are just jealous. The WWF's reports are nothing like as good, being concerned entirely with dreary old pandas and boring old natural habitats.

* * *

Election notes

I am slightly terrified of people who believe in only one thing. The only important thing about the Green Party is it exists. No other justification is necessary, and neither are votes.

Looking around for someone worth voting for in this great election year 1997, I opened the manifesto of the Green Party. When I woke up, all I could remember before falling into a doze was some stuff about persecuting drivers and reducing our 'emission levels'. I do not know whether Green Party activists have particular problems with their emissions, although most of them seem to drive cars. The trouble with these earnest, bearded vegetarians with their bobble hats and badges is that they haven't the faintest idea how to rake in the votes. Their only hope is to pander to the mixture of sentimentality and misanthropy that might be lurking in any drop-outs or thickos tempted to vote Green.

The Green Party's cue was in fact staring them in the face in the morning newspaper: *Save the Squirrel* This exciting project is going to rescue the endangered red squirrel from approaching extinction, it says. The project is wittily entitled Megalab Red Alert. Participants are encouraged to go

outside until they spot a squirrel, then fill in a form and post it, before returning to their television sets. The best time to spot red squirrels is at sunset, when all squirrels tend to turn red, whether or not they are really brown, grey or some other colour. In this way, the squirrel will be saved, and the good news will be broadcast on *Tomorrow's World*, the television programme about the exciting future.

Even the least imaginative, most tongue-tied Greenie should have had no trouble in conjuring up a wonderful vision of tomorrow's world teeming with these innocent jumping creatures, with happy mums and kids looking on. With the prudent example of the squirrel before us, we might become a nation of savers, not borrowers. Many might even be tempted to climb a tree. Some of the happiest days of my life were spent clambering about in trees. Megalab Red Alert is exactly what the Bobble Hats are looking for, did they but know it.

As it was, I decided that the Green Party was too stupid to vote for. Perhaps the red squirrel should be allowed to become extinct. Sooner or later the time is up for all species, and the fossil record shows that newly evolved animals are nearly always more beautiful and interesting than the ones they replace (try studying early mammals if you want to see some really hopeless plugs). I think the solution of not knowing who to vote for is to stand myself under the banner of The Right to Die Out. We will be known as the Bone Party.

* * *

New hope for harvest mice

Twitcher's mild objection to Simon Lyster, then head of the Wildlife Trusts, was his determined optimism: whatever he wrote, the message was always the same: The Wildlife Trusts can save the world with your support. And very boring it was, especially from a body that believes the word 'Trusts' is singular.

This week we take out our worry beads for the harvest mouse, *Micromys minutus* (which means, amusingly enough, 'smallest tiny mouse'). When, thirty years ago, mouse-lovers made a concerted search for it, they found, rather to their surprise, that the countryside was swarming with these tiny mice, swinging acrobatically from their tails and eating everything in sight. But now there has been another survey, and, it seems, most of the mice have gone.

Harvest mice ask for very little from life. They eat practically anything, and so long as there is a bit of tall grass and a few hedges left they are quite happy. They don't mind, either, if the numbers of stoats and weasels go down, which, indeed, they have done. Possibly the mouse-seekers of the 1990s are not as bright-eyed and diligent as their predecessors. But if the harvest mouse is really dying out, then large amounts of the countryside must be pretty well lifeless.

It is in this context that we should consider the latest review of the Wildlife Trusts. In it, the Trusts' 'director general' Simon Lyster, sums up 1996 as another terrific year for wildlife (pretty much like 1995 in that respect). 1994 was pretty good, too. It seems that the Trust has once again achieved wonders all over the place, and that it cannot wait to fulfil the challenges of the new year. 'Keep supporting us,' he tells the troops, 'and 1997 could be *even better.*' But surprisingly there is not a word about the poor old harvest mouse and its difficulties.

Is it possible that Simon is so busy achieving targets in his London office that he didn't in fact have much time to check on how the harvest mouse is getting on? In general, 'director-generals' seem more interested in putting the best gloss on events for their ssubscribers and shareholders than with surveying small mammals. I feel we owe something to the harvest mouse for exposing the hollowness of their claims. I see that Mr Lyster's review is made of non-toxic recycled paper, and so is presumably edible.

Perhaps if each of the Wildlife Trusts' quarter of a million members could tear their copy of his message into tiny bite-size pieces and scatter them in likely harvest mouse habitats, the mice would at least find something to eat. I would call this a really positive way forward, and Simon could tell us all what an amazing success it had been in his next review.

Next time I shall be explaining how excellent shelters for earwigs can be made out of Corporate Plans.

* * *

Woolly hats

Back into 1986 I got into trouble for an insulting piece about anglers published in Natural Selection, *the Nature Conservancy Council's 'unofficial' staff magazine. The* Angling Times, *a wonderful tabloid-style fun sheet for Sun-reading fishermen pretended to regard my little* jeu d'esprit *as NCC's official policy. Ah, if only it was.*

Whatever is happening to the fishermen of England? One week we read of a vicious assault on a river bailiff by a gang of anglers. The next we learn that the former editor of *The Angling Times* has been charged with inciting his readers to slaughter a protected species, namely the cormorant. The newspaper's front page displays a masked man, a gun and a pile of dead cormorants under the banner headline: *'This is a picture every angler wants to see'.*

He seems to take a very dim view of the average angler. But if fishermen really do harbour such thoughts, it can only strengthen the growing lobby of people who want to outlaw fishing, along with hunting, shooting, picking mushrooms and country life generally. Personally, I think their argument is over-stated. While there can be no doubt that the poor fishes suffer tremendous pain and humiliation as they dangle from the hook, most would argue that fishes don't really count as wild animals, being silent, cold-blooded and bereft of feet.

An extra consideration might be the nature of the modern angling journalist. Years ago I had the misfortune to cross swords with the editor of *The Angling Times* over an article criticising the messier sort of angler and the fishing lines he left behind, ready to lasso and throttle any passing water bird. What seemed to have caught his eye was a reference to his newspaper's pictures as 'piles of dead fish, generally surmounted by the porcine grin of some woolly-hatted oaf'. His response to this playful banter was a series of screaming headlines – 'Fury at Pigs Jibe' – 'Outburst Staggers Chiefs' – and, best of all, 'BETRAYED' – accompanied by an appeal to his readers to write to the Prime Minister about it. The effect was like prodding Mike Tyson with an umbrella. Unfortunately for him, the upshot was that, while some people see a fish-eating bird and think of shotguns, others now see *The Angling Times* and think of woolly hats.

Still, in the light of this experience, I should advise everyone to leave the anglers alone and ignore the poor suffering fishes. Otherwise they might find themselves inside another picture every angler wants to see.

* * *

The rocks remain

In the 1960s, taxpayers' money was spent on taking stones out of a stream. Thirty years on, Lottery money was spent on putting them back in again. In this piece I looked ahead to the happy day when the stones that were taken out and then put back in again were taken out again.

Many, if not most, conservation projects are concerned less with doing something new as with undoing something old. And, as often as not, both the doing and the undoing are paid for by you and me. I was reminded of this fact when I visited the Nant Ffrancon valley in Snowdonia, snooping about on behalf of the Heritage Lottery.

You may remember Nant Ffrancon from O Level geography as the classic example of a U-shaped valley, carved out by glaciers in days gone by. It is a magnificent place, a lost valley among the mountains dominated by the brooding presence of Tryfan, on whose distant frowning cliffs rock climbers hang like baby spiders. Through the valley runs a little stream, the Afon Ogwen, many sizes too small for it.

After a moment or two, it dawns on you that something is missing. Where is the gurgle and splosh of water? Not here, is where it is. Or rather, isn't. There are all too few wild corners where the stream ripples round a bend and creates a steep bank on one side, and a marsh on the other. This is because there aren't many bends either. Back in the 1960s, the tenants of the valley persuaded the local river board to straighten and deepen the stream. This meant taking out all the boulders with a big mobile crane. Never mind that the land was owned by the National Trust and was also part of Snowdonia National Park. Out they came anyway, because that was the way things were then. The river immediately flooded all over the place, but, heck, progress is always a struggle.

Now the National Trust has had a change of heart. Always conscious of what it perceives to be the public mood ('ooh, let's ban stag hunting. *That'll* be popular '), it has decided to borrow another mobile crane and put all the boulders back in again. It even hopes to recreate the odd bend. Naturally the Trust doesn't want to pay for this work itself, and that is why I am snooping about in the Nant Ffrancon. As far as I can see, it seems a reasonable idea, which will bring in some wildlife and the better class of tourist, in place of all these starving, worthless sheep. But we snoopers are trained to take the long, cynical view. What if the National Trust has yet another change of heart, and decided it would be a terribly good idea to take all the boulders out again? One has to consider all the wear and tear on these boulders, as well as the health and safety aspects involved. It is one thing being a political football, but chucking political rocks about sounds like a dubious use of the lotto-players hard-earned money.

* * *

Conserving the newts

English Nature's solution to the problem of Peterborough's 30,000 surplus newts was to build them a customised home nearby. Everyone was happy, except miserable old WWF. Oh, and possibly the newts.

Do you remember the crested newts of Peterborough, 'translocated' by the bucket-full across a busy highway to make room for a housing estate? It seems that the newts, known as the Peterborough 30,000, have now been settled into a new 'home' nearby. Everyone involved must be hoping that newts do not have migratory instincts, or indeed any kind of instincts, and will oblige everybody by sitting still in their new pond and not moving around too much.

Hanson, the multi-national builders, are now in line for 'a prestigious national award' for all their efforts in 'mobile newting'. Theirs is one of 200 green schemes to be put forward for the Millennium Marque, a Euro-award to be made in the year 2000. But everything depends on the newts staying in their new home and breeding.

'We are confident that the work will convince the assessors that the reserve is worthy of the Millennium Marque, ' said an 'extremely pleased' James Hopkins, managing director of Hanson.

Let us hope so. If I were him, though, I would leave nothing to chance. I would raise watchtowers around the newt compound, with orders to recapture any newt seen heading back to its old place. Rapid breeding

would be compulsory, and we would know how to deal with any slackers. With the right kind of attitude, I have no doubt that we'd be heading for the prestigious award with the largest newt colony in Europe.

* * *

Notes on fungi

The programme was Country Tracks, *later, just* Tracks. *Though strenuously funky and 'yoof' in style, it was still too cerebral for BBC's programme managers, and axed.*

I'm on the telly again to explain why puffballs puff and why stinkhorns look like willies. A pretty tough assignment I think you'll admit, especially as the alternative name for puffball is vesse-de-loup, that is to say the fart of wolves. The programme presenter is a well-bred Irish girl who won't want to listen to that kind of smut (incidentally, another kind of fungus). I think I'll explain that the stinkhorn is keen to date the puffball, which responds negatively in the definite but unfortunate manner just described. Or so we believe in Wiltshire.

* * *

A birthday pet

Triops was one of those Nineties wonder-animals sold in packets like seed, but which burst into life when you added water. It was the idea of an American entrepreneur, whose biggest success was the 'Sea Monkeys'. They looked great on the packet, but turned out disappointingly small and not very monkey-like.

When I was very small, the animal I most wanted to see above all the whales and tigers in the world was a beast called Triops, also known as the tadpole shrimp. In the book, at least, it looked weird and compelling, like a sort of horseshoe crab which had grown a tail like a dolphin's, and the grabbing arms and boggle-eyes of the beast from the Planet Arg, as seen in one's Dan Dare comic. But though I longed to catch one, I doubted that it really existed, especially as Triops was said to come from a place

called Kirkcudbrightshire, which obviously didn't exist either.

It wasn't until many years later that I saw the real thing, and there it was, a mimsy little shrimp not much bigger than a wood-louse, and not looking the least bit fierce or alien. Frankly, it was a bit of a disappointment and you felt a little childhood dream suddenly burst, like spent bubblegum.

Now, it seems, some entrepeneur is marketing the Triops as a pet for the kiddies: 'Step back in time to the Weird World of Triops'. For your £9 you get a sachet of Triops eggs, some 'Triops food' and a little plastic tank, together with a promise that 'you are about to embark on a biological adventure that will take you back to prehistoric times, and give you weeks of enjoyment as you grow your own 'living dinosaurs''. Dinosaurs, already. We are also told that Triops is a really fierce animal that 'will eat any living creature in its environment'.

I think that may be pitching it a bit far. If Triops really eats anything it finds, that can only be because it swims around with its mouth open. In point of fact Triops can survive in the wild only in puddles and temporary pools where there are no fish or other creatures to eat it. I would have taken a different line, marketing the malformed shrimp as the most useless animal that ever lived, known only from Kirkcudbrightshire, which probably doesn't exist. This strikes me as more interesting, as well as more honest, and less likely to produce tears at a birthday party. After all, what would you rather see – happy, laughing kiddies curling up at the sight of their pathetic new pet, or sad, wistful ones, feeling their secret dreams pop like perished rubber balloons.

At the Loch

I approached the two burly men at the loch side who had fishing rods. I faced their backs, they faced the loch, which was flat which looked as if it was water. I knew it was, because I saw a duck.

People ask me how I can tell the difference between a duck and a squirrel. I know I have lots of experience, but it isn't difficult after a bit of practice. I was really lucky to have been taught by a talented old man from the MacMiller unit, and it was a bit strange us walking around looking at creatures, him in a long white gown. At least mine had ties at the back.

Suddenly Stenga brought me back to reality more than usual and the fishermen were packing up. I went down and said to one of the men as they were packing, what have you been doing, showing the inquisitive mind of the successful naturalist. Fishing, you idiot, he said.

By the way, next time you see something up a tree quacking, ignore it. Squirrels and ducks can be a bugger to separate sometimes.

Loch Morlich
March 1953

1998

Bye-bye Pool Frog

The British Pool Frog became nationally extinct within a few years of its discovery, which suggests that it might be safer to stay undiscovered.

Full legal protection can be the kiss of death for a native species. Occasionally they even manage to protect a species *after* it has become extinct. The latest animal to slip down the plug-hole is the Pool Frog. It was only discovered a few years ago, and, of course, was immediately protected with all the force and majesty of the law. Shortly afterwards, it died out. Were the protection police sleeping on the job? Or, more likely, were they overdoing it again? Frog lovers, or herpetologists as they like to be called, are noted for their irresistible urge to tattoo toads or photocopy frogs. You think I'm joking, don't you? I told you, I never joke. Go read a comic if you want a laugh. It's on page 28 of the official manual.

The last Pool Frog, whose name, ironically enough, was Lucky Jim, was caught and taken to London Zoo 'for its own safety'. In its final days, Jim could hardly lift his pea-green snout from the aquarium without seeing some drooling newt-fancier with his tattooing apparatus and photocopying gear. Frogs are gentle creatures, easily hurt by the wrong sort of attention, as Hilaire Belloc reminds us:

> *Be kind and tender to the Frog*
> *And do not call him names,*
> *As 'Slimy Skin' or 'Polly-wog',*
> *Or likewise 'Ugly James',*
> *Or 'Gape-a-grin', or 'Toad-gone-wrong',*
> *Or 'Billy Bandy-knees',*
> *The Frog is justly sensitive*
> *To epithets like these.*

What could be more likely than that the Pool Frog, whose hearing is not of the best, mistook some piece of conservationist's jargon for an insult. Jim probably thought 'SSSI' was a snake hissing at him. For a frog already feeling depressed and lonely, this might easily have been the last straw. For the tragic spectacle that undoubtedly followed, we must turn to Mrs Leo Hunter's delightful Ode in *The Pickwick Papers*:

> *Can I view thee panting, lying*
> *On thy stomach, without sighing;*
> *Can I unmoved, see thee dying*
> *On a log,*
> *Expiring Frog!*

We can only hope there will be a full inquiry that unshrinkingly points the finger of blame.

On the other hand, the sad story of the Pool Frog suggests a possible replacement for the popular but, alas, now un-PC television programme, *One Man and His Dog*. 'One Man and His Frog' will replace the unacceptably rural component of *One Man and His Dog* with a human-interest drama, exploring the relationship between the male person and the protected species, with particular emphasis on any social issues that might arise and consequent demands for instant legislation to deal with them.

My only concern about this is that the rumbustious Robin Page might not be the ideal presenter. As Belloc reminds us, the relationship here is a most delicate one:

> *No animal will more repay*
> *A treatment kind and fair;*
> *At least so lonely people say*
> *Who keep a frog (and, by the way,*
> *They are extremely rare).*

Biodiversity action

The current vogue for 'reintroductions' began in the Nineties. You reared your beast on the finest delicacies, in a nice warm zoo, and then, once fully grown, booted them out onto some windy down or dune to fend for themselves. Whether they survived was neither here nor there. It 'delivered a target'.

'It's a remarkable come-back for an animal once threatened with extinction, ' exclaimed the reporter. As he spoke, a beaming biologist from London Zoo emptied a bin full of field crickets into the grass. Some 4,000 of these endangered chirping creatures had been raised indoors at the zoo, all squeezed out of just three heroic pairs of wild-caught crickets. Whether any of them survive the current nasty, cold, wet weather remains to be seen, but one can't help feeling it may come as a nasty shock to them.

The crickets are sponsored by Volvo cars, who are naturally keen to tell us all about their latest model, the V70 XC. Apparently it proved ideal for transporting the insects to their new home, with its useful off-road capability and exciting accessories. Perhaps in recognition of its insect-friendly capabiilities, the car should be renamed the Bugmobile or possibly the Grub-dumper. For the greener sort of customer, the horn could be replaced by a plaintive chirrup, which would amuse us all, I'm sure, when we are stuck in traffic jams.

Well, field crickets are nice, harmless things (though – careful kids – I believe they bite), and I hope they survive. But even if they don't I expect the zoo can always manufacture a few more. The press can be relied upon to report the dumping of captive-bred insects into the wild as a tremendous achievement. They assume the project is going to be successful, and so get the hurrahs in early. If, as seems possible, the end-result is 4,000 dead crickets, you can be confident it won't be reported. Do the reporters scale their praise according to the numbers involved? If 4,000 captive-bred bugs somehow represents a 'remarkable' recovery, what might 40,000 be? A sensational recovery perhaps? And how about if a full four million crickets, reared in huge thermoregulated vats, had been tipped onto the down from a dump-truck. Surely it would be nothing less than a truly miraculous come-back for the weakly chirping beast.

It crosses my mind that all this raising and carrying and dumping might be rather expensive. Surely it would be cheaper in the long run if we just rounded up the remaining wild crickets, shoved them into a Volvo and dumped them all at London Zoo?

* * *

Eco-warrior

A hero for our times, this young zealot, with his waist-length hair and expression of a hibernating squirrel. I wonder what became of him.

Matthew Morris-Steward, the 11-year-old eco-warrior perched up an oak tree somewhere in Surrey, knows a thing or two about the environment. Though unable to read or write, he preaches ecology from his tree, like St Simon Stylites, the noted hermit who lived on top of a pillar. Matthew's message is simple. Trees give us oxygen. Therefore we must save the trees, notably the one he is sitting in. Oddly enough, the Forestry Commission was saying much the same thing recently. 'Out of the mouth of babes, ' they will say, though this particular babe probably got it from them in the first place.

It would be a terrible tragedy, of course, if young Matthew fell out of his tree, or was mistaken for a squirrel by a passing owl – as, given his waist-long hair and blank expression, he well might be. By coincidence, I find that a well-grown oak tree supplies just about enough oxygen for a boy of about Matthew's age. One could argue therefore that the tree is needed only for as long as he is sitting in it. Naturally we must hope that Matthew stays on his perch in order to delight us further with his ecological messages. But if a predator did carry him off, we could at least console ourselves with the thought that both the tree and its oxygen were now redundant, and get on with building the bypass, or whatever.

* * *

Poor taste

WWF was one of the first bodies to become a pure acronym. It changed its name so often, always with the same combination of capital letters, that eventually no one could remember what WWF stood for. The Wonderful Worldlife Fund, or whatever they are called this week, had mutilated the report about English Nature I did for them, removed my name, and lied to me about it. So I was out for revenge.

The confusingly renamed Worldwide Wildlife Fund (WWF) is cross about a Japanese television programme, which showed three Geisha girls tucking in to braised tiger. Though they had pronounced the tiger delicious, a man from the WWF thought the programme was in bad taste. 'It sends the wrong message,' he grumbles, and sets 'a terrible example' to the programme's thick viewers. Lest there should be any misunderstanding about this, I should make it clear that the WWF is not in favour of eating tigers. Most definitely not. If you see a tiger, you must try to refrain from eating it, even if you are Japanese, say the WWF. Tigers are off the menu, OK? Just leave that tiger alone.

I do not know the WWF's opinion on whether tigers should be allowed to eat Geisha girls. In this country, whenever a tiger has eaten someone, or even parts of someone, the tiger concerned has got into serious trouble. But since pressure groups like the Wideworld Fund for Wildlife (WWF) like to reduce the whole spectrum of ethical debate to 'right' and 'wrong' messages, I daresay they are against that too. They seem rather hard to please, these earnest crusaders at the Wildworld Fund for Widelife (WWF).

I mention this controversial matter of eating endangered species because I have myself encountered a similar case in this country. On behalf of various conservation bodies, I am investigating the whereabouts of a rare mushroom called the Royal Bolete, which the government has in its wisdom decided to protect by law. The reason they have done so is that the Royal Bolete is said to be edible, and so, like the tiger, liable to be eaten by unenlightened people who have got hold of the wrong message. Fortunately there cannot be many Royal Bolete gourmets in this country, for, according to the national database for fungi, only four persons have set eyes on one in the past fifty years. Did they eat the evidence? To find out, I managed to track down and interrogate two of them. One says he avoids temptation by bringing sandwiches to fungus forays. The other claims that mushrooms disagree with him. I was obliged to release them, with a stern warning, for want of evidence. But I shall certainly report the matter to my friends at WWF, who, I am confident, will want to release a statement containing the words 'message', 'wrong', 'unacceptable' and 'community'.

I have just been informed that I have got the WWF's new name wrong. It is the Wildwild Fund for Wildlife. I am happy to put this right.

* * *

Extinct possibility

Twitcher seems convinced that wildlife would get on better if we just ignored it.

According to my copy of the latest Whitaker's Almanack (I do the environment pages), the Environment Agency has managed to breed the 'endangered' Twaite Shad in captivity for the first time. (The Twaite Shad, as *British Wildlife* readers will know, is a migratory fish, and not, as many young persons believe, a sort of grasshopper from outer space.) This was a bit of rare good news among the other events of July 2000, which included a plague of mosquitoes in Italy, a fire in Australia that killed over 1,000 crocodiles, and news that ice melting in Greenland is 'causing a seven per cent rise in sea levels'.

Perhaps it is just coincidence, but quite a number of rare British plants and animals became nationally extinct shortly after scientists started taking an interest in them. The coincidences began in the 1970s when the Large Blue butterfly died out just as we had worked out how to save it, to be followed in quick succession by the Stinking Hawk's-beard, Ivell's Sea Anemone, Essex Emerald moth and the Pool Frog (*q.v.*). Against these losses, there is the magnificent example of the Mauritius Kestrel, which staged a recovery, despite being festooned with rings, radios and other apparatus. Perhaps it is just a matter of timing.

I suspect that what has upset the Twaite Shad is the persecution of Britain's smokers. In the days when everyone smoked like chimneys and collected cigarette cards of freshwater fish, everyone had heard of a Twaite Shad. According to Players, it could be caught by ' 'whiffing ' at the river mouths with a slip of mackerel'. Wills cigarettes told us that the Twaite Shad enjoyed musical sounds, and so fishermen eager to catch it carried chiming bells on their bows. Very nice they were, too, served with a bit of lemon and some *pommes frites*. The fish, I mean, not the fishermen.

Now the Twaite Shad is just another endangered species. Heigh ho. If only people had showed a touch more tolerance about smoking we might be eating them still.

Gladys

While my heavy but friendly wife Gladys was boiling the spinach, Stenga and me thought we would pop on our jackets, well not Stenga who has a coat, and go out for a walk. I knew that the geese would be on the stubbles after they had come from Iceland that autumn day in the fields where we would be, Stenga and me.

The geese were too far off as they often are, so we went back for the Allegro. Gladys was still boiling and there was a smell at the window. The spinach, not Gladys.

Stenga sat on the passenger seat while I drove. He has no license so I have to do all the driving. It's alright because he makes up with the vacuuming. Anyway, in the dark I drove with Stenga watching but I missed that nasty bend at Dalnavert. We awoke among the wreckage. Alone and not a goose in sight.

Strathpeffer
January 1957

1999

Spot the squish

Some wildlife sells, and some doesn't. Foxes sell so well that Reader's Digest wanted us to mention them at every opportunity.

With my colleague, Robert Burton, I am writing an exciting new book about how to find wild animals for Reader's Digest. Knowing that most of them sensibly keep out of the way of your average Reader's Digest reader, stomping along in his orange anorak, we have decided to describe the clues they leave behind as they dive for cover. Our publishers are keen that we say lots about foxes. When I point out that few people ever see a fox, apart from dead ones on the roads, or the occasional mangy dustbin-raider, the Reader's Digest lady replies that for many of her readers the fox is the only wild animal they care about.

So, we are writing about squashed foxes. A good clue to a squashed fox is that it is usually found at the side of the road. This is because foxes are quite light, and will fly some distance after being hit at 80 miles an hour. Badgers, on the other hand, are heavier and have a lower weight-distribution ratio. Hence, they are more often to be found on the tarmac, where they quickly assume a greyish, mat-like appearance.

Another animal to look out for is the squashed otter. County trusts have reported a recent increase in this beast, especially near places where otters are being reared in pens to fulfil a target for the Biodiversity Action Plan. It seems that these production-line otters spring gleefully from captivity only to dash straight on to the nearest main road for their appointment with a speeding 40-tonne Euro-truck.

I suggest to the Reader's Digest lady that squashed otters are still quite rare, rating the same I-Spy score as, say, an eclipse of the moon or a Victorian letter box – and perhaps even meriting a special Brownie Point from the Big Chief. But she shakes her head and tells me that her readers would not be very interested, unless the otter was reddish and had a big bushy tail.

* * *

Country matters

The process by which people are elected to Government councils is cloaked in mystery, even, or perhaps especially, after the Nolan report was supposed to have 'democratised' the process. In the old days, the Chairman invited you to join them. Today the Minister invites you, and, in my case at least, his Council tells you to 'Sod off'.

As a rule politicians' attempts to intervene in country matters are about as welcome as a revolving door in a prison. They always get it wrong, and someone – never them – ends up getting the stick for it. All the same, it would be grudging of me not to put in a good word for Minister Meacher, the environment man, who has done two things to deserve the thanks of at least a few of us.

The first was to invite us to wander all over other people's private property. His opposition number, Gillian Shepherd, objected, saying that this would annoy the 'country-dwellers', but nothing, in fact, annoys country-dwellers more than being called 'country-dwellers'. I suppose she thinks we live in holes, like hobbits. My own reservations are different. I find myself wondering what we could do on all this private property once we get there. I think I would like to celebrate my new-found freedom by chasing butterflies, catching a few fish, picking mushrooms for supper and taking pot-shots at a pheasant afterwards. But all these activities are either proscribed or subject to dreary 'codes of conduct' that allow you only three egg-sized mushrooms on alternate Wednesdays.

Moreover, there is the risk of inexperienced 'ramblers' injuring themselves and sueing the landowner for damages. In support of this possibility, *The Times* accompanied Meacher's surprise announcement with a picture of a typical party of ramblers, spread out in a row, each with a leg raised and clearly *goosestepping* along the path. Never mind that goosestepping ramblers will cause soil compaction, annoy the country-dwellers and risk stepping on a goose. Anyone who tries marching stiff-leggedly over moorland or marsh is going to come a cropper. Possibly it was a kind of victory march, and they will now revert to the usual straggling line, all busy complaining about the state of the footpath and the lack of wildlife. Still, I think it is the sort of thing Meacher should keep an eye on, in case he has to pay for all the twisted ankles and bruised bottoms.

But enough of ramblers, it is time we moved on to Meacher's more important decision. This was to invite me, Twitcher of the Swamp and snatcher-up of unconsidered trifles, me, I say, to put my name forward to join the ruling elite of English Nature! English Nature, my regular readers will know, is the noted supplier of 'natural-style' toiletry products, based at some reeking dump in the Midlands. Unfortunately, instead of simply walking on to one of these bodies, as in the past, and proceeding to push one's weight around, one is now expected to go through the most degrading series of hoops – forms, interviews and what-not – as though one was some jobbing boy scout looking for a chimney to clean. Not surprisingly, government quangos tend in consequence to attract *Guardian*-reading bus conductors, legless running instructors and pterodactyls from the planet Tharg. Still, my information was that Meacher, or possibly Meacher's creature, Maule, had chosen me to goosestep over to English Nature's fragrant soap factory and deliver them all a jolly good scrubbing. And so,

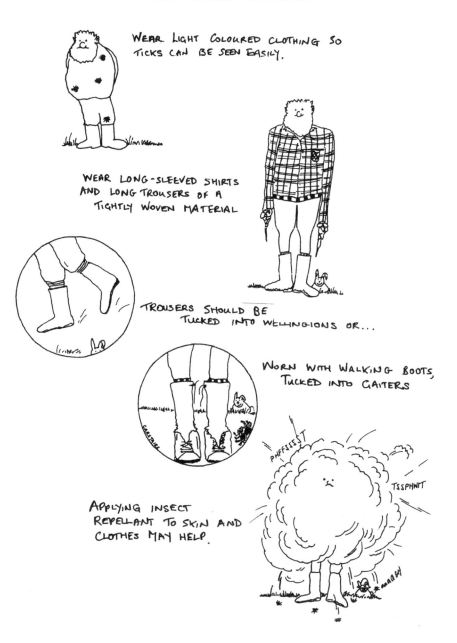

WEAR LIGHT COLOURED CLOTHING SO TICKS CAN BE SEEN EASILY.

WEAR LONG-SLEEVED SHIRTS AND LONG TROUSERS OF A TIGHTLY WOVEN MATERIAL

TROUSERS SHOULD BE TUCKED INTO WELLINGTONS OR...

WORN WITH WALKING BOOTS, TUCKED INTO GAITERS

APPLYING INSECT REPELLANT TO SKIN AND CLOTHES MAY HELP.

PHFFSSST   TSSPHNT

although the proferred fee was not quite what one might have hoped for, I laughingly filled in his pathetic form and awaited my free pack of bath salts, and anything else I could get.

Instead, I was sent a curt rejection slip, signed by Meacher's creature's minion, Plopp. Obviously someone had blundered. I learned later what had happened. One of the pterodactyls on English Nature's so-called Board had kicked up a tremendous squawk about the richly deserved scrubbing that was coming his way, and somehow got Meacher's order rescinded. And so the democratic will is flaunted, and the government's good intentions brought to naught. Well, I don't care. I didn't want the rotten job anyway. But doesn't it make you wonder what this country is coming to when some reptilian quangocrat can dictate to the mighty Meacher, opener of gates and herdsmen of the ramblers.

As Blackadder once remarked in a similar situation, 'This is the last time I interfere in politics'.

* * *

Stick to the bunnies

In Twitcher's view, the Wildlife Trusts support for the Right to Roam was pure Nimbyism. Anywhere but on our land is what they meant.

'My idea of what heaven is like,' said nine-year-old Sam, 'is mostly going for walks in the countryside.' Young Sam's views on the afterlife were presented on the religious-affairs page or 'God-slot' of a daily newspaper. He expected heaven to be 'green and beautiful and full of plants and stuff, and really good'.

Almost certainly the reason why Sam imagines the countryside in this way is that his parents (or parent) never allow him to set foot in it. The country may look like the Garden of Eden, but sensible mums and dads reckon that the grass is full of snakes (and worse). When you do see the odd child out of town, corralled up in some sanitised country park, that child generally looks bored out of its mind. But don't worry, Sammy. I doubt if heaven is like the countryside. I expect it will be more like watching Disney Channel and stuffing your face with pizza and chocolate.

Still, the law will soon allow Sam and his chums to wander pretty well where they like, whether they want to or not. What do the Wildlife Trusts have to say about that? In a forthright leader, entitled 'Walk on', the Trusts' Director-general has hope in his heart. The more people roaming about, the more members he thinks he will have, and this 'really will have the politicians eating out of our hand', he says. On the other hand, 'access needs to be managed', he warns, so that the roamers aren't tempted to stray onto sensitive sites. 'It's a question of balance.' To sum up – the Trusts think that everyone should have a right to roam so long as they do what they are told and keep their dirty feet off its property.

I find myself wondering whether the Wildlife Trusts' view on this matter might be about as worthy of note as young Sammy's. From where I sit in my swamp, I see that another load of rotting cartons and plastic bottles has been emptied on the verge, possibly by a burglar doing his rounds. The narrow road is also used by a local lout as his private racetrack. He has accumulated a fine assortment of squashed ducks and toads this year, and, yes – oh my – he's just bagged a grass snake. That's the trouble with rights: when you give them to nice middle-aged ramblers you also give them to yobs. If the Trusts really want to 'hand-feed' politicians, they should try to see modern Britain as it is, and not as they would like it to be. But I'd advise them to stick to fluffy bunnies and raffle sales. People join wildlife societies to escape from everyday realities, not to mix with seedy backbenchers, pap-babbling under-secretaries and similar riffraff.

* * *

Domewatch

Twitcher offered Blair's government a clear way out of the increasingly obvious impending disaster represented by The Dome. Typically, they failed to listen. And they broke the law. Policeman, arrest that Prime Minister.

I was looking forward to Tony's big party at The Dome, and the opportunity to meet the carefully-picked 'ordinary people' he says he has invited. I'm not sure that the young people most likely to enjoy 'doming out' at Tony's expense will take too kindly to being described as 'ordinary', but that's his problem. Another of his problems is that a pair of Black Redstarts have built a nest in The Dome. No doubt the birds realised instinctively that there was little likelihood of being disturbed, since the site is almost impossible to reach.

Now that a protected species is nesting there, all work must stop immediately, says Ralph Gaines of the London Wildlife Trust. He warns that Body Zones and Spirit Levels, or whatever rubbish they are planning to put in there, will be in direct contravention of Section 1(5)(a) of the Wildlife and Countryside Act, and expose the perpetrators to prosecution and a consequent fine of up to £2,000.

For some reason, the RSPB's Mike Everett takes a more compromising line. He suggests that Dome work could still go ahead, so long as it was all done very quietly and everyone spoke in whispers. He claims the law *does* allow for some disturbance so long as it is 'the incidental result of a lawful action that could not have been avoided'.

I fail to see his point. This action can be avoided very easily, *by not building The Dome*. What would it say about this supposedly environmentally-aware age if The Dome were to be founded on the corpse of a protected species? Quite possibly, anyone visiting it would lay himself or herself open to prosecution as an accessory. The entire Dome and all its contents would have to be confiscated and taken away to the RSPB's remote country estate at Sandy Lodge. There it would be painlessly destroyed.

I think that Black Redstarts are among our most attractive species, with delightful habits and a song to gladden the heart of the most stressed-out, downtrodden office worker. Why not look for one on **your** local housing development, and have a word with the council about it. Anything small, blackish and vaguely bird-like will do.

* * *

Badger girl

Twitcher admitted to an unexplained fondness both for badgers and for the Spicegirl, Geri Halliwell, who had lately dropped off the Spice Rack, as the newspapers wittily reported it. I have since rather gone off Geri. She's a bit of a show-off, really, don't you think?

The great West Country Badger Massacre isn't going to plan. In the interests of reducing disease in cattle, the Ministry of Agriculture had decided to kill every badger they could lay their hands on in certain areas to find out whether it made any difference. These areas are called 'Total Cull Zones'. In other places, they have decided to obey the law and protect the badgers, and see what difference that makes. Depending on the results, they will either slaughter or protect the badgers, as the case may be.

This must have seemed a brilliant idea from the MAFF office at Smith Square. But, as Julian Pettifer discovered in his television documentary about the great Experiment, it took no account of human perversity. Sure enough, animal liberation activists are rescuing badgers in the killing fields, whilst angry farmers are slaughtering them in the protected areas. This, of course, invalidates the great Experiment, and makes it a complete waste of badgers.

Unfortunately Julian Pettifer's investigation clashed with another interesting documentary I wanted to watch, about Geri Halliwell, the former Spice Girl. Since I have never acquired the knack of adjusting video appliances, I was reduced to flicking channels, watching well-meaning scientists murdering badgers during the *longueurs* when Geri was sitting at her kitchen table staring into space, which she seems to do quite a lot. I was hoping she would entertain us with her throaty, baritone singing, which

"I like a man with a beard"

always puts one in mind of a red-sailed, barnacle-bottomed tugboat, butting through the sleet on a bad day in Essex. But no, it seemed Geri was taking a day off, *sans* songs, *sans* jokes, *sans anything.*

Between juggling badgers and Geri, my notes might have got confused. I am not sure now whether it was the badgers or Geri who wondered whether life had lost its meaning. Possibly it was Geri who warned us about population control, while the badger's merely suffered from it, but the two did seem to find certain interests in common. I found myself wondering whether Geri does her legs with a badger-hair shaving-brush. This would establish what the former TV personality, James Burke, used to call 'A Connection'. In that event, the controllers could have saved us a lot of bother and put them both on the same programme.

The badgers would, I'm sure, agree with Geri that true happiness can be elusive. I think the best solution would be for Geri to become a spokesperson for Badger Power. Not only would this give her something to do, but it would probably result in a popular uprising in the West Country. We would chase the scientists back to Smith Square where they belong, brandishing pitchforks and roaring Spice Girl hits like 'Too much' and 'Who do you think you are'. Come on, everyone, let's have Geri to spice up our dreary old environment. Come on down, Geri, the badgers need you!

* * *

A use for pickled serpents

Since entrance charges were wickedly introduced, the Natural History Museum has gone ever downmarket. Of course, like everyone else, I want it to be exactly as it was when I first saw it, back in 1873.

As the dreaded Millennium approaches, our thoughts turn naturally to the nation's growing criminal underclass. Wondering what to do about the 'rough diamonds' and 'loveable rogues' in our midst is exercising the best minds here in Swampville. We're not allowed to shoot the brutes, or even dust down the man-traps, and modern policeman interpret 'reasonable force' in terms of polite requests to leave.

A possible answer has been hit on by the staff of a Tesco supermarket. When their store was invaded by a gang of thugs intent on mischief, did these till-girls flinch, did they blink? Blink they did not. Instead, by making a crafty outflanking manoeuvre to the fruit stall, they forced the villains to retreat under a hail of malignant melons, vicious pomegranates and truclulent bananas. So far none of the staff have been arrested for fruit abuse, and we can only hope that their action remained within the constraints allowed by the law.

Perhaps the Natural History Museum has taken note of this encouraging story. As we know, its present managers have little use for the original fabric of the museum, truly described by its designer, Alfred Waterhouse, as a 'Cathedral to Nature'. Realising that old-fashioned educational museums make very little money, they cleared out all the old stuff to make room for a really, really modern facility with plenty of cafés, junk shops and rent-a-space displays about lesbianism in chimpanzees. But in the wake of the telly-success, *Walking with Dinosaurs*, the museum must surely be anticipating a spate of bone-lifting in one of the few good displays left (never mind that all the dinosaurs are made of fibre glass, the thieves won't know that). The fruit-hurling exploits of the valiant shelf-fillers of Tesco may suggest an obvious means of deterrence. It would be nice to see the museum putting to some good use all those sad old specimens collected from around the world by the likes of Wallace, Darwin and Captain Cook.

Twitcher's A to Z of the year

The idea of these alphabets was for Twitcher to summarise events at the end of each year (which, for British Wildlife *magazine, ends in August). Unfortunately no one ever did anything that started with K. Oh for some Kangaroos, or Koalas.*

A is for **Amphibian**, slow-moving, defenceless beasts you can shovel up and remove in buckets whenever their presence becomes inconvenient. The perfect conservation animal really.

B is for **Bogs**, a former habitat delivered to your door in a sack, to help you with your geraniums. The craters left where the bogs used to be are to be declared nature reserves.

C is for the **Countryside**. Undeveloped land between towns, variously reported stolen (Marion Shoard), killed (Graham Harvey) or ended (Bill McKibben).

D is for **Darwin**, a keen beetle collector who discovered evolution by accident. There are probably more things awaiting discovery out there, but no one collects beetles any more.

E is for **Environmental Task Force**, that is, a group of people cutting hawthorn bushes. Other groups cut hawthorn under Reserve Enhancement or Habitat Restoration Programmes. Particularly zealous cutters are called Eco-Action Volunteers.

F is for **FWAG** (the Farming and Wildlife Advisory Group), an eco-friendly group of farmer's daughters, guaranteed to cheer up a damp field corner or hedgebank. I am a regular attender of FWAG meetings, along with most of the young farmers of Wiltshire. Often we bring a little present, such as an amusingly shaped vegetable. It shows we care.

G is for **Gummerisation**, the means by which we are ruled by computer predictions, notably Gummer's brilliant decision to build 4.4 million new 'homes' at a time of nil population growth.

H is for **Heather**, a component part of a habitat called Heathland. According to the literature, there are other things, too, to be found in Heathland. This, as anyone who has struggled through heather will know, is not true.

I is for the **Institute of Terrestrial Ecology**, the unpronounceable rent-a-scientist organisation, last heard of in about 1987.

J The original dictionary definition of conservation was the process of making sweet, sticky conserves, or **Jam**. It still is, in a way.

K is for the **Kennet**, a former trout stream. Although designated as a SSSI it is currently a muddy, fishless trickle. 'Next year could be even better,' promise the Wildlife Trusts.

L is for the **Lottery**. The Romans appeased the poor with free bread and circuses. We make them pay for Bitterns and Action Plans. Let's hope they are suitably grateful.

M is for **Management**, that is to say action done to prevent nature from behaving naturally.

N is for **Nature Conservation**, a unique enterprise in which industry (staff, money spent, etc) expands as the resource diminishes.

O is for **Otherness**, the notion of nature as something separate from ourselves. Clearly a laughable idea, until the next storm or flood comes along.

P is for **Partnership, Programmes and Proactive**, all much misused words meaning something quite different. The P word of the year, however, was Pivotal, meaning nothing at all..

Q is for **Quackwak**, the last utterance of my duck, coincidentally named Quackwak, before she was squished by a lorry last June.

R is for the spirit of Rio, a ghostly green figure which urges you to think globally when putting up a nest box or planting a sapling.

S is for **Sustainable, Set-aside, Stewardship, SSSIs** and **Success**. Count the S's. What *is* it about that hissing sound we seem to like so much?

T is for **Target**, a thing for biodiversity planners to aim at. Unfortunately we are poor shots, and usually fix the score.

U is for **Urban Environment**, a temporary open space stocked with people-friendly objects such as surplus newts and non-toxic plants. Shame about the vandals.

V is for **Vision**. Formerly the revelation of a transcendent truth through a glimpse of the divine. More recently a hackneyed statement of purpose cobbled up late at night by tired managers after a fortnight of team-building. Ideally it should sound good but be completely meaningless. It usually does.

W is for **Wilderness, Wolves** and **Wheelchairs**. I hope that they can be combined somewhere, preferably under a big Welcome sign.

X was, of course for **Tony**. Conservationists never vote conservative. To both parties, their cognate similarities are pure coincidence.

Y Young People. Zealous guardians of those invasive sycamores, which destroyed most of the wildlife before they were born.

Z Two useful words are **Zugzwang** – an irresistible need to do something even when every alternative is bad; and **Zwitterion** – a self-important little body which faces both ways at once. Do you know any Zwitterions?

The Gorge

Stenga ran ahead of us both as we neared the gorge. The old man and I had spoken of this moment for a moment, as we approached Stenga was at the edge, looking at us approaching.

'There!' The old man pointed with his hazel stick. We stood and looked below where we stood by the edge of the gorge. I knew then that something exciting was down there where the three of us stood. We looked for a while; it seemed like an age, but it was only a while. Stenga barked and answered a call of nature against an outcrop of schist. I laughed, and the old man rebuked me with a silent gesture of rebuke. 'Where?' I said, finally. He pointed. I looked. Stenga looked. There, far below us, way down at the bottom, far, far away, was the bottom of the gorge. I sat down in the rock-rose and wept.

Strathpeffer

2000

Remembering them

By the latest reckoning, a quarter of the world's species will be wiped out by 2050, to make way for another zillion human beings. Twitcher suggests that a suitably grandiose monument should be the least we can do to show our appreciation of their sacrifice. Carstairs shows us an example.

I see London is about to receive one more war memorial before we all turn our faces towards Tony's fun-filled future. This is to take the form of a 'monumental' sculpture commemorating all the various animals 'from elephants, mules and camels to horses, dogs and pigeons', which supported the armed forces during the two World Wars. 'They died that we might live'. They think it would be fitting if the monument was placed at Hyde Park Corner, next to the Wellington Arch and the Artillery Memorial. One can only hope that the descendants of these heroic pigeons will have the decency to crap somewhere else.

Perhaps it is time we gave thought to building an even more monumental memorial for all those unfortunate species we have wiped out during the past thousand years of human progress. The extinction rate, says Sir Robert May, the government's chief scientific adviser, has been a thousand times greater than it would have been had mankind not existed. And it is set to get worse, he thinks. Much worse.

On the other hand, leading British wildlife charities hold a much rosier vision of the future. Not only can we save the biodiversity, but the year 2100 could be even better for wildlife than 2000, claims the Wildlife Trusts, so long as we keep sending them money. I don't know, you just don't know what to believe, do you?

All the same, I think we should get on with this monument to our Departed Species. Not only would it be an act of reparation for past misdeeds, but it would also remind the tourists of Britain's proud record of heroic failure, one of our gifts to the world. It is only right that we honour those unsung species that have died out so that we have more room to park the car, or can get from A to B just that bit quicker.

* * *

Restricted view

The BBC were busy promoting Titchmarsh, another TV gardener, as 'the new Attenborough'. Helpfully, Twitcher drew attention to his obvious hatred of sycamore trees.

Meanwhile on the Isle of Wight the pressing conservation issue is whether Alan Titchmarsh should be allowed to cut down his sycamore tree. Titchmarsh, who is, apparently, a television personality, claims that the tree spoils his view and is out of scale with its surroundings. The picture bears him out – his sycamore is a hulking great brute, and the scene would be much better without it. But, typically, the local council has clapped a tree preservation order on it. 'We try to keep and protect as many trees as we possibly can,' says Matthew Chatfield, a senior countryside officer. Local conservationists agree that the tree is sacrosanct. 'It's wicked,' a neighbour chimes in.

I wonder whether these people know what it is they are protecting. When your train arrives late, thanks to leaves on the line, blame the sycamore. Unusually, its fallen leaves turn to slippery pulp, causing the train's wheels to skid helplessly. Did you park your car under the shade of a sycamore on a hot day? Say hello to sticky 'honeydew' all over your windscreen. Oops, granny has slipped again, and it looks expensive. Better sue the local authority which planted the offending sycamores. One might have hoped that any senior countryside officer would know that conservation groups spend half their working lives battling with invading sycamores.

The solution to this problem is somewhat complicated. First the Council must cut down the offending sycamore since it threatens Alan's safety as well as his car, which I imagine might be quite an expensive one. Next his busty colleague, Charlie, should help Alan to erect a harmless plastic replica in its place, so meeting the Council's landscape objectives. And finally, senior countryside officers should all be assigned new duties on a conservation corps in, say, the Avon Gorge, or in any one of the thousands of sycamore-struck woodlands in northern England.

Of course, the whole thing could be just another television stunt, in which case I may decide to sue the whole lot of them for wasting my time.

* * *

Keeping the score

At some stage in the Nineties, objectives became 'targets', though they are by no means the same thing. An objective is an aim; a target is a circular pad or card used for archery or firearms practice. This outbreak of violence in the hitherto placid conservation world clearly worried Twitcher.

I wonder how the biodiversity industry reconciles the vast number of targets it has set itself. Every rare beast or plant, and some of their habitats, has been assigned a target, and there are local targets as well as national ones. Everybody, from the smallest county trust to national agencies seem to be churning out targets as though they were in the archery business, preparing for a second Hundred Years War. Presiding over this mountain of targets is the Department for the Environment, Transport and the Regions (DETR), which itself has produced some 500 performance targets during the past year alone, some of which set targets for achieving targets. So many, indeed, are the targets that ministers are said to be losing track of them – it is like one of those fairground shooting galleries where the endless targets flash past too quickly to take aim.

I suspected this might happen when I refused to draw up a target for my own bit of biodiversity, the Royal Bolete, on the grounds that it would be completely meaningless. My impression was that all concerned were immensely relieved. Possibly they feared that any Bolete target I drew up might compromise the contradictory target of some rare bat or beetle. It would be sad if all this hard target-making started a target war in which rival conservationists shot at one another's targets. Not least because they would almost certainly miss the targets altogether and whang one another in the foot.

ANOTHER BREAKTHROUGH IN BIRD-WATCHING: THE 20-FOOT HIDE

Letter from Down-under

This piece wasn't really a Twitcher. I had been on a birdwatching holiday in New Zealand, and wanted to tell somebody.

It was when a wild kaka parrot landed on my head with a flutter and gently removed my grip from a sandwich that I realised New Zealand's birds are not like ours. Birdwatching in Britain is reduced mainly to a glimpse of the cowardly little sods legging it, or speeding off into the foliage. Or it is when I do it. Here in God's own country of New Zealand the birding is of superior quality. The little ones appear from nowhere to check you out for any bugs you may be attracting or stirring up (to the Fantails and Tomtits you are just another big smelly mammal, or possibly a giant penguin). And, as I say, some of the bigger ones may wish to part you from your lunch. Minutes before the parrot incident, my companion Jamie had a dishevelled look. As far as I could make out, a mad one-eyed kaka had attacked his rucksack, smashed up a couple of polystyrene cups inside and then bit him on the ear. We had been warned about this. We were also advised to avoid any weka wearing a white leg ring (a weka is a flightless rail about the size of a chicken). These wekas were persistent troublemakers, on some sort of probation. They don't just take your sandwiches: given half a chance they steal the bag containing your entire rations. This little failing of theirs can lead to disaster, since, having gulped down your sandwich, scones and Moro bar, they will then try swallowing the bag, and that don't do them no good at all. The white ring is their last warning. One more squeak out of them and they risk being deported from their comfortable predator-free island and dumped in some bush country on the mainland, seething with stoats and cats.

All things considered, it is amazing that these adorable birds still trust human beings. Consider the plight of the kaka. The kaka gets its meed of protein and fat by eating beetle grubs. But unfortunately it uses up more energy locating and digging up the grubs than it gains from eating them. So it needs lots of sugar. It is here that its problems start to pile up. Plague numbers of introduced wasps lap up all the available honeydew, while introduced possums account for most of the nectar and sap. Sugar, in other words, is what it can't get. Meanwhile introduced stoats eat the kakas. Let's look at the arithmetic here. There are about 10,000 kakas and about a 100 million possums competing for the same food, that is 10,000 possums per kaka. And that is why that kaka wanted my sandwich. His need was probably greater than mine.

What are our gallant Antipodean chums doing about all this? Well, while there was some incentive to trap possums for their fur, possum numbers could be kept down. But the animal rights lobby has managed to ban the fur trade. Meanwhile any kind of trapping or poisoning, even to take the pressure off New Zealand's remaining native birds, is fast becoming socially unacceptable. So what can be done instead? Though dead possums are a common sight on the roads (they just sit there and stare transfixed at the approaching lights) it is a case of 'the more and more I knocked 'em down, the more they multiply'. Reproducing the way they do, they can afford the casualties.

The latest idea is to develop a genetically-modified carrot that will reduce the fertility of any possum happening to eat one. Somehow I can't see that one working either. I think our friends in Greenpeace would be sending another Rainbow Warrior to New Zealand if they gone wind of GM crop experiments of that sort. Short of some Pied Piper of possums appearing and taking them all back to Australia, I'd say they have managed to hit the buffers on this one.

It is a sign of the general hatred for the possum, despite its cuddly face, that the beast has no native name. Nowadays people are encouraged to refer to native birds by their Maori name: Kereru for the New Zealand Pigeon, for example, or Titi for the Sooty Shearwater or Muttonbird. Some of these names are rather confusing. As well as the Kaka, there is the even more endangered Kakapo or Owl Parrot (as a last-ditch attempt to preserve the Kakapo, they have resorted to artificial insemination) – the Kakapo is not to be confused with the Kokako, a wattlebird, or the Katipo, a kind of spider. I'm not sure whether some of these names are particularly dignified either. OK, we didn't exhaust our imaginations with the Brown Creeper, but surely even that is better than the alternative of 'Pipipi'? And what kind of joke are we playing on the seriously endangered Stitchbird by calling it a Heehee? It bears an uncomfortable echo of the native Laughing Owl, which laughed all the way to global extinction by 1914. Still, for the record, we did manage to see Titi, Pipipi, Heehee and even

Hoiho (formerly Yellow-eyed Penguin), though my hopes of finding Pukupuku (Little Spotted Kiwi) were dashed by a touch of gippitummi. And now I suppose it is time to return to the land of the whinging Poms. New Zealand is a beautiful and friendly country, which seems relaxing even when you are toiling through the tree-fern looking for a Pipi. It makes you realise what, fundamentally, is wrong with England. There are too damn many of us. That is the long and the short of it. Perhaps we should be force-fed with GM carrots.

* * *

A future for Wales

I love small countries: they don't have the hang-ups of the big ones, and get away with saying the most outrageous things. Corsicans and the Welshmen should, I thought, get together at bit more.

Oliver Walston, the boisterous farmer, predicts the spread of 'useless unattractive' scrub over the hills if public farm subsidies are withdrawn. Most hill farms would go out of business and the land will return to wilderness, he warns. But this need not be all that bad. I have just returned from a place where this prediction has come true: the island of Corsica. People often remark about the invisibility of British farmers, except when you're stuck in the traffic queue behind one. But our countryside is a beehive of activity compared with Corsica's. Corsica is a place where you see bracken growing up among what little corn there is, where crops are confined to the odd tattered row of vines, or the occasional net is optimistically draped under an olive tree. The rest is scrub, horizon to horizon. Though Corsica has fewer residents than Swindon, I am told that most of its food is imported.

The locals seem quite happy about all this. The scrub, or maquis, which looks like a rose garden in May, is full of scented herbs which you can press into lavender bags, delicious free-range pigs that gorge themselves on chestnuts, and hidden streams teeming with trout. Your typical rugged independent Corsican will drive a bus or man a bar for a few months in

the summer, then grab a fly rod or gun and head for the hills. They have changed the subsidy system, you see, from supporting farming to supporting people. This is why the fiercely nationalistic Corsicans, who chalk the word 'Libertas' on every gatepost and doorway, and fly their very un-pc flag – a black man's severed head (it's a long story) – from every village hall, seem in practice to spend most of their time eating and drinking and watching the world go by.

It looks a lot more fun than chasing sheep over rainy hillsides. I wonder whether this might be the solution both to the farming crisis in Wales and to the resurgence of Welsh nationalism. It might also encourage the Welsh to do something about their bloody awful cooking, said to be the worst in the civilised world.

* * *

Pushing up bluebells

Simple folk think that being buried in a cardboard box enables them to give something back to nature. Does it ever occur to them that nature might not want all the poisonous chemicals accumulated from a lifetime's over-indulgence?

Perhaps it is a morbid subject to bring up in the sweet spring, but someone has to comment on this new fad of being buried in wild places. A trust has now been set up to bury environmentally-aware churchgoers in a plot of land in Cambridgeshire, and then plant trees on top. Its slogan is: 'Go Wild When You Die'. 'I love the sound (sic) of being buried among the bluebells', murmurs one prospective client. The vicar who runs the show believes that people have become uncomfortable about being buried near a church and prefer 'giving something back to the environment that has nurtured them'.

Yes, but what these deluded people will give back most of is phosphate. Mankind, as Oliver Rackham has observed, is a phosphate-accumulating animal. Old woods and pastures are naturally short of phosphate, which is why they are rich in wildlife. What is destined to flower over these recycled environmentalists is not bluebells but stinging nettles. Although a few of us might rather like the idea of being remembered in that way, it would be a shame if the outraged relatives sprayed all these 'green graves' with Roundup. Defeats the point of it all, really.

A much better idea would be to encourage more country churchyards. Not only are they pleasant places in which to sit and muse about the transience of life, but you can't beat a nice old-fashioned bone yard for wild flowers, lichens, bats, waxcap fungi, etc. Let's give these people their traditional seven-feet-by-two and leave the bluebells in peace.

* * *

Well done!

You get the impression reading these 'Action Plans' that rare species are all out there heaving and straining to lay enough eggs to fulfil their quotas or targets. I liked the idea of urging a bird to lay an extra egg for nice Mr Meacher.

Let's have a big round of applause for the Stone Curlew. Not only did it exceed its breeding target this year, but it seems it was the only species of farmland bird to do so (come on, you farmland birds, lay another egg for nice Mr Meacher). According to the latest figures, the Stone Curlews are 50 pairs up on what was expected of them this year, which I think we're all agreed is a jolly good effort, especially with all the wind and rain we've been having. Their next challenge is to build on this success to achieve the 'golden goal' of their Ten Year Plan with 'at least' 300 pairs by the year 2010. With the right spirit, I'm sure they can surpass this target too. I hope so. I really do. Otherwise we might have to consider bringing in the men from the research units with their tubes and their needles. But I'm sure this won't be necessary, and that the birds know what is good for them.

At this moment of celebration, I'm sure we'll all want to pay tribute to the teams of carers and supporters that have made it all possible. First, let's have a big hand for the DETR, with its multiple departments, directorates, agencies and commissions; next the local authoritieis, both regional and urban, and the stalwarts of the RSPB, BTO, BAP, HLF, JNCC,

CA, EA and EN, and their Scottish and Welsh counterparts, who've teamed so tirelessly to get a result; and last but not least, you, the taxpayer and lottery gambler, for financing them all. It shows just what can be done with a few dozen plans, unlimited money and an army of busybodies working at creating visions, implementing targets, rationalising priorities, making the tea, etc. Let's hope that far away on some beleagured heath, a small knock-kneed bird will be laying an extra egg in gratitude.

* * *

Weather notes

Don't you just love those chirpy weather girls: 'clards are thweatening the sarf, and that's yer weather!' It would be good if they could be trained to weep when it's raining, and take their clothes off when the sun comes out. They're nearly there.

I'm sure the BBC did not intend to alarm its viewers when one of the weather girls told us it was raining '20 centimetres an hour' in south-east England last October. Twenty centimetres in an hour really is quite a lot of rain. But millimetres, centimetres, they are easily confused. The important thing is to sound metrically-correct. No weather girl would

dream of talking in inches, though if she had, she might have realised that eight inches of rain per hour would soon drown the lot of us. On the same day another BBC hackette told us that Stamford Bridge, then underwater, was the scene of the famous English victory over William the Conqueror. Personally I'll believe anything I hear on television.

Some of these weather girls don't look old enough to have seen much bad weather, and perhaps this accounts for Mr Prescott's solemn warning of imminent eco-catastrophe: 'It's a wake-up call for everyone'. But if anyone is thinking of building an ark, I'd say: go back to sleep. Sure, it has been pretty wet down here, but nothing we have endured so far compares with the floods of 1947 or 1953, to say nothing of the summer of 1316, when it rained non-stop from April to October, and everybody starved. What has changed is not so much the climate as the reporting of it, and also the level of insurance pay-outs. Bad weather is certainly more expensive than it used to be, but isn't everything? Of course it doesn't help that since the war our brilliant planners have encouraged building in places notorious for flooding.

With travel becoming ever more frustrating and chaotic we will eventually learn to stay at home and spend most of our lives indoors. There are few quiet pleasures left to compare with watching the pelting rain and bending trees through double-glazing with one's knees resting on a nice warm radiator.

* * *

Twitcher's A to Z of the year

Another alphabet. Thank heaven for Kestrels.

Another year, another volume. Twitcher looks back alphabetically at some of the highlights.

A is for **Afforestation**. The hated State Forests are being replaced by some lovely, fluffy things called Community Forests. Amazing the difference a word makes.

B is for **Badger**, a short-lived animal. Each year some 50,000 badgers are squashed on the road, and thousands more shot by MAFF trappers or sent packing by the builders. Any survivors are fully protected by law.

C is for **Controversy**, like the proposal to ban hunting, something never mentioned by 'country-style' magazine or wildlife bodies in case they lose money over it. C also stands for Cowards, of course.

D is for **Designations**. Good news: St Kilda is to be made a Special Area of Conservation (SAC), in addition to its existing status as a WHS, NNR, NSA, SSSI and SPA. Collect the lot and you win a fridge.

E is for **Earth Day**, when we set aside a few hours 'to help the Earth get better', before continuing to mess up the planet on the other 364 days. It's an American idea.

F is for **Farmer**, formerly the provider of the nation and salt of the earth, now either a sidelined bankrupt or a hired lackey paid £6 per hectare per year to 'protect the environment'.

G is for **Global Warming**, a mystic belief which, for the Faithful, has survived years of freezing springs, washed-out summers and the odd gale. We're all Guilty.

H is for **Hedgerow**, defined by European regulations as a linear barrier no more than 2m wide, preferably made of EU-approved hawthorn from Hungary.

K is for **Kestrel**, a fastidious bird with a taste for endangered species, such as Snipe or Little Tern. Then the Foxes eat the Kestrels.

L is for **Leaflet**. One on wildlife gardening I wrote years ago has just surfaced as a booklet for 'Beazer Homes', whose 'superbly built houses' and bug-friendly gardens are just the thing you need for your new hobby.

M is for **Move**, what the conservation agencies routinely do to their field staff to prevent them from ever knowing too much about the areas they administer. Knowledge worries senior managers.

N is for **Norway**, a flexible country. According to something called the Global Economic Forum, Norway is 'the most sustainable nation in

Europe'. But the WWF says 'Norway? No way'. Actually, it is the least sustainable. Well, that's clear then. Terrific work all round, chaps.

O is for **Optimism**, embodied in a leaflet from Countryside Alliance entitled *Hunting in the 21st Century*. It's a short leaflet.

P is for **Prohibition**. Anything that's not compulsory should be forbidden, that's my view. Personally, I think Tony is wonderful.

Q is for the **Queen Mum**, Gawd bless her. A recent survey found that the garden of Buck. Palace is one of the best places for wildlife in London, thanks to its high walls. There were immediate calls from 'environmentalists' to have them pulled down.

R is for **Roaming**, the right to, so long as we don't get up to anything incorrect, like collecting beetles or picking mushrooms. Please don't confuse rights with liberties. The fines are awfully steep.

S is for **Sustainability**, that is, your ability to sustain interest while reading Agenda 2000. I'm very proud of my personal best of ten minutes.

T is for **Tomorrow**, that hallowed dawn when the ultimate fulfilment of all the red tape and regulation will keep every Briton in a state of blissful impotence.

U is for **Utilitarian**. Professional environmentalists routinely divide all creation into indicators, or elements in a system, or targets for recovery. Taking any interest in the wonders of nature is the mark of a rank amateur.

V is for **Veteran Trees**, gnarled but experienced trees that have been round the block a few times. Wisely, foresters chop them down before they corrupt susceptible young conifers.

W is for **Whales**, large, blubbery things, formerly useful for making margarine, now the object of blubbery humans, eager to take endless snaps of an empty ocean distinguished only by an incomprehensible greyish lump in the distance.

X is for **X-rated**, for example, the bits of Twitcher's column in *British Wildlife* you don't read, thanks to Branson's snappy scissors.

Y is for **Yesterday**. *The happy highways where I went and cannot come again.* The past is frowned on by Tony, who is more of a Tomorrow type, on the whole.

Z is for **Zander**, a fish. Wildlife agencies told the Burns inquiry that natural predation is not a problem (since it is natural), evidently overlooking the Zander is it chomps its way through our native fish. Still, out of sight, out of mind.

Some wax

At this time of year in winter when they are cold ones, people phone and tell me about their waxwings. These special birds, which are Arctic, have no wax, but people who phone me are adamant and I spend hours telling them that, just as goosanders are not crested like the merganser, which is red breasted, that they aren't covered in wax. Candles are though, and Stenga and me spent the whole of Tuesday eating them in the kitchen, where we could without making a mess. Stenga loves the curly ones from Woolies. Me? A couple of straight cake ones are fine for me after my dinner.

It is bird feeding time again and my time to tell you what to do. Go to your petshop, buy a huge sack of shelled peanuts, go home, mix them with water and feed to the dog. Sod the birds. They never survive the winter anyway.

Strathpeffer

2001

Consoling thought

Twitcher often writes about rhinoceroses, invariably in a tragic context. Of course, one would like to be upbeat and gung-ho, like Chris Baines, the ubiquitous gardening pundit, for instance, and talk about 'joined-up' rhinos or 'weaving the rhinos back together'. But let's face it, 'rhinoceros' and 'good news' are not words you often see together.

Is this the ultimate conservation programme? Extinction threatens the Black Rhinoceros of Cameroon, of which barely a dozen have survived the poachers. As a result, each one is to receive a 24-hour armed bodyguard until a special rhino sanctuary can be built. Then they will all be tranquillised, trussed up and bundled inside a security fence with built-in searchlights and watchtowers. This is called an Intensive Protection Zone. It's the best that the scientists can do for what American veterinarian Mike Loomis calls 'these amazing prehistoric creatures', most of which have been recycled into Yemeni dagger-handles.

Meanwhile, any similar plans they might have had for the recently discovered Mountain Buffalo of Cambodia were halted on the reasonable-sounding grounds that it doesn't exist. The buffalo hunters were looking for a beast with unusual lyre-shaped horns which they had seen in local

markets and assumed belonged to an unknown beast. But they forgot to ask local craftsmen, who had made the things from ordinary cattle horns, heated and twisted into shape. With their customary ingenuity, scientists had managed to deduce a great deal about this non-existent animal, including its numbers ('less than 2,500 mature adults'), weight, diet and habits ('lives in small herds'). Needless to say, it was in urgent need of Intensive Protection Zones and translocation procedures.

I wonder why over-excited scientists invariably refer to rhinoceroses as 'prehistoric' creatures. Leaving aside the obvious fact that prehistoric animals are, by definition, extinct, Black Rhinos are no more ancient than many other animals. They just happen to have big horns on their noses, which are the ideal thing for making Yemeni dagger-handles. All the same, one has to agree that rhinos do look a bit improbable. When poachers finally kill the last one, perhaps we can make ourselves happier by believing that their curiously shaped horns were only an artefact of Yemeni craftsmen. Obviously, the creatures never existed.

* * *

Dustbin of history

It is one thing being dictated to by do-gooders, but what I really can't stand is being bossed about by morons. Here, Twitcher acknowledges his debt to the late, great Auberon Waugh, who fingered lettuces as the probable cause of increased moronism in our midst.

In 50 years' time will anyone remember that we used to hunt wild animals? Among the demonstrators outside the Palace of Westminster on 17th January, as the Commons 'debated' the Hunting Bill, was Wendy Turner, who presents a television show called *Pet Rescue.* Wendy, a vegan, posed with three men dressed up as wild animals before delivering a letter to MPs demanding a full and total ban. 'The time has long passed for hunting with dogs to be consigned to the history books along with bear-baiting and cock-fighting,' said Wendy, cuddling a man dressed up as a fox.

What Wendy seems to be saying is that it is too late to ban hunting. But I expect that she knew what she meant. Where I part company is in doubting whether it is safe to consign things to history books. To some people, history and dustbins are more or less interchangeable words. They see history as a dumpster or trash can for all the incorrect stuff we did in the old, unenlightened days. As for real history, a survey commissioned by Osprey, the educational publishers, finds that many children of secondary-school age believe that Hitler was our prime minister during the Second World War. The battle of Hastings was won by Oliver Cromwell, and Nelson probably sailed to his famous victory at Waterloo in the good ship *Mary Rose*. One day, children will believe that the toffs hunted horses using foxes, and finished them off by throwing dogs at them. Then they ate the fox, the rotten swines.

I wonder whether this confusion has anything to do with all the vegetables we eat nowadays. We ignore at our peril the health risks involved, which, if Wendy is any guide, include the inability to form coherent sentences, an unexplained need to cuddle foxes in public and an insatiable desire to find out what people are doing in the countryside and then trying to stop them. Unfortunately, the one person who constantly warned us about lettuces, the journalist Auberon Waugh, has died. Now there may be nothing to stop these lettuce-worshippers from filling their dustbins with more and more prohibited activities from the past. Well, never mind. We can always watch repeat episodes of *Pet Rescue*.

* * *

Gaby shows the way

More about morons, this time in a televisual context.

The latest casualty in the onward march of 'dumbing down' is Anglia TV's famous wildlife series, *Survival*. Yes, *Survival* has failed to survive. Although it normally makes enough money, *Survival* was mildly in the red last year, which unfortunately coincided with the arrival of a new management team from Granada. In the world of budget telly, you don't get a second chance. Now, *Survival*'s team is about to be disbanded and dispatched to sink or swim in the freelance pond, or sent to Bristol, home of the BBC's Natural History Unit. 'There are a lot of people who are very upset, hurt and angry,' one of *Survival*'s ex-producers told a *Guardian* journalist.

'So what?', you might well ask. The trouble is, by telly standards, *Survival* really was quite good. The programmes were relatively expensive to make, but that was all right because *Survival* films sold all around the world – they even won a Queen's award for export.

Survival's real crime, it seems, was to make programmes that are intelligent. 'We don't want to make programmes that send people to bed feeling depressed,' moaned some lobotomised TV executive. What they think the viewer prefers is 'presenter-led series following international animal-welfare workers, a kind of *Animal Hospital* on the road'.

Oh my, that's an original idea isn't it? Any dearth of content or point of view will be more than compensated for by the sight of some tearful Gaby or Tabby or Blabby restored to radiant joy by the sight of some injured beast stuck back together again and restored to the wild. A happy Gaby, a better world for us all, is the wholesome message. The important thing is that we don't go to bed feeling upset, hurt or depressed.

* * *

Mad cows

The sight of bonfires of burning farm animals upset a lot of people though it wasn't very different to what was going to happen to them anyway, roasted in the oven for two hours at 180°C or sizzled in the pan for breakfast. Most farmers did all right out of compensation. It even helped to bury MAFF, for which there was, by then, hardly a moist eye to be found.

When people are allowed to roam in approved bits of the countryside in about eight years' time, I wonder whether they will any longer want to. Ever since they closed the footpaths in Ramsbury after the foot-and-mouth outbreak, I have been dying to do a spot of roaming. Once they open them again, I dare say this urge will leave me. Forbidden pastures always look sweetest. Forced to stay indoors, watching the plumes of black smoke from the burning cows and piggies, one is inclined to brood about the state of the countryside. The lives of farm animals are pretty unenviable really, even when they are not being taken all the way from Wallow-on-the-Wall, Northumberland, to Buggeridge, Essex, to be slaughtered.

'What has it all been for?', one broods. The strategic aim of intensive home-grown food production was achieved long ago. If continuing subsidised agriculture was meant to prop up farm incomes, it has obviously failed miserably. The only other possible reason for subsidies is to keep food prices low. But many of us nowadays prefer quite expensive food from relatively happy animals, in the hope that it tastes nicer and is less likely to be infected with foot-and-mouth, BSE, *Salmonella* and nasty things they haven't discovered yet. In other words, it seems that we have ill-treated animals and laid waste the countryside in vain, unless it was to enable people with no money to eat more.

The trouble with this policy, as George Orwell noticed all those years ago in *The Road to Wigan Pier*, is that people with no money often eat far too much. It is the rich, pop stars, for example, or TV presenters, that eat very little, and none of that from farm animals. It seems to me that the men from MAFF may be suffering from some as yet undiagnosed illness, not unlike that of mad cow disease. They are still living in the world of the 1950s, when chicken was a Sunday treat, and a sandwich was a curly thing with a tile of processed cheese inside. As the excellent David Starkey pointed out on a recent *Moral Maze*, if MAFF ran the car industry they would produce nothing but Ladas. I think the time has come to give reluctant consideration to slaughtering the entire MAFF herd. A few of the more intelligent ones could be vaccinated and kept on for breeding, under nice Mr Meacher's supervision.

My wooden farm

Many of us spent the plague-ridden summer of 2001 looking wistfully over gates and brooding about the farming industry.

There's silver lining every cloud, or so think our leading conservation bodies. All right, so 3.5 million livestock have been slaughtered, and it is becoming hard to find a cow to grace a field. But what tomorrow's countryside needs, says the 'Rebuilding Biodiversity Group', is not farmers but planners – you know, the guys that brought you tower blocks and made you live in a zone. They have a beautiful vision of how 'to bring back Britain's wildlife'. Among the lovely things shimmering in this vision are community forests around every town (how delightfully Swedish), 'targeted agri-environment schemes at (sic) biodiversity priorities' and, take a deep breath, 'effective implementations of the Rural Development Programme as a mechanism to maintain the rural environment in Less Favoured Areas'. Obviously, visions of this quality do not come cheap. But there will doubtless be plenty of CAP money sloshing about looking for a new home once they've slaughtered the last sheep. I think that we can trust the conservationists to lasso quite a lot of it.

Perhaps it's about time I stuck my own bucket under this Euro-cow. Having finished what I was doing earlier this year (another damned thick, square book), I have decided to join my fellow conservationists in building for the new tomorrow. Specifically, I'm going to make animals. Farm animals. Out of wood. This may surprise you, but wooden animals are superior in every way to plastic or fibre-glass ones, like the famous model cows of Milton Keynes. The 30,000 people who attended the recent East of England show, where the only livestock on display were two wooden cows, can't all be wrong. Very life-like rare breeds can be made out of choice woods, such as cherry or maple. Stick on some cotton-wool, and you have a convincing sheep, while good workaday pigs can be created from little more than a roll of cardboard, an old mackintosh and some sausage skins.

My wooden farmyard will be the perfect alternative for a country no longer capable of farming real animals. I can't wait to unveil the puppet squirrels which I have ready for the community forests – they tell old Forestry Commission jokes in a variety of amusing dialects. 'Wooden wildlife for a lifeless wood' will be our motto. The project as a whole is called Animal Challenge: alternative animals for a disease-free tomorrow. Does any reader know where I can get hold of some coconut matting? It's holding up my work on Aberdeen Anguses.

* * *

Noise tax

Twitcher continues his plans to become a 21st century-style farmer. I doubt they came to anything.

One of the advantages of wooden animals is that they do not make annoying noises. Newcomers to the countryside are often driven mad by cockerels crowing at unreasonable hours, or cows and sheep ruining a relaxing day out. Not only are these noises irritating, they are also boring. It would be the work of a moment to introduce more vocal variety in my farmyard, for example by making the sheep honk like geese or the Rhode Island Reds low like tethered bulls. The important thing is to amuse the kids and attract the foreign tourists, neither of whom know anything about animals.

There is also the ozone layer to consider. In New Zealand, they are levying a new tax on livestock to offset the environmental damage caused by dangerous gases erupting from cows. Each cow will henceforth cost the farmer seventeen hard-earned pounds, or roughly two pence per fart. This may rebound on the public if, after some culpable tax-dodges involving corks or balloons, the hills of New Zealand echo to the sound of exploding cattle, with heaven knows what harm to the environment. Fortunately, New Zealand is a long way from here.

For my part, I am becoming anxious about vegetarians, who are said now to number about a fifth of the population. The ozone layer must be shuddering in anticipation. I fear that a tax on baked beans may not go far enough. What is needed is a charge on oxygen, a valuable and finite gas of which we lose a little every time a vegetarian blows off. Those of us who still eat decent food, smoke and enjoy a gin-and-tonic before dinner would be exempt, it being well known that we are killing ourselves anyway.

* * *

A choice of bustards

The fruits of another birdwatching trip, in which bustards were twitched.

Having at last set eyes on a Great Bustard, strutting along on the plains of Extremadura, I now see that it would be wrong to reintroduce it to Britain. This bustard is Spanish through and through, from the tips of its magnificent moustachios to the flamboyant sweep of its tail. Indeed, it seems to me that your better sort of Spaniard probably models himself on the Great Bustard, copying the cool way in which it swaggers back and forth, head held high, like a grandee on the plaza, or flashes its feathers like a flamenco dancer. Why, stick a hat on it and a cane under its wing and you could pass it off as your eccentric relative from the provinces. In the wind and rain of Salisbury Plain it would just look silly.

Instead, I propose that we introduce the Little Bustard, which we also saw out on those Extremadura plains. While the Great Bustard swirls its feathers in extravagant foaming displays, the Little one tries to draw attention to itself by jumping up and down. First it takes a deep breath, stomps its feet, and then – up we go – does its little jump. Boing! 'Here I

am!' Boing. 'Look at me!' Boing. 'It's me again!' Boing. 'No, don't go away, I'm interesting. Look, I'll do another little jump.' Its call is a grating 'knerr'. In flight it makes a noise like a rusty bicycle. Yes, the Little Bustard's the one for us.

* * *

Team spirit

This next one was a rare piece of straightforward reportage. I hardly needed to change a thing.

The fourth of May 2001 may go down in history as the day they caught the Beast. As you may remember, there have long been rumours of a large animal on the loose in north London. It was one of those shadowy Beasts one reads about in the tabloids, generally from somewhere starting with B, like Bodmin or Barnet. Suddenly, as domestic cleaner Carol Montague found early on that fateful morning as she peered through the kitchen window, there it was, in clear view, sitting on a garden fence in

Cricklewood (thereupon becoming the Creature of Cricklewood, I expect, but I digress). 'I thought it was a Leopard or something', she told reporters. Nearly right, Mrs Montague. It was in fact a Pardel, or Iberian Lynx, which does indeed have a spotted coat, though to be scrupulously accurate it is not nearly 'as big as an Alsatian'. Very properly, she phoned the police: 'I don't think they believed me at first. They just laughed'. Next to see the Beast was Mrs Newman, returning from the shops: 'What I was worried about was getting our Staffordshire bull terrier, Samson, safely locked away indoors'. Very wise, Mrs Newman. Police officers Green and Leech arrived on the scene, perhaps still laughing. They took one look and sensibly took cover in Mrs Newman's kitchen, along with the dog, Samson. Discussing what to do next, they decided to call the RSPCA. An 'animal collection officer' duly turned up, but he was not prepared to tackle the Beast, either. 'It's not often you see something like that in north London,' he explained afterwards. So, they discussed it a bit more, and decided to call London Zoo, which sent its top man, the guy who looks after the big cats, who has encountered a few Beasts in his time, no doubt. From cover, the big cat guy eyed the Creature of Cricklewood, still sitting on the fence, yawning and licking its paws, and called for the assistance of a senior veterinary officer, Mr Sainsbury, who turned up armed with a tranquilliser gun. By this time, one imagines the kitchen as starting to resemble the crowded ship's cabin in the Marx Brothers' film *Night at the Opera*, at the moment when the steward pulls open the door and they all fall out in a heap.

Mr Sainsbury took a shot at the Beast but only winged it. The startled lynx hopped off the fence and took off over some playing fields with the team in hot pursuit, Mr Sainsbury and his gun, the big cat guy, the RSPCA officer, Mrs Montague and Mrs Newman, PCs Green and Leech, and probably Samson the dog, all shouting out 'stop, stop!'. Eventually, Mr Sainsbury cornered the Beast in the stairwell of a block of flats, took aim and shot it. The Beast, a thin, slightly lame Pardel Lynx the size of a small dog, was later said to be recovering behind bars at the zoo. 'It's a dangerous animal', said an RSPCA spokesman.

As I write, the hunt is on to find out where it came from. I suppose that it is unlikely to be a descendant of the old line of British lynxes that roamed our ancient forests. For one thing, it is the wrong species. However,

recent evidence from carbon-dating reveals that lynxes survived in Scotland at least until Roman times, and could probably do so again. They would be a useful means of controlling all those beavers they are intent on releasing. If they do reintroduce the lynx, it would be wisest to do it in secret. Rumours of ferocious Creatures of Caledonia lurking in the northern forests could spark a useful job-creation scheme for veterinary marksmen, RSPCA inspectors and big cat experts in places where they have pretty well run out of other employment ideas.

* * *

Neoteny

There was some animated correspondence in British Wildlife *about whether the word 'neophyte' meant anything beyond a reference to novices, nuns and Julie Andrews. Once again, Twitcher's warnings were ignored.*

Since the dawn of history, field botanists have by custom referred to introduced species as aliens. Hence the title of Sir Edward Salisbury's classic book, *Weeds and Aliens*. Today, he would probably be made to call it 'Arable Flowers and Non-natives', especially if this curiously-named new government department, DEFRA, (aka Department for the Environment, Food and Rural Affairs) had anything to do with it. DEFRA has told botanists producing the forthcoming plant atlas that the word 'alien' is unacceptable. Nor are they allowed to call it *The Atlas of the British Flora* or even *Atlas of the Flora of the British Isles*. There is no such thing as the British Isles under DEFRA's rule. Instead it must be *Atlas of the Flora of Britain and Ireland*. Catchy title, huh? Except that it leaves out Northern Ireland, the Channel Islands and the Isle of Man.

DEFRA's heart-warming sensitivity extends even to the origins of our wild flora. Ancient introductions, like Cornflowers, must not be called aliens or even non-natives but *archaeophytes*, a word borrowed from Europe, and so extra-correct. More recent introductions, such as Giant Hogweed or Skunk Cabbage, are to be termed *neophytes*. Unfortunately, whoever decided that this was a good idea cannot have glanced at a dictionary lately.

Neophyte means a novice or candidate for priesthood. Julie Andrews in *The Sound of Music* was a neophyte. I imagine that Julie would object most strongly to being compared with a Skunk Cabbage. When I was at university, an archaeophyte was the name given to primitive fossil plants from the antediluvian swamp. The only place where you'll find those is preserved in a lump of coal.

None of this is likely to bother DEFRA, which obviously agrees with Humpty Dumpty that 'a word means just what I choose it to mean – neither more nor less'. There is another word that accurately describes bossy, stupid officials who are forever ignorantly meddling in matters that don't concern them. The word is *bicaudal*. In the dictionary, you'll find this used for a kind of mutant fruitfly that has an extra arse where its head should be. It's a sort of double-bummed creature which serves no useful purpose, and which flies uselessly around in circles, bumping into things and annoying people. Besides, if DEFRA is serious about its PC mission, it could start by changing its name, which is bound to offend anyone with hearing difficulties. The Bicaudal would be a good new name, which wouldn't offend anyone.

* * *

You know where you are with an aardvark

Art, as they say, anticipates truth. In suggesting that were were too many molecular biologists and not enough plumbers, Twitcher could not have forseen the news in today's paper (24 February 2004) that a molecular biologist has quit for 'a better future' as a gas-fitter. Was it just the money, or does he read British Wildlife?

The great thing about an Aardvark is that you know exactly where you are with it. The ant-loving beast has no living relations to confuse it with, and surely no other animal is likely to make a little mistake and mate with it. The Aardvark, you can be pretty sure, is a good species. Unfortunately, other beasts are not so lucky. Since molecular fingerprinting became all the rage, increasing numbers of animals have been split into two or more look-alikes, more or less the same on the outside, but with slightly differently arranged molecules deep inside their reproductive bits. So, as molecular researchers dissect their way through the animal kingdom, pairs of beasts are emerging as if from Noah's ark – two gorillas, two chimpanzees, two wood-white butterflies – and up to 13 chiffchaffs.

The latest candidate for splitting is the African elephant. Investigators from Kenya and America taking 'tissue samples' from elephants, using a nasty-looking dart, have decided that there are really two different elephants, one smaller than the other and living in denser forest. Of course, if true, this changes their conservation status considerably. 'They are both more endangered than we presumed,' said Dr Georgiadis of the Mpala Research Centre in Kenya. I thought they might be. Wouldn't it be so much worse if there were 13 different elephants instead of chiffchaffs?

Some are starting to wonder whether all this molecule-inspired splitting serves any useful purpose. Is it any of our business if one group of chiffchaffs doesn't mate with another identical group of chiffchaffs for some impenetrable reason of their own? There is surely something a bit self-serving about all these new species. I find myself wondering not only whether there are twelve too many chiffchaffs, but whether there might also be too many molecular systematists, each one eager to find a new elephant or chimpanzee. By contrast, it is a devil of a job finding a decent plumber around here.

I'm afraid it is no use *British Wildlife* readers hoping that they might prove to be a different species from, say, DEFRA officials or Posh Spice fans – and definitely more endangered. DNA research shows that we are all exactly the same, from the palest Eskimo to the blackest aborigine. Pretty much like Aardvarks, really.

* * *

Germs in disguise

More about warped reality. Television's 'enhanced' images of anthrax reminded one of Hilaire Belloc's microbe, which was:

So very small,
You cannot make him out at all.
But many sanguine people hope
To see him through a microscope.
His jointed tongue that lies beneath
A hundred curious rows of teeth.....
His eyebrows of a tender green;
All these have never yet been seen –
But Scientists, who ought to know,
Assure us that they must be so.

Oh let us never, never doubt.

The BBC television news programme broadcast another scary story about anthrax last night. Apparently a New York journalist had opened a letter

containing some suspicious-looking powder, and what did she do? Why, she did what anyone would have done, she hurled the letter and its contents high in the air with a yell of fright, then fell over backwards and ended up with the stuff all over her face. Fortunately it turned out to be harmless, no doubt just a sample of some organic medication or environmentally-friendly body product in the regular junk mail. Still, it must have been a nasty moment.

What has struck me the most about these news pictures is the appearance of the anthrax bug. Real *Bacillus anthracis* is a drab object, resembling nothing so much as a string of sausages. The television version is much more shapely, with various inner organelles and what looks suspiciously like hair. In fact it strongly resembles my old friend *Paramecium*, the slipper animalcule, beloved by microscopists down the ages. *Paramecium* wouldn't harm a flea, let alone a New York journalist, though it probably would make short work of any anthrax bacilli it came across. The TV pictures of the spores were another puzzle. Surely those rotating green balls were none other than *Volvox*, one of the loveliest green algae and found in any pond near you. What is going on around here?

One possibility is that the news reporter decided that anthrax does not look sexy enough. We learn from the redoubtable Kate Adie that in the modern telly industry the medium is more important than the message, so that cute bottoms and sexy ankles count for more than accurate news stories or any possible proficiency in reporting them. If *Bacillus anthracis* doesn't show any cute little poison glands or sexy rows of teeth, 'then get me something that does!'.

A more sinister possibility is that some fiend may have bred mutant forms of anthrax that do indeed mimic forms of pond life. If so we may soon be threatened by waves of anthrax frogs or water voles, jumping about leaving suspicious looking piles of powder all over the place. If anthrax can look like a *Volvox*, there is no reason why it could not look like an elephant.

That being so, some might conclude that the only safe thing is to kill all forms of life on earth, except for those that have been tested and pronounced anthrax-free. Personally I think this would be an over-reaction. The trick is to disbelieve anything read to you on the news by some po-faced bimbo of less than, say 35. Me, I have taken the precaution of listening only to old trouts on the radio. You can hear Kate Adie every Saturday morning, at 11.30am on Radio 4.

The outing

Sunday, my favourite day, and Gladys and I go for our run. Soon we decide to go back for the car. Reg is smiling from the window as we look back from the car where we smile through the window. Stenga looks as well, but shows no emotion as dogs do.

We watch as Reg turns his tall, rather shabby frame into the unrelenting darkness of the oak-lined unlit sitting room. We look away and set off on our outing. After all, it is Sunday.

2002

Twitching on-line

Isn't it amazing how quickly and completely people have become willing slaves to their computer? Or is it worship? I'm not sure.

Welcome to the real world, they tell me. Life will never be the same again. Yes, Twitcher has been given a computer. In place of the row of calf-bound reference books and antiquated card index sits The Machine, with its tangle of cables, its modems and printers, and its glowing, malevolent 'window'. Facing the Machine is a horrid little swivel-seat, and a keyboard with buttons of strange command: Pg Up, Ins, Esc and End. I press 'End' but unfortunately nothing happens.

Obviously, this is just the start of a long and meaningful relationship, but I'd have welcomed a set of instructions. Apparently these are locked up inside the Machine. I'm told that it is no use shaking it until they fall out. Instead I have to creep into W H Smiths and buy a special book. The

choice here seems to be between *The Idiot's Guide to PCs, Windows for Thickohs* or *This Computer Belongs to Stupid*. I learn from one of these that my Machine is operated by clicking a piece of plastic, and then waiting for orders to appear in the window. Sure enough, here they come, in a parade of little boxes. Do I wish to debug? I certainly do. How about deleting the programme menu? Hit that tab, Window Boy.

As I'm probably the last person in the known universe to discover the joys of www.clickme.com, you'll have noticed that I was probably wrong to delete that menu as I now realise from the hilarious in-joke on p 575 of my copy of *Doh! Done it Again, Dummy?* for no-hopers who should have stuck to the Parker 61. What I was hoping was that The Machine would give me the answer to wealth, fortune and life as we know it. Let me explain. When I was born, most people did things that even a child could understand. They built ships and cars, or went out to sea and caught fish, or dug coal and other useful substances out of the ground. But hardly anyone seems to do real work any more. Instead, they imitate the cartoon hero, Dilbert, and spend their working lives sitting on a little swivel-seat, staring at a screen and clicking a bit of plastic. I could never make out exactly what Dilbert was doing as he clicked away. Perhaps he was creating special cyber-fish or cyber-coal with the help of his amazing machine. If so, this is good, because it saves on resources, and seems a much safer way of working – though I have heard of some troubling cases of thumb strain from over-zealous use of the Mouse.

Conservationists are, of course, among the most zealous Mouse-clickers on the planet. Most bodies have set up special 'websites', presumably to trap cyber-money as it whizzes through space. But how is all this cyber-wealth created in the first place? As far as I can make out, it must be done by the simple action of clicking. Could I do that, I wonder, instead of writing, which is, frankly, hard work? Could I, too, become a web-spinning cyber-spider? Well, it looks worth a try. And so I must leave you, as shadows lengthen over the stricken Wiltshire countryside, swivel-seated in front of the glowing window, clicking hopefully.

* * *

Sounds of spring

This rather rambling piece was the result of skimming through the Wildlife Trusts cheery magazine, Natural World. *When stuck for a subject, it never fails.*

Spring at last! And once again you sense the sap rising in the nature conservation world. All around are little messages of hope and confidence, 'calls' for action as upbeat and predictable as the little birds singing in the tree-tops. The Wildlife Trusts' call this season is for 'an end to road schemes and housing development that damage wildlife'. Well, cock-a-doodle-doo to that, we must all agree. Meanwhile, from another sonorous bough, the Woodland Trust is calling for 'dynamic thinking on a landscape scale', which, I suspect, might come to mean yet more community forests. We also hear a mighty 'tweet tweet' from Jonathan Porritt's perch in *BBC Wildlife* magazine. Jonathan thinks that those wildlife shows on the BBC just go on getting better and better: 'To be honest, I've lost track of the number of lion films I've seen over the years'. As it happens, I have been more careful and kept an exact log of my own experience of lion-orientated entertainment. It comes to more than 100 films, but I find I still know nothing about lions. It was all a bit of a waste of time, really.

The only discordant note I detected in this chorus of love and pineapple trees was (ironically enough) from the RSPB in its quarterly magazine, *Birds*. Packed away in its pages is a useful mathematical expression of a problem ignored by the others. As easy to remember as $E=mc^2$, it can be rendered as follows:

$$\text{People} = \text{sewage} + \text{rubbish}.$$

Perhaps it should be rubbish squared: $P=sr^2$. For, in the same magazine, I learned that people are throwing away their refrigerators at a rate of 6,500 *every day*, that is, at over two million fridges per year. This is a terrifying number of fridges. Nor, in a time of global warming, does it seem a prudent thing to do – especially when the apparent reason for it is to make room for a parrot. According to the RSPB, some 21,000 wild-caught parrots were imported into Britain in the past five years – and that's just the ones that passed through a customs shed. The problem can be summarised as follows:

P (people) = parrot minus fridge = CFC gas + toxic metal + fewer parrots.

The conservation world would probably like to do something about this, but its hands are tied. In order to save the fridge, they naturally need more money. Lots of it. But to get more money, they need more members, and that means paying at least some attention to what the members want. Unfortunately most of them don't know what they want, apart from banning hunting and planting even more trees.

For my part, I am more interested in an exciting initiative from Norfolk by the newly formed Fairyland Trust. 'Once upon a time, the countryside was *ancient,* **magical** and natural,' says the Fairyland Trust. 'We intend to **rekindle** ancient countryside, **recreate** habitats and make the land *fit for fairies*.' Activities will include wand-making, a certain amount of prancing through the wild flowers, and the discovery of 'sprites fantastical'.

I suspect Fairyland of having latched on to a seriously good idea here: that nature is there to be enjoyed, through play and imagination. Let those who want to campaign against fridge-hunting, or whatever, do so. You'll find me with some of my younger friends, down in fairy dell, making a tree house, laying traps for the crayfish and engaged in fierce sword fights with hogweed stems.

Junk mail

County Wildlife Trusts make a significant part of their income from landfill tax credits. For every landscape you fill with trash, the Trusts can buy another nature reserve. Sounds fair? At least no one's complaining.

As a member of several wildlife charities, I have long become resigned to shaking their magazines free of junk before opening them. If, like me, you are often deluged with unwanted flimsies and glossies, here's a useful tip. Don't even think of opening the envelope without taking proper precautions. Grasp the hind end of the thing between finger and thumb. Then, steadying a wastepaper basket between your knees, give it a sharp tap. With luck, the shiny nature of the junk will ensure it a short, expeditious journey to the bottom of the basket. Then you can get on with reading the journal's thrilling contents.

It has to be said that, on recent form, it may not be many minutes before the magazine itself has joined the weepy appeals and tempting offers in your basket. Most of the charities seem to be using a kind of rose-tinted dream language that has everything to do with keeping the members happy, and very little, unfortunately, to do with the real world. For example, the Wildlife Trusts are 'Waiting for the green shoots starting (sic) to come through (sic)'. It will be a long wait, mate. The Woodland Trust is 'Planting the seeds of hope'. Keep planting, garden-boy. 'Larks singing over every home in the land'? Nice try, beardie.

Be that as it may, the latest copy of RSPB *Birds* magazine caught even this cautious trash-shifter on the hop. I should have noticed the danger signs. The plastic bag containing it had developed a nasty bulge. *Birds* looked as if it was about to have chickens. Yes, *Birds* was loaded. As I say, keen as I was to learn about the green shoots of hope etc, I forget to string a safety net beneath the bag. Seconds later, I was deluged by an appalling cascade of special offers. *'Quality vitamins for a healthy life.' 'Hot packs for happy hikers.' 'Party at YOUR historic chateau.' 'Visit Wales for space to breathe.'*

Struggling hard to find my own space to breathe, I swept up the mess and binned it. Along with that copy of *Birds*. I gave up hope of finding anything to read after wading through no less than 46 more pages of ads, from porcelain owls to nestboxes that tell the time. Somewhere in there may have been an article on the RSPB's latest doings, but I couldn't be bothered to find it.

I know what the RSPB will say: that ads pay for the magazine, and so release more funds to pay for conservation. But a suspicious mind might find something funny going on here. Tax credits from landfill companies are a currently lucrative source of income for the wildlife charities. So, in theory, the more junk there is, piling up in the country, the more the trusts benefit from it. Could this be the sinister truth behind the ads for Badger-snacks and the plastic toy for your frog?

In the meantime, the RSPB knows where it can stick its hot packs for hikers.

* * *

Rural dangers

The grass is greenest on the far side of the hill. Anyone else's wildlife sounds more exotic than our own.

Germaine Greer, with whom I occasionally share a page in the *Daily Telegraph*, says that she has bought 145 acres of outback in central Australia. Perhaps she is getting bored with living over here, and, if so, one can see why. Her 145 acres will be home not only to Germaine, but to 13 kinds of dangerous serpents, two water-dragons and several bird-eating spiders, not to mention the Duck-billed Platypus, which, as many readers will know, has a venomous bottom.

La Greer is one of the best of today's writers on nature and rural life, and she would be wasted in the outback, among a bunch of guzzling Aussies. What home-grown dangers can we offer her to stay here? What horrors could lurk in a comparable 145 acres of central England? Stinging nettles are too common to frighten anybody, but there is a promising newcomer in the form of a fungus called *Schizophyllum commune* or Split-gill. This is a toadstool that really gets up your nose, quite literally so in the case of the farm-worker who was found with one sticking out of his

nostril. Split-gill grows on burst silage bags, whence it will send spores spinning up your nose, and then EAT YOUR BRAINS. Or so say the tabloids, and people will believe anything nowadays.

I think that I would recommend Germaine to give birdwatching a try. Though they are superficially attractive, a lifetime's close observation of birds has convinced me that they are all monstrously selfish, mean and cowardly, and not given to elevated sentiments of any description. My chickens are a possible exception, but there's no denying that even they are often consumed with greed.

* * *

Sour grapes

I am an old hand at coming second at book prizes.

'No furniture so charming as books' wrote some silly old fool. He should get a load of my books, perched on sofas, spilling over the floor, climbing up the wall. You can hardly see the dang furniture. You have to punt pyramids of paperbacks across the room every time you use the bathroom. This place is, as it were, fully booked. I need a barn. I'm booked out.

As a conscientious reviewer, I have to start reading them soon, and I shudder at the thought. I knew that the reading public had been struck another body blow when Edward O Wilson won this year's Natural World prize. He certainly wrote the most famous book, the one that made the headlines. He was of course not there in person to collect his cheque. I doubt whether a double Pulitzer winner like Wilson would have much time to spare for small-time Brit awards from people in any case more interested in bolstering their corporate egos than rewarding talent. Interestingly, the press release described him as the 'new Darwin', which is exactly what was said about Jones, the genetics guy from UCL, who won the time before last. Next time, I suggest that they do not bother with books at all. Just track down the latest Darwin and hand him the dosh.

The unshakable fact about Edward O, the irony in the nutshell as he might put it, is that he is completely unreadable. The natural history world, in search of a guru figure, a neo-Darwin, found Wilson at about the time of the Rio summit in 1992. His big idea was that life forms on earth are so interlinked that, if you could pull out one species from the system, the whole lot would come tumbling down. But no idea big or small could prepare you for the unadulterated Edward O. Experience, the Full Wilson. Nor could the soft-spoken guru guy you see on the telly. You've got to read him. Here is a sample (let's call it a Wilsilience, or an Edwarsity) from his acknowledged masterpiece, *The Diversity of Life* (new edition 2001):

'For what, in the final analysis, is mortality but the command of conscience seasoned by a rational examination of consequences?'

Excuse me? In what analysis? Seasoned with what? Yes, OK, one gets the drift after mulling it over a few times, but bear in mind that the next line is going to say something equally portentous, like *'Is there not a common body of inherent principles underlying the entirety of human endeavour?'*

To which the intended answer is yes, and that Wilson found it. Bear in mind that there are two dozen similar chains of words on every page. And that *Diversity of Life* has 406 fun-filled pages. You really have to hand it to the BP-Subbuteo-Book Trust crowd, who had obviously read every

word of the latest Wilson, *The Future of Life*, with utter joy.

The attractive thing about Wilson, I suppose, is that he is an optimist. He makes an assumption that is common among tender-hearted environmentalists, namely that everybody else is like him, ploddingly earnest, internationally-minded and dreaming of sunlit uplands. Personally, I would have given the money to Michael Boulter, whose book *EXTINCTION: Evolution and the end of man* posits an original and rather refreshing view of mankind as a greedy, selfish and exploitative little git.

* * *

Corned beef

Praise is never something that should be left to other people.

This season, two home-grown elder statesmen of natural history published their memoirs. David Attenborough's *Life on Air* celebrates the great man's life in the front of the camera, hobnobbing with gorillas and so forth. The other David, D Bellamy no less, writes about the 'hilarious and sometimes disastrous events that have shaped his life'. His book is called *Jolly Green Giant*, (and, please, no sniggering there at the back. Jolly Green Giant is a most respectable brand of tinned corn. I'm thinking of calling *my* memoirs *Heinz Baked Beans*). One hopes this does not mean that the two Davids are about to disappear and leave us to the tender mercies of Titchmarsh.

I write this with some feeling, since a wildlife magazine recently saw fit to publish a profile of my good self that looked remarkably like an obituary – even though I had taken the precaution of sending the editors a portrait of me in my golden youth, splayed half-naked on a rock. Worse, they had talked to the wrong people. Here I am, in the swamp, surrounded by charming birds and happy amphibia, without a care in the world. And the rotters present me as some village Wilson, haggard with anxiety about the fate of the world in general, and the performance of 'English Nature' (English who?) in particular. Davids Attenbee and Bewamee were quite right to do the job themselves.

Twitcher's A to Z of the year

Another alphabet. Plans to do more were sabotaged by conservationists, who sat on their hands and refused to do anything that started with J.

Well, here it is again, Twitcher's trusty A to Z of another wild, wild year.

A is for **Administratium.** A new chemical element, currently taking over the world. Completely inert, it consists of 1 neutron, 12 assistant neutrons, 75 deputy neutrons and 23 deputy assistant neutrons. These are held together by weak forces called morons. Every three years, all the assistant neutrons, deputy neutrons and deputy assistant neutrons exchange places.

B is for **Bittern.** An invisible bird specially trained to honk from any patch of ground on which the RSPB has planted reeds.

C is for **Cornish Chough.** For ten years, zoos, conservationists and Cornish nationalists toiled and plotted to reintroduce the Chough. Last year, five birds arrived in Cornwall of their own accord. Someone should shoot them.

D is for the **Dipstick Award 2002.** John Birt ('Lord' Birt of TV) wins the oilstain of the year for his exciting plan to double the size of the motorway network by running toll roads next to freeways. No wonder the television is so terrible.

E is for **Extinct.** The bad news is that the earth is in the throes of a mass-extinction of species. The good news is that it's confined to species that haven't been discovered yet.

F for the **Future.** It's funny, isn't it? Conservationists dream about all the wonderful things that will happen when we get there. But whenever we do, it always seems to be the same old problems, the same half-baked solutions.

G is for **Gardens.** Let's hear it for Titchmarsh, 'the new David Attenborough'. We are obviously about to turn the countryside into one big garden. But I fear for the poor sycamore (see 'Restricted View', 2000).

H is for **Holistic.** Holes are where the landscape used to be. Some excellent examples were offered to conservation bodies by Hanson PLC, the river floodplain and limestone-pavement specialists.

I is for **Infinitude**. Quite a number of bees, flowers, meadows, etc have been declining by 95% for a long time now. It's not maths, it's magic!

K is for **Kite**. That large predatory bird you saw just feet away on the M40, seconds before crashing into the lamp-post.

L is for **Logorrhoea**. An area of tropical forest the size of the Isle of Wight is felled every year to create paper for Conservation Action Plans.

M is for **Motorway Madness**. See DIPSTICK AWARD.

N is for **Nature Conservation** by Peter Marren: 'The most brilliant book ever written about anything' – P Marren. Only £19. Hurry, hurry!

O is for **Organisation**. A new one, Songbird Survival, has declared war on raptors. Is there anything *you* don't like? Why not form a society?

P is for **Payments**. New 'far-reaching' CAP reforms propose to pay farmers for not producing anything, but maintaining their fields. I like it. If it helps, I offer to stop writing for £250 a non-article, while guaranteeing to keep the paper in useable condition for future eventualities.

R is for **Reports**. It was another vintage year for conservation reports (see LOGORRHOEA). On the one hand, there were LIVING LANDSCAPES, SPACE OR NATURE and GREEN SPACES, BETTER PLACES. On the other, BITTER HARVEST, PETERING OUT and GREEN UNPLEASANT LAND. Perhaps we should let them fight it out.

S is for **Spring**. A br ief spell of fine weather before the rains start, generally around February, but on target for Christmas in 2050.

T – Another trying year for **Trees**. There was SOD (Sudden Oak Death) and ongoing DED (Dutch Elm Disease). Note the catchy acronyms. What next? Conifer Annihilation Disorder (CAD)? Beech Unwelcome Malignancy (BUM)? New disOrder Now Over (NO! NO!)?

U is for the **United States**. A quaint country across the water that doesn't believe that global warming is caused by human activity. Actually, it's done by fairies and their tiny ovens.

V: the **Vocal Minority**. Minister Alun Michael pretended not to understand what the Countryside March on 22nd September 2002 was about. 'I'm listening, but I'm not sure what I'm hearing.' So listen some more: IT'S ABOUT HUNTING, you sanctimonious twerp.

W is for **World Summit.** There was another one on BIODIVERSITY this year. Biodiversity! I get so excited whenever I hear that word that I just want to lie on my back and have my tummy tickled.

X, Y and **Z** have been recycled.

J and **Q** were not found this year, but will be reintroduced from Aztec stock as part of AAP (Alphabet Action Plan), sponsored by Oxford English Dictionary.

A wiser man

After all, I did recognise the old man's skills as he took me and Stenga ever deeper into the pines. I noticed Stenga was not with us, suddenly remembering he was at home by the roaring fire, and how stupid I was not knowing and everything that I forget these days.

The old man walked without a sound, staying perfectly quiet as he led me ever further into the silence of where we were going. In the gathering evening of hardly any light, I felt a feeling of great respect for the stone-deaf old man as I went with him ever deeper into the already out-of-depth forest.

I knew then that we were totally lost, and that the old man, although a prolific reader, was completely insane.

Strathpeffer

2003

Vote, vote, vote

I can't believe they didn't make Michael Crawford the Top Brit. What's the matter with them?

The whole nation, we hear, is in a ferment over who is to be made the Top Brit of all time. Will it be Michael Crawford or Princess Di? Or perhaps it will be John Lennon, whose place in the Top Ten rests, surprisingly, not on *Strawberry Fields*, nor *Imagine*, but in the contention that 'he really believed in peace'. In true modern Brit style, the BBC presents all this not as a relaxed discussion over a port or three, but as a gesticulating mob shouting at one another and waving their fists. They really believe in John Lennon, or possibly Michael Crawford. You had better believe it, too.

My own choice of King Harold (famous last words: 'I spy with my little eye, something beginning with 'A'...') failed to make it to the top million. In fact I myself was ahead of him, thanks to some sly tactical voting by mummy and her gang down at the Hungerford thrift shop. Possibly there was a confusion in the public's mind about which King Harold it was. It wasn't King Harold Harebrush, who, so far as I know, did nothing at all, nor Harold Hardrada, who was nine feet tall and conquered Russia – and therefore might have been a contender except that he was foreign and not very nice. No, my Harold was the hero of 1066, described by Simon Schama as a really caring sort of guy. He was funnier than Michael Crawford (his catchphrase, 'ooh, Etheldreda', kept the Witan in stitches), made a better clothes-prop than Di (doubters had better check out the Bayeaux Tapestry – he's *hot*), and was so keen on peace that he ended up in pieces. If Harold isn't made Top Brit, there's something wrong with this country.

Meanwhile, the gates have now closed on Plantlife's Top Flower competition, in which we are invited to nominate a wild flower to represent one's home county. Here, different qualities are needed. Most people seem to have voted for something rare or pretty, or both: oxlips, pasqueflowers and orchids. These are understandable choices, but also, I fear, wishful

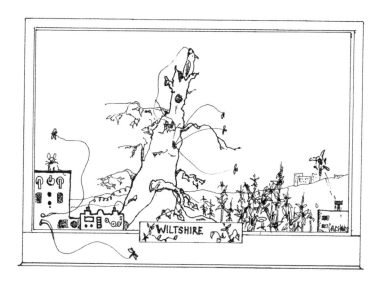

ones. If the pasqueflower has any relevance beyond its own botany, it is for the downland landscape of the century before last, with its rolling acres, wandering sheep and shivering shepherds. Recently, I revisited the corner of Wiltshire where Richard Jefferies was brought up, transferring his own boyhood to fiction in *Bevis*. It was then a pasqueflower kind of place, I suppose, though the scenes of boyish irresponsibility conveyed in *Bevis* would make any modern parent shudder. For today's Bevis-land, let's zoom in on the suburbanised Country Park, now wedged between the hospital and the bypass. Here you can hear the sounds of bees murmuring in the remains of a hollow tree. This tree plays a part in the book, but these bees are a big improvement on the original in that they never stop murmuring and don't ever sting. This is because these bees are *electronic*. Well, actually, they are not really bees at all, only a recording. In fact, I don't suppose they were ever actual bees, only a kind of humming noise made in a sound-effects workshop. That's the beauty of these modern bees: we don't need their honey, only their hum, and if all we want is a hum, who needs the whole bee? An appropriate choice, surely, for an age of illusions, and a neat reminder of the distance between contemporary Britain and wild nature. Oh all right, a bee isn't a flower, I know. A bee orchid, then. An electronic bee orchid. OK?

Dream on

Perhaps, like John Lennon and Harold Harebrush, conservationists believe in an imagined world. At least, they tend to write as though they do, using soppy words like partner, target and 'shared vision'. In a short review of my 'surprisingly readable' book *Nature Conservation* in *Plant Talk*, Hugh Synge remarks that it comes thrillingly to life when describing conflict – and, by implication, anyway, drones on like a sleepy buffalo whenever the partners are chalking up another strategy. Could Hugh have lifted the lid on a rarely acknowledged truth here – that conflict is invariably more exciting than agreement, hence the old Chinese curse, 'may you live in interesting times'? Essentially, what Hugh is saying, I think, is that to write a good story you've got to seek the enemy, identify him, and then *kick his ass*. By coincidence, this is exactly the advice which my ex-agent gave me: stop being nice, find your enemy and then put the boot in, *obliterate that villain*. Is this why so much conservation talk has you reaching for the smelling salts: too much licking and not enough kicking? I don't know. What I do know is that Lennon would soon have got tired of his imagined world of universal peace and started breaking windows.

* * *

Don't cry for me, Oxyura

For reasons best known to himself, our editor showed this piece to a duck conservation expert who promptly demanded it be 'binned', if not publicly burnt. Yah, boo, sucks to him, whoever he was.

Will no-one shed a tear for the American Ruddy Duck *Oxyura jamaicensis*, destined to be wiped out in the next ten years by DEFRA marksmen? Though it may have annoyed the Spanish by mating with their native White-headed Duck, the Ruddy Duck has certainly pleased plenty of British birdwatchers. It has been the symbol of the West Midlands Bird Club, the largest local bird group in the country, for 27 years. What does the club's current President, Bill Oddie, have to say about this?

What seems to have escaped the attention of the duck-murderers, including the wretched Wildfowl 'n Wetlands Trust who started all the trouble in the first place, is that the Ruddy Duck is the obvious prototype of Donald Duck, the popular cartoon character. The key features of Donald – his broad beak and upstanding tail-feathers – are plainly taken from the Ruddy Duck, as is his amusing adenoidal quack. Some might argue that calling attention to this can only strengthen the case for complete extermination. All the same, when I am called upon to lead the resistance to what the charity Animal Aid calls 'this shameful crusade', I shall go straight to Euro Disney in Paris to tell them of this naked insult to the American Way. I suspect that it will require only one phone call from the White House to convince Mr Blair's Government that the Ruddy Duck is a charming and beautiful creature that deserves full protection.

Until then, Animal Aid's advice, that 'if you see one of these, don't tell a soul', seems a bit lame. A more positive course of action, which may appeal especially to the 'human shields' lately returned from Iraq, is to take up a new cause as human 'duck decoys'. This could involve living in a giant inflatable duck on a lake frequented by the Ruddies. Or some might decide to tie a model duck to the top of their head and sink beneath the water. Knowing Ruddy Ducks as I do, this could lead to problems during the mating season but, heck, anyone who is frightened of a little amorous attention from a loud duck should not be in the conservation business.

Another idea would be to get the Ruddy Ducks to cohabit with animals that no-one is allowed to molest, such as hedgehogs. There are, of course, more potential difficulties here. Perhaps the most practical course would be to enlist some of the hedgehogs 'rescued' from the Outer Hebrides by animal-lovers, and set them among the ducks. The hedgehogs may not enjoy being tied up, painted red and blue, floated out into a lake and shot at. On the other hand, they may be glad to repay a little of the vast amount of fuss and sentimentality poured over them by drooling animal lovers.

* * *

Cuckoo rumbled

There is good news from Australia, where a small bird has finally put two and two together, and realised that it was not the cuckoo's mum. The transparent confidence trick played by cuckoos down the ages forced us to recognise, reluctantly, that birds are not very bright. One might have hoped that some pipit or warbler would have had the odd moment of doubt when faced by a gaping baby six times its own size. Perhaps they are like young human mums, believing their own hideous, puking baby to be the most beautiful thing in the universe. Be that as it may, top marks to the Blue or 'Superb Fairy' Wren for rumbling the imposter and kicking it out of the nest.

Now that birds are at last showing a little intelligence, we must hope that they will uncover that other confidence trick being played on innocent avifauna, the 'biodiversity action plan'. Skylarks, for example, may be alarmed to learn that they are unwitting pawns in the Government's plans to 'enhance the quality of life' on the ghastly estates they are building all over the remaining countryside. That nice Mr Meacher plans to have them carolling and chirping over every roof in the land. Having evicted the cuckoo, the larks might want to think carefully about all this. Perhaps they will start rehearsing a new song, a series of cacophonous grunts and groans, followed by a bloodcurdling shriek, before leaving the universal avian trademark all over the washing.

* * *

Toad of joy

This sudden interest in toads came about after Trevor Beebee, the authority on amphibians, took issue with my views about reintroductions and general toad-pampering. Only kidding, Trevor!

If any football fans read British Wildlife, they may be interested in a new sport from Western Australia called quokka soccer. It gets the name from an animal, a sort of wallaby, called a Quokka, which by ill luck is almost the same size and shape of a football. The Quokka has the added misfortune of being extremely stupid. 'They wander down the streets and into cafés and bars,' explained PC 'Cobber' Wear, a policeman. 'You can get right up to them'. What Quokkas do when they see some footballing lout swaying right up to them is to curl up into a tight furry ball. The rest, as they say, is quokka soccer. Other sports fans belt them one with a stick. This is called quokka hockey. 'I don't understand human beings sometimes,' commented wildlife ranger Sallyann Gudge.

While many, I am sure, would condemn such callous, abuse of café-going marsupials, those of thoughtful bent realise that the only future for many animals on earth is to serve humankind in some way. British sports fans might show more interest in nature if there were animals that could be drafted in as temporary goalposts, say, or a makeshift wicket. For my part, I have no sympathy with sports fans, and would like them all to go away. But the problem remains: how are all these expensively 'reintroduced' Dormice and Natterjack Toads going to pay their way in years to come?

A possible solution is suggested by a recent article on the Wellbeing Survey sponsored by Boots, the well-known chemists. Psychiatric scientists have made the fascinating discovery that people are made happy by the simple things in life, a toad at your feet, for example. In the past, we might have glanced at the wretched toad, smiled at this sign of the approaching spring, and passed by. But, say the scientists, it is harmful to button up our feelings in this way. We should 'notice the moment', and shout with joy, wave our arms, jump up and down. The general idea is shown in an accompanying picture of a comely young lady leaping into the air with joy, and she certainly looks as though she likes a good time.

It occurs to me that the savings thus made on aspirins and anti-depressant drugs might pay for any number of conservation projects. The obvious danger is that people leaping into the air to express their feelings would very probably land on the object of their joy and squash it flat. But many would say that this is a small price to pay for releasing the inner person, or developing one's caring side, or whatever it is that we are supposed to do.

* * *

Love toad

As we consider ways of strengthening our relationships with the natural world, I wonder whether anyone has yet suggested marriage. Apparently, marriage to an animal is legal in the state of Missouri, and, as we know, where America leads, Britain tends to follow. Few politicians are prepared

to stand up for traditional values any more, and marriage to an endangered species would, it seems to me, hit many desired 'targets' – happiness within a caring relationship and protection for a threatened animal all in one.

In Missouri the knot is normally tied between a person and his or her faithful horse, but over here we preserve our strongest feeling for animals in the Biodiversity Action Plan – Natterjack Toads, for example, or Field Crickets. In his poem 'Uncle Arly', Edward Lear wrote most touchingly about the lifelong love between a lonely man and his ever-faithful cricket:

Clinging as a constant treasure
Churping with a cheerious measure
Wholly to my uncle's pleasure

Admittedly, there are legal quibbles to overcome. It is not clear, for example, whether marriage would infringe a rare species' right to be rounded up, marked with paint or a tattoo and 'reintroduced'. Nor whether the union would entail an attachment to a particular toad or a platonic bond with an entire species. This is a matter for our legislators, and I, for one, look forward to the debates. Many conservationists take a rather dim view of the human race. A new life with a favourite toad might bring a little sunshine into an existence which is all too often cold, dark and always raining.

* * *

Otter crap

This next one was pretty straight reportage, apart from the bit about badgers and jam sandwiches, which at least seemed plausible.

Ever on the lookout for cheerful news, Twitcher was naturally intrigued by the newspaper headlines celebrating the return of the otter. 'Otter Joy' was the favourite one, followed by 'Otter Claw-back' and 'Otterly Amazing'. Closer inspection revealed that otters have not, in fact, done anything particularly newsworthy. The headlines were based on an Environment

Agency report that told us what we already knew – that otters are slowly recovering from a low point in the 1970s, when their breeding performance had become reduced by pesticide poisoning. Now, eager otter fans, snuffling up and down the riverbanks, are finding more and more piles of otter poo, or spraints, as they are known. In fact, all things considered, 'Otter Crap' might have made a better headline.

Never slow to pat themselves on the back, conservation bodies are claiming most of the credit for this modest recovery. But the animals are not trying hard enough, it seems. 'Otters are not increasing as fast as we would like in some areas,' complains Andrew Crawford, the report's author. It is a pity that we are stuck with the facts of mammalian reproduction, as it would clearly be more efficient, more satisfactory all round, if otters could multiply by cell division like an amoeba. All the same, otter experts are doing our best to hurry things along with a programme of releases, riverbank 'management' and the constructing of special otter houses to tempt them to stay. Some 40 of these new 'homes' have been provided in Nottinghamshire alone as an 'environment service'. Now we have reports of otters in city centres, climbing in and out of supermarket dustbins, and pacing the streets at night in search of fish-and-chips.

No doubt this will endear them to animal-lovers, but otters are not really suited to city life. Most of them will only end up squashed on the roads, or die of the mange or some other nasty disease, much as urban foxes do. In fact, if otters were of a reflective disposition, I doubt that they would regard humankind among their friends and benefactors. A clue to what they may really think of us may lie in the behaviour of a badger named Boris, who went on the rampage in Evesham for two days after escaping from a local Wildlife Rescue Centre. Badgers, I should explain, have a particularly nasty bite. It is something to do with the way in which the jawbone fits into the skull, allowing the animal to snap its teeth together with tremendous power, crunching through flesh and bone with quiet efficiency. Fed by images on the telly, people tend to assume that badgers are like small doggies, and like nothing more than a friendly pat on the muzzle and a jam sandwich. What Boris thought of this can be judged from reports of people fleeing in terror, jam sandwiches abandoned, and pursued by an infuriated badger. A squad of policemen called to the scene was forced to take refuge on the bonnet of a car. Five people were bitten, one of them quite badly, before Boris was finally cornered and 'destroyed'.

As it happens, I have been bitten by an otter. It was only a playful nip by a tame dog-otter called Benjy, but it hurt like hell, and was sore for days. No doubt otters should feel grateful for all the well-meaning attempts to welcome them to our suburbs and cities. All the same, I think that these are misguided. Otters belong to the wilder parts of Britain, as far from people and their cars as possible. The sight of otters pilfering from dustbins like giant rats dignifies neither them nor us.

* * *

Test ban

Meanwhile, the great debate continues over whether or not fish feel pain. Dr Lynne Sneddon, head of animal biology at Liverpool University, has tested this by injecting fish with bee venom and acetic acid. The fish showed every sign of disliking this treatment very much, and furthermore went right off their feed 'until the effects of the experiment subsided'. However, other fish biologists deny that the fish felt pain. They were just exhibiting 'behaviour'. No brain, no pain, they say.

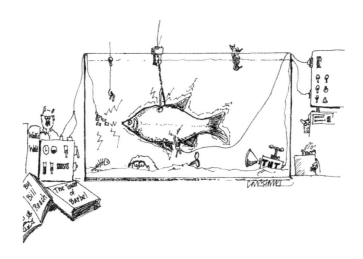

On the other hand, no absolute proof has been offered to show that hunted foxes suffer much pain either, or at least no more than from being shot, poisoned or dying of the mange. If hunting is to be banned on no more than a suspicion, then it is surely time to remove the three and a half million anglers from their fishing rods. Some might suggest we should start locking up gardeners too, given their manifest lack of compassion for poor little slugs and greenflies. As for Bonfire Night, we are urged to get right behind the RSPCA in its campaign for quiet, boring fireworks. 'We are not complete killjoys,' protested its spokesman.

Oh yes you are, Mr Spokesman. As Macaulay once observed, 'The Puritans hated bear-baiting, not because it gave pain to the bear, but because it gave pleasure to the spectators'. Soon, anyone spotted observing nature with a smile on their face had better look sharp.

* * *

Fantasy gardens

When, eighteen months ago, Twitcher acquired a computer, I had no idea of its awesome power to transcend reality and create a parallel universe. It was first brought home to me when I was asked to edit a CD-ROM about wildlife gardens, into which a few bugs had inadvertently crept. The designers had decided to link each species to its main enemies, as well as to its favourite food. Unfortunately, they seem to have let the computer do most of the choosing.

The result was a wonderful imaginative 'wildscape' in which the most unlikely things went on in the herbaceous borders and shrubberies. Gangs of linnets got together to mug stag beetles. Over there a dunnock was quietly grazing on a patch of poppies, while on the lawn something called a snake millipede was emerging from its lair to pursue flying insects. Casting a shadow over the whole proceedings was the most terrifying animal of all, the one that eats everything, long or tall, strong or swift ... the firecrest!

I would spend many happy hours in such a garden, marvelling at the ability of grass snakes to slither up vertical walls in search of their favourite prey, jumping spiders, or at how bats tiptoe about lifting up stones in case anything tasty lies underneath, or how house martins return secretly in the dead of winter to feast on a certain kind of gnat. It would probably not take very long before this food-web had worked itself out to the inevitable conclusion, leaving us only with the firecrests burping on their sagging branch, surrounded by a great pile of empty shells, spat-out bones, stag beetle carcasses, etc.

The advantage of this conceptual garden is that, with a bit of refining, you could create a whole new scenario at the press of the button. If, for example, you wanted a less aggressive scene, you could relax with the alternative Sentimental Garden, a kind of ecological love-in where the fly doth lie down with the bat, and lovely newts dance about drinking nectar from pink flowers.

The beauty of the thing would be that you wouldn't need to do any actual gardening. There would be absolutely no danger of being bitten by a cleg, or stung by a nettle, or risking tetanus or hay fever by messing about with plants. As I constantly remind people, gardening is not only boring and potentially dangerous, but a complete waste of time.

In all fairness, I should add that the CD-ROM is now perfectly reliable and fantasy-free, and is, indeed, highly recommended.

Historical context

Here we are, pretty much where we began, with another claim that urban development is good for wildlife.

Can we help wildlife by building more houses? Keith Porter, English Nature's 'environmental information manager', thinks we can, which presumably means that English Nature thinks so, too. The farmed countryside has become so barren that houses and their gardens would actually be an improvement, he says. 'If we get this right, it's not just biodiversity that benefits, it's people that benefit.' This will be music to the ears of John Prescott, who does indeed plan to cover much of the south and south-east with houses. But whether Prescott will provide the sort of nice houses with big gardens that Keith wants remains to be seen. It seems unlikely. The Government has recently changed the rules to make it possible to build more homes, not fewer, in a given space.

Funnily enough, when English Nature's predecessor, the NCC, was under political pressure in the late 1980s, it, too, tried to please the minister by making surprising claims. The message then was that prosperity was good for wildlife. In theory, the richer we became, the more money we could spare to help the birds and bees. Perhaps Keith is making much the same point: that the bigger the garden, the more room there will be for animals escaping from the 'degraded' countryside.

The NCC, as I recall, said that golf was pretty good for wildlife, too. As it happened, quite a few of its senior staff played golf, and so did the minister. Shooting wildlife was also good for it, at least for as long as Ridley was Environment Minister. I cannot remember whether the NCC agreed with the Transport Department that roads were good for wildlife. It may have dodged the question by saying that it welcomed the right kind of road in the right sort of place, which also happened to be its policy on Sitka Spruce.

In my opinion, nothing could be better for wildlife than a strike by an asteroid of considerable size. Agreed, it would cause a lot of short-term problems, including the total elimination of Prescott's housing estates, Ridley's duck shoots, and the NCC's wretched golf courses. Indeed, it would probably wipe out human life altogether. But I think that most people would now admit that the 'K-T Event' which brought about the extinction of the dinosaurs was a good thing in the long run. Perhaps a really honest appraisal of current environmental problems would conclude that the whole thing is a hopeless cock-up, and that it would be best to start again.

$$* * *$$

A dog's job

No wildlife body, official or voluntary, had much to say during the 'hunting debate'. They were presumably too frightened of annoying the minister, or the members. Whatever happened to the British bulldog?

Announcing that the Government will ban foxhunting irrespective of anything the House of Lords says or does, 'Lord' Whitty, the Minister for Rural Affairs, suggests that the estimated 20,000 thereby doomed hounds might be retrained for farm work. He did not particularise, and it is hard

to imagine them learning how to drive a tractor, milk a cow or fill in a DEFRA form, perhaps the most onerous of all duties on the modern farm. And even if the hounds could learn some other useful task, there is always a danger that they might forget the new dispensation and chase a rabbit – in which case a Government Inspector would pop up out of the hedge, and the dog would be shot.

Perhaps nobody outside the hunting community really cares about the poor doggies. It is only when one gets to know an animal by teaming up with it in some way that a rapport develops. We in the conservation community should make amends for our sorry performance in the great hunting debate by employing these dogs. I do not know what work can be found for them. But if a beagle can be redeveloped to help a farmer, then one of their number should be a director of English Nature in no time at all.

Five, four, three, two, one ...

Are you keeping up with the great Cornish Chough project? Of the six released by Paradise Park Bird Sanctuary in August, two were found dead within weeks. *'Six little Cornish Choughs, one found dead in a cattle trough. Five little Cornish Choughs having quite a lark, one soon got eaten by a predatory hawk. Four little Cornish Choughs ...'*

Jellybabies

The British Mycological Society had been busy making up new names for mushrooms and toadstools in the hope it would make them more popular. Needless to say, this was yet another opportunity for political-correctness to poke its nose in.

I yield to no-one in my admiration for Liz Holden's proposed common names for toadstools. Her succinct and often witty 'Lemon Discos', 'Burgundydrop Bonnets' and 'Stinking Dapperlings' will certainly help to keep the troops amused on those long, dripping walks in search of 'mushies'. But with the new name 'Jelly Ear', the long nose of political correctness seems to have been poking around again. The fungus called

Auricularia auricula-judae has been known as 'Jew's Ear' for as long as fungi have had names – hence the scientific name, which, for those of you who bunked off Latin at school, means 'Jew's ear'. At the 'steering group' there was reportedly heated debate between the 'jew's ear' traditionalists and the 'jelly ear' reformers, which the 'jellybabies' won. Jew's ear is off the menu.

Well, the jellybabies have got it all wrong. This unusual name is not a slur on the Jewish religion, but rather a reference to the legend of Judas Iscariot, who hanged himself on an elder tree. Jew's Ear is particularly common on elder, where it represents the lug-hole of Judas Iscariot himself. If every bit of folklore is to be censored in this way by self-appointed sanitary inspectors, we might be better off sticking to scientific names. But if we are to be denied Jew's Ear, then we should take a closer look at the fungus called *Verpa conica*, which Liz has dubbed the 'Thimble Morel'. But *Verpa* does not mean 'thimble'. It has nothing whatever to do with soppy thimbles. Verpa is one of those cryptic words which the describer apparently borrowed from one of Horace's Odes. It means, roughly, 'one that has been shorn', and one look at *Verpa conica* will tell you exactly what feature the describer had in mind. Let there be no circumscription about this, *Verpa conica* must henceforth be known by all and sundry as 'Jew's Willy'. There is nothing insulting or antisemitic about it – indeed, quite the opposite. For the operation, though associated since Biblical times with the Jewish faith, is in fact a wholesome and sensible surgical precaution, which is widely held to improve the proportions of the person's manhood.

* * *

Faith that moveth mountains

It's all about faith isn't it? If we stuck to observable facts, we would probably give up.

In his masterly new edition of *Ancient Woodland*, Oliver Rackham is gloomy about the future. 'Woodland will increase in quantity, but get worse in quality,' he predicts. A few woodlands will be strenuously protected. 'The rest will have the guts eaten out of them by deer or sheep.' It seems to me that this is not so much a prophesy as an accurate observation of the state of things. However, the book's publisher has rounded up a collection of chairmen, chief executives and assorted wiseacres in the woodland business to insist that 'it ain't necessarily so'. We are more optimistic than Oliver,' smiles the chairman of the Forestry Commission. We must rise to the challenge and prove him wrong, proclaims the chief executive of English Nature.

Since Rackham has been comprehensively proven right in almost everything he said 20 years ago, one admires their apparent confidence. Perhaps, they know something we don't. More likely, like religious zealots down the ages, they believe that anything can be overcome with enough faith. To doubt is to err; faith will move mountains. Surely only blind faith, allied to money, can explain the spreading plantations of broadleaves up and down the country, under such grandiose titles as 'millennium forests' or 'community woodlands'. It is expected that 'the wildlife' will take eager advantage of them as they grow up into tall stately forests. But will the plantations last that long in the face of gales, drought, floods, deer, squirrels and fungal disease? Experience says: 'Sorry, guys'. Faith says: 'Of course, absolutely. Here come the new New Forests. Glory Alleluia, we've done it again!'.

Faith thrives on the absence of fact. There may be a clue to how it all works in a recent article in this very magazine. Describing how a landscape and its natural inhabitants are to be rescued by action-planning, it includes the following phrases in a single action-packed paragraph: 'Biodiversity Action Plan', 'implement a shared vision', 'project officer', 'audit', 'partner organisations', 'workshops' and 'steering group'. The piece struck me as a prolonged prayer to the god of the clipboard. All will be well, it implied, so long as everyone obeys the great plan, with its mighty assembly of targets, measurable outcomes and – be warned – 'regular scrutiny' of any waverers. Perhaps what they were really telling us, in a roundabout way, is that the whole area is about to disappear under planted trees. Part of the appeal of millennium forests, I suppose, is that you do not have to bother any more with cows, ploughs, farms and hedges.

Well I, for one, don't want to live there. If I had the time, I think that I would form an Anti-faith League, with the great W H Hudson as our hero. Hudson it was who once remarked that 'the world is a shambles, but I wasn't born to set it right'. The man to whom he said this was Edward Garnett, the novelist and critic. And, as it happens, Garnett's great-grandson and namesake is a good friend of mine. I really must have a word with Ned about all this.

Jim, son of Old Countryman

We had been watching seals all day, me and Uncle Stan. I noticed them bobbing in the firth as the tide was coming in again, now that it had been out for most of the day.

We walked across the frozen landscape and I realized how eager I had become to get home and have my dinner. Uncle Stan was hobbling along behind. 'Come on you old fart,' I rejoindered, hoping it would be sausage and mash.

2004

Well, we had a couple of pages left over – so here's a contribution from the February 2004 edition of British Wildlife *that ruffled a few feathers here and there.*

'Now all the youth of England are on fire.' In Shakespeare's Henry V they were eager to sell their pastures to buy a horse and set off to give those Frenchies the licking of their lives. Today, if youths are on fire, it's more likely to be caused by carelessness with a lighted banger, or dozing off with the gas mains on. But in fact they are incandescent for another reason. They have straightened their baseball caps, tightened their disgusting smelly trainers, and given us their views, with passion and only a hint of tantrums to follow. 'The game's afoot!' The nation's youth has spoken at last. And what they have spoken about is pheasants.

In the green corner are the pupils of the appropriately-named St George's Middle School in Sandringham. Outraged by the sound of guns on the nearby estate, and stunned by the sight of a dead pheasant landing near the playground, the children were encouraged by their teachers to write to the Queen about 'the killing of our wildlife'.

'Lots of us were extremly (sic) upset, especially our wildlife teacher', wrote one of them. Another asked Her Majesty, 'What have pheasants ever done to you?' The estate apologized for upsetting the children and promised to arrange to shoot only when the pupils were indoors about their lessons, but will that satisfy them? 'We spend a lot of time helping and saving our wild life and environment', protested a tearful 10-year old. How tragic, if the pheasants are being sheltered and fed tit-bits on one side of the hedge, and being blasted from the skies on the other. Most confusing for the pheasants, I should think, though in my experience, pheasants are not of a reflective disposition.

Meanwhile, in the red corner, we have 11-year-old Tom from Essex. Lucky Tom is one of many youngsters taking advantage of 'a major initiative' by BASC, the British Association for Shooting and Conservation, to introduce more young people to the joys of shooting. In 'a brilliant day' just before Christmas, Tom downed 10 pheasants in the morning, and another nine in the afternoon. There are many similar stories in a special youth issue of *The Shooting Times*. It's clear that pretty well everybody had a good time, with pheasants raining down all over the place in varying states of disrepair.

A charity called Animal Aid found these stories 'disturbing', and one sees what they mean. Many of today's cage-reared pheasants can hardly lift their sagging bellies off the ground, let alone offer a sporting target to schoolboy marksmen. And there are other dangers. In her last Conservation News column, my esteemed colleague Sue Everett admitted to being 'pheasant-unfriendly': 'if one gets in my way, I run it over and then put it in the boot for dinner'. Shortly afterwards she was on the receiving end of an email from the BASC press officer pointing out that she had admitted publicly to a criminal offence. But what was the offence – running over the bird or eating it for supper? And where does the youth of England stand on this? Was Sue spoiling young Tom's shooting or was she harming the Sandringham school's environment? Either way, I fear she will be given a stiff sentence. The one thing nobody seems to condone is actually eating the things.

* * *

Jethro Tull

THICK AS A BRICK

In-depth

Laura Shenton

The phrase "thick as a brick" is a North English colloquial term meaning "stupid" — Like the religious themes on *Aqualung*, the theme of *Thick As A Brick* came out of my adolescent feelings about society and how it tries to bend you away from your will and toward its will, as if you're not bright enough to make your own choices. I wasn't a precocious child, but I knew how it felt to be one of the more academically gifted people; I knew what it felt like to be ostracised, despised and feared by the rank and file, who weren't terribly bright. Nobody likes the clever kids. So the album came to represent the gulf between growing up clever and the social discrepancy that results from that: the fact that you were really disliked by some of the kids.

- Ian Anderson (Guitar World, September 1999)

Jethro Tull

THICK AS A BRICK

In-depth

Laura Shenton

WP
WYMER
PUBLISHING
Bedford, England

First published in 2021 by Wymer Publishing
Bedford, Englandwww.wymerpublishing.co.uk Tel: 01234 326691
Wymer Publishing is a trading name of Wymer (UK) Ltd

Copyright © 2021 Laura Shenton / Wymer Publishing. This edition published 2021.

Print edition (fully illustrated): **ISBN: 978-1-912782-57-4**

Edited by Jerry Bloom.
Proofread by Lin White of Coinlea.

eBook formatting by Coinlea.
Printed and bound in Great Britain by
CMP, Dorset.

A catalogue record for this book is available from the British Library.

Typeset by Andy Bishop / 1016 Sarpsborg
Cover design by 1016 Sarpsborg.
Cover photo © Gijsbert Hanekroot (Alamy Stock Photo).

Contents

Preface

There's a fair bit that has already been written on Jethro Tull, both biographically and from a music analysis perspective. On such basis, you could be thinking, "Another Tull book? Really?" But here's the thing; I do think there is a gap in the literature whereby the biographical stuff out there doesn't talk in length about the music and the music analysis stuff out there often makes a lot of connections between Jethro Tull's music and theories that haven't actually been put out there (or indeed corroborated) by the band themselves.

So I'm not trying to reinvent the wheel here; what I want to do is offer an insight into *Thick As A Brick* in a way that discusses the music in detail in relation to what the band's intentions were. I want to offer something factual rather than something that is peppered with my own opinion and interpretation of the music. You won't see any of that whole kind of "this section is in the key of C and it therefore means X" or "I think this lyric means Y". For of course, the beauty of a lot of Jethro Tull's music is the ambiguity. As author of this book, it is not my place to throw a lot of my own opinions out there because it won't add anything to the literature if I do that.

The purpose of this book is to look at *Thick As A Brick* in detail; an extent of detail that has been put out there by Ian Anderson in terms of what was intended by the album and detail as in how the album was perceived at the time. As a result, throughout this book you're going to see lots of quotes from vintage articles. I think it's important to corroborate such material as there will probably come a time when it is harder to source.

In the interest of transparency, I have no affiliation with Jethro Tull or with any of their associates. This book is based on extensive research and objective commentary.

Chapter One

Why Thick As A Brick?

T*hick As A Brick* was a big deal. Musically, it defied a lot of convention, even in comparison to other progressive rock albums at the time. It is one long forty-three minutes song and very quirky. From America's (and indeed anywhere else's) point of view, Jethro Tull were an eccentric British band and commercially, *Thick As A Brick* could have been something of an underdog in such regard.

As was reported in American magazine, *Creem* in May 1973, "*Thick As A Brick* rocketed straight to number one on the charts, and so far the band has done two sell-out tours on the strength of it. On the second tour they sold out Madison Square Garden for a straight week. All this on the basis of an album — and a style — which on the surface would seem to tax anybody's attention span."

Some people think that *Thick As A Brick* is the ultimate Jethro Tull album, and not just because it is ambitious as a one-song progressive rock epic; *Thick As A Brick* has the flow of a masterfully composed short song and everyone in the band gives a stellar performance of gorgeous melodies played with technical expertise, especially in the complex changes in time signature throughout the piece. Ian Anderson's lyrics and the delivery of them are provocative, memorable and unique in their fascinating mix of silly and serious.

Although the overall themes in *Thick As A Brick* are known due to what Anderson has stated in many interviews over the years, the specific meaning behind each line of lyric is largely ambiguous, but that is a point of fascination rather than frustration in much of Jethro Tull's music. As an assembly of words, they sound good and Anderson delivers them convincingly; it sounds like a story worth listening to, regardless of what that story (perhaps) actually is. The album has a tremendous extent of replay value in such regard.

In the days of vinyl records, *Thick As A Brick* was divided across two sides of the LP, and on CD releases of the album exists as two tracks connoting side one and side two but ultimately, it is one long song. The whole thing is dominated by interesting interplay between a wide range of instruments and changes in mood. All in all, *Thick As A Brick* presents a fascinating soundscape that covers both acoustic and heavier styles. The way in which the different sections interweave is an excellent vehicle through which everyone in the band gets the chance to sparkle. Performed with conviction, the musical rapport in the *Thick As A Brick* line-up of Jethro Tull is evident. An ambitious and fun album, *Thick As A Brick* showcases Jethro Tull at a strong point in the band's tenure. A pleasurable and unique album to listen to and one that is certainly worthy of an entire book's worth of exploration into it. *RPM* reviewed *Thick As A Brick* in May 1972; "With that familiar amalgam of rock, the classics and acoustic instrumentation, Jethro Tull presents us with one of the best packaged, best written and best performed albums we've ever come across. It's a mindblower."

By the late sixties and early seventies, British progressive rock bands were broadening their horizons in terms of musical output. Gone were the days of predictable verse, chorus, middle eight, repeat. Groups were experimenting more with structure, texture, harmony and instrumentation. To name just a few groups, such exploration was prevalent with Yes, Genesis, Emerson, Lake & Palmer, Curved Air and certainly, Jethro Tull. Combined with advances in what was possible with studio technology and the record-buying public's willingness to embrace this, all such ingredients are very much present on *Thick As A Brick.* The song features short songs that are all interspersed with instrumental passages linking them (see the appendix in the back of this book for a breakdown of the structure). Abundantly inventive, *Thick As A Brick* is musically complex and yet accessible. With the original LP packaging being a twelve-page newspaper full of Monty Python style humour, the album stands out as something that was very much in a league of its own creatively. Ultimately, it is an important milestone in progressive rock music history.

Creem reported in May 1973; *"Aqualung* was a giant and the follow-up, *Thick As A Brick*, was over a year in the making and even bigger. Bigger in every way: the only time in rock history previous to this that a single song had covered two sides of an LP was Canned Heat's 'Refried Boogie' on *Livin' The Blues*, and that was just an extended jam. *Brick* was a moose of a whole other hue: a series of variations (though they really didn't vary enough to sustain forty minutes) on a single, simple theme, which began as a sort of wistful English folk melody and wound through march tempos, high energy guitar, glockenspiels, dramatic staccato outbursts like something from a movie soundtrack and plenty of soloing by Anderson, all the way from the top of side one to the end of the album."

Rolling Stone reviewed *Thick As A Brick* in June 1972; "For all its intricacy, the "theme" or poetry of *Thick As A Brick* is its least important aspect. Anderson's language (in *Aqualung* as well) is often wordy and ponderous, and its bitter condescension and breadth of denunciation can be unpleasant. What marks this album as a significant departure from other Jethro Tull work, and rock in general, is the organisation of all its music into one continuous track. Albums like *Sgt. Pepper* or *Tommy* were complete entities in themselves, but still chose to use songs as their basic components. While sections of *Thick As A*

Brick are melodically distinct, they all inherently relate to each other. What connecting there is, is uncontrived and is often the occasion for some of the album's boldest playing. The lyrics, clever and dense as they are, are chiefly valuable as a premise for the music. The album's opening is sprightly, with Ian's flute poking in and out; a more introspective, minor key digression follows, then a stalking bass line, accompanied by horns and John Evan's excited Rick Wakeman-like organ. The relentless and mechanical gives way to something very stately and regal, as English as, yet less folksy than, the opening passage. The piano plays arpeggios; Anderson overlays a jazzy flute. Some overdubbed guitar yammerings follow. Anderson takes to the violin and creates a whirling, macabre setting for the combative son's announcement, 'I've come down from the upper class...' As the other son begins to speak, the music becomes milder, then sunnier. A bell-like organ rings out behind a jig, performed in almost telegraphic rhythm. This, and its reprise on side two, is the album's most attractive section. An ominous heraldic organ shatters the calm, and the side ends with the electric guitar shrieking helplessly, like a wounded bird."

The review continued; "Side two reintroduces side one's second statement. It merges into an energetic though hollow, unemphatic drum solo; then some free jazz, over which a set of lyrics is recited. A rather fine English folk melody emerges. Anderson's voice becomes more severe, a classical guitar is introduced, and the music takes an Iberian turn. A harpsichord plays as a guitar repeats the riff from George Harrison's 'Wah Wah'. The writing becomes very linear, with rapid harmonic shifts. This alternates with a vaulting melodic figure. Then a sudden whoosh, and we return to the closing theme of side one, now strongly reinforced by the organ, only to be momentarily interrupted by some expansive strings. As almost a postscript, the initial theme is recalled, and with it the sentiment, (the reviewer quoted the final lyrics on side two here). The members of Jethro Tull were hand-picked by Anderson (several are old school chums); no one, save Ian, remains from the original band. The playing, not surprisingly, is tight as a drum. Martin Barre's guitar and John Evan's keyboards especially shine, and Ian's singing is no longer abrasive. Whether or not *Thick As A Brick* is an isolated experiment, it is nice to know that someone in rock has ambitions beyond the four or five minute conventional track, and has the intelligence to carry out his intentions, in all their intricacy, with considerable grace."

Melody Maker reviewed *Thick As A Brick* in March 1972; "As the album is already brilliantly reviewed on the elaborately produced sleeve, there is hardly any point in adding our own comments. Ian Anderson's latest work consists of a poem wrapped in a newspaper. And a local newspaper of doubtful authenticity — the "St Cleve Chronicle" — I have heard informed observers remark: 'This is the silliest cover ever seen' — one can merely add that the joke at the expense of a local newspaper wears thin rather rapidly but should not detract from the obvious amount of thought and work that has gone into the production of *Thick*. There are some twelve pages of painstaking material in the cod newspaper, which must have given Gerald "Little Milton" Bostock and Ian Anderson a lot of fun, and a considerable headache to the staff of Chrysalis, who spent a lot of time preparing the sleeve and photographs. But what of the music? It's a lot to take in a brief test run of the album. It needs time to absorb. Heard out of context of their highly visual stage act, it does not have such immediate appeal. But there is not quite the same doomy quality that *Aqualung* had; the ideas flow in super abundance, making me suspect this will receive similar if not greater acclaim. An intense level of performance is maintained throughout this long work, while not quite as battering as some of the extended works of, say, ELP. Ian's flute playing seems greatly improved. Not to say that it was below standard before, but he does seem to have taken care over increasing his ability on the instrument. Barriemore Barlow is a fine drummer who roars around his kit with lightning dexterity, and punches home the arrangements, while the Tull sound blossoms forth under the combined efforts of Martin Barre's reliable guitar and John Evan's excellent keyboard work. The band seem to be more co-operate now and each member pulls his weight most effectively. As the sleeve note says: 'Not blatantly commercial then, but a fine disc which although possessing many faults should do well enough.' We'd like to add that only time can Tull."

Thick As A Brick was reviewed in *Sounds* in March 1972; "One of the most disillusioning experiences of my musical life occurred when I saw Jethro Tull for the second time. It was three weeks after the first time, when I'd enjoyed them a lot — they were musically strong, and Ian Anderson had a fine stage presence, cracking lots of little comments and asides. I took it for a clever spontaneous performance. Then I saw them again, and everything was exactly the same — practically every note of the music (bar the goofs) and all the jokes and asides. I can't help feeling that someone who has his ad-libs rehearsed that carefully needs watching a little carefully, and I've been a little wary of Jethro Tull ever since, especially when I found successive albums breaking little new ground and doing little more than refining down and adjusting slightly a concept stated on the first album. Ian Anderson has borrowed and created his own clichés and stays with them — even on this new album. Apart from him, the band is completely changed from the first record, and there's no doubt that it's good — but limited, I think, by the Tull format. Martin Barre and John Evan especially come through with some fine playing, but they don't really break any new or particularly exciting ground; they get so far and seem to hit an undefined but quite recognisable wall of policy. I get the feeling that the band is being used as an effects box, as sidemen to a central idea that isn't really strong enough to justify its role.

That central idea is Ian Anderson's new monster work *Thick As A Brick*, a long, related sequence of songs which reflects a bitter, cynical view of the world around him and the people who run it — businessmen, the church, schools... you know the things. That obviously is a vast over-simplification of the work, but I think Ian Anderson too is guilty of over-simplification — somehow *Thick As A Brick* sounds to me like a bit of an empty gesture, a hollow threat. There's nothing in there that hasn't been said before — though he does put it quite well — and I don't find much in there to jolt me, to catch my imagination. Maybe these things need saying over and over again, but does it really need a whole album to say it? I think not, but doubtless thousands will disagree."

What a weird review! Weird as in, the reviewer seemed to spend more time complaining about the band overall than actually passing much comment on the album they were meant to be reviewing. Still though, the review is certainly demonstrative of the fact that people who didn't like Jethro Tull, and indeed *Thick As A Brick*, *really* didn't like it. Historically, I would suggest that this is actually part of what makes the album so fascinating.

During a period in popular music where what was possible was expanding, *Thick As A Brick* is a fascinating album in how even though it was so quirky and unique, it still achieved tremendous commercial success. It got to number five in the UK in March 1972 and reached number one on the US Billboard 200 album chart in the June.

New Musical Express reported that month; "*Thick As A Brick* only recently deposed after three weeks at number one in America (it reached the top in an incredible three weeks)." This was such a noteworthy achievement for an album consisting of a forty-three-minute-long song. *Thick As A Brick* is fascinating because whilst it came to prominence at a time where the possibilities within popular music were expanding, it was still a big deal in terms of how, overall, it still did so well as something that went so much against the grain.

In March 1986, it was stipulated in *Billboard*, "What does Barbara Streisand have in common with AC/DC, Led Zeppelin, Pink Floyd, Bob Dylan and Jethro Tull? Give up? Those are the only six artists since the early seventies to earn number one albums without the benefit of a top forty single." The article then went on to list *Thick As A Brick* and *A Passion Play* as the Jethro Tull albums that applied to the trend. Anderson was quoted in *Ultimate Classic Rock* in March 2017; "It was a blessed bit of luck that it (*Thick As A Brick*) did okay. It spent a number of weeks at number one in the *Billboard* chart, which came as a surprise to everybody — including Mr Bill Board."

Record World reported in June 1972; "*Thick As A Brick*, the recently released album by Jethro Tull, has been certified gold by the RIAA, signifying sales of over one million dollars. *Aqualung* and *Benefit*, Jethro Tull's last two Reprise albums, were also certified gold."

Cash Box reported in May 1975; "Jethro Tull's latest Chrysalis album, *War Child*, has sold over one million units, qualifying it for a Warner Bros. platinum record award. The platinum award comes on the heels of a resurgence of sales activity on the entire eight-album Jethro Tull catalogue. All of the albums are RIAA gold award winners with *Aqualung*, *Thick As A Brick* and *Living In The Past* having previously attained platinum status."

It was in the spring of 1974 that the band collected platinum awards for the American sales of *Living In The Past*, *Aqualung* and *Thick As A Brick*, as was reported in *Billboard* in March 1974.

***

The first three minutes from *Thick As A Brick* have been included on the majority of Jethro Tull compilation albums. This edit has had radio play and ironically perhaps, has become a well known Jethro Tull "song" in its own right, even though it's really just a cut off of the entire *Thick As A Brick* piece. Being in the moment of the whole thing — whirlwind tour schedules and promotional interviews, perhaps the enormity of *Thick As A Brick* was somewhat lost on Ian Anderson at the time. He was quoted in *Prog* in August 2016; "It's only in recent times that I've appreciated how complex the music is, I was only twenty-four at the time we began to put this together. Yet there are so many weird time changes and musical innovations on the album. I would never compare what we did back then to jazz rockers like Weather Report or the Mahavishnu Orchestra — they were really amazing musicians — but we were a little more sophisticated than the usual riff rockers you'd find on the scene."

It wouldn't have been particularly surprising perhaps, had *Thick As A Brick* been popular just among fans of progressive rock. Fans of progressive rock would have been likely to have been open to the musical oddities of the album anyway due to the very nature of progressive rock and its penchant for the long song. What is remarkable about *Thick As A Brick* is that not only did it grab the attention of progressive rock fans, but also that of the record buying public on a larger scale. Structurally it was very much outside of what was on offer with popular music at the time and yet, it still rose to popularity on such scale. One of the key reasons as to why *Thick As A Brick* was such a landmark album for Jethro Tull, is that it was very clearly a move away from the twelve bar type of stuff that the band had been doing at the start of their tenure in the late sixties.

Anderson was quoted of *This Was* in *Guitar World* in September 1999; "When we went in to make *This Was*, I felt okay that we were playing blues, but I also felt that we were just being somewhat imitative of other groups. By the time we finished the record, I was aware of the difficulties I would have working with Mick Abrahams, and not only because of his limited ability outside of playing blues guitar. He was content to play three or four nights a week in pubs, but the rest of us saw the record as a steppingstone to something bigger — as a chance to travel abroad and go to America. One very good thing did come out of our association, however: I had been a guitar player since I was sixteen or seventeen, and it was only when I met Mick that I quit playing guitar and started working on the flute. And obviously, the flute is the thing I'm best known for. I owe that to Mick."

It could be considered that the experimental nature of *Thick As A Brick* wasn't explicitly different to what other artists at the time were doing in terms of creativity. Regarding long songs, structure and vast varieties of melodic ideas, Frank Zappa, Miles Davis, The Doors and Pink Floyd were all putting some amazing work out and yet, it was Jethro Tull's *Thick As A Brick* that had such prominent success commercially.

Now, whilst commercial success is not necessarily an indicator of quality, it is nevertheless a noteworthy achievement. It wasn't that common for a band to put out a concept album and/or extended pieces of music that were both of interest in the mainstream and more complex than the type of music that was more typically commercially successful. With the exception of The Beatles, other progressive and experimental rock bands who had number one albums in the sixties and seventies were in the minority. As well as Jethro Tull, only Emerson, Lake & Palmer, Pink Floyd, Yes, Rick Wakeman and Mike Oldfield managed to do it in the UK albums chart. In the US, it was only achieved by, as well as Jethro Tull, The Doors, The Jimi Hendrix Experience and Pink Floyd.

Not only was *Thick As A Brick* a landmark album generally, it was also a big deal for Jethro Tull in terms of their musical journey up to that point in how it signified a stylistic change. In July 1972, *New Musical Express* offered an overview of Jethro Tull's pre *Thick As A Brick* albums; "As a writer, Anderson has always sailed his own course, unaffected by the trends and tastes of his contemporaries — he rarely listens to other bands either live or on record. This refreshing originality was the key stroke of *This Was*, on which the uneasy alliance of Anderson and Mick Abrahams concocted a beautifully loose mixture of jazz and blues. A lack of frills and a naïveté of approach were the album's strongest factors. Numbers like 'My Sunday Feeling' and 'A Song For Jeffrey' were startlingly out of the mainstream of popular music at the time, and have lost very little over the years. By *Stand Up* — the second album and a number one seller — Abrahams has vacated the stage solely to Ian Anderson, who wrote whenever his flights of fancy took him. That was the point where outside influences were rejected in favour of unfettered self-expression. *Stand Up* introduced a more riffy Jethro, with guitar (Martin Barre) solos crisp and compact. Typical numbers were 'New Day Yesterday' and 'Nothing Is Easy'... punchy, concise, little miniatures, reaching very tight peaks of dynamics. Anderson was then only dabbling in tonal colouring. Beside the riffy stuff, *Stand Up* also allowed plenty of space for the more sensitive side of Anderson's composing ability. 'Fat Man' remains a gas, humorously sad; 'Jeffrey Goes To Leicester Square' has a madrigal quality, and 'We Used To Know' and 'Reasons For Waiting' are flowing, lyrical compositions. At this stage, the most noticeable facet of Anderson's writing was his lack of pretension. Lyrics dealt with simple personal statements and reminiscences. There was none of "the social message" that was to blight many of Jethro's contemporaries. Anderson restricted his lyrics to songs about him, Jenny his wife, and his experiences, because that was the area he knew. He felt then he lacked the qualifications to broaden his horizons any further than his immediate basic surroundings."

The article continued; "*Benefit*, the third album, is a personal favourite of mine, and one that received least attention of any Jethro set. Musically it was mellower than *Stand Up*, although Anderson's ability to pull quirky riffs out of thin air, and coax equally quirky chord changes of Martin Barre, remained intact. 'Nothing To Say' and 'Play In Time', both lyrically alluding to group lifestyle, represented the riff side, but overall the album reflected a delicate feel. Standout tracks 'To Cry You A Song', 'Son', 'For Michael Collins Jeffrey And Me' and 'Sossity' possessed several common characteristics pointing to Anderson's future development, including growing appreciation of light and shade in the music and a blossoming out lyrically onto wider subjects. 'Son', with a neat twist, explored a father-son relationship. 'Michael Collins' was a sympathetic lament for the astronaut left behind in the mother ship at the time of the first moon landing. *Benefit*, to my mind — because it contains some of Jethro's most melodically attractive songs — brings to issue the regrettable fact that Anderson is widely ignored when contemporary songwriters come under discussion. Had he chosen to sing in the fashionable manner of the acoustic guitar soloist, there is little doubt in my mind that he would be ranked among the most important in that field. *Benefit* also introduced John Evan to Jethro, but it wasn't until the following *Aqualung* set that Evan got a real chance to spread out. Also new on *Aqualung*: Jeffrey Hammond-Hammond replacing Glenn Cornick on bass. Perhaps the most significant points concerning *Aqualung* are (a) that it was released a whole year after *Benefit* and (b) that, by then, Jethro were well into the American scene, spending much of their time on tour there."

Still from the same article; "Both may explain why *Aqualung* is a good way removed from *Benefit* in overall feel, the former being much harder and more aggressively riffy — American audiences like their rock that way — than its predecessor. *Aqualung*, in the main, represents Anderson fully in control of the tonal colouring he'd been aiming at since *Stand Up*. Heavy, rasping riffs that give way to delicate acoustic or flute work are typical characteristics, although to my mind the fine sensitive songs on this set tend to be lost against what I feel is a total impression of oppressiveness. Both 'My God' and the title track are almost ugly in that oppressiveness, taking away a great deal of the sentiment expressed in the first instance and the compassion one should feel in the second. There's no denying, however, the meticulous ear for detail that Anderson brought to every facet of the *Aqualung* presentation, nor the fact that the lyrics represent an important new departure. For the first time, significantly, Anderson allowed the words to be printed on the sleeve, and lyrically *Aqualung* is a powerful, heartfelt statement. Yet although it was a new departure in that Anderson was no longer restricting his scope of writing, the lyrics remain highly personalised to the writer. Not just harking back to Sunday boredom in Blackpool or having to face the press in LA., though, but going further into Anderson's sincerely held belief that society abuses God by manipulating him as a figurehead, instead of as a concept of love… From a production angle, this was Anderson the professional in full control. And if one hankered nostalgically for the naïveté of *This Was*, then there was compensation in the impressive maturity of Ian's composing ability."

I've quoted a lot from the above article but it is a really important one in the sense that it explores Jethro Tull's musical journey up to the point of *Thick As A Brick*. It is an example of how Jethro Tull were viewed before some of their later classics even existed and thus, I feel it is important to document how people viewed *Thick As A Brick* before it became iconic, historic and part of a discography that would ultimately go on to include classics such as *Minstrel In The Gallery* (1975), *Songs From The Wood* (1977) and *Heavy Horses* (1978).

When it came to *Thick As A Brick, New Musical Express* advocated in July 1972; "Most recent Tull album — ignoring the retrospective *Living In The Past* — is *Thick As A Brick*, which Ian obviously regards as Jethro's most important set to date. Musically and lyrically there is a definite lineage here with *Aqualung* — the points regarding America are again relevant. Yet whereas with *Aqualung* it was the lyrics that returned to a common idea, on *Brick* both lyrics and music have a linking theme. The degree of success varies enormously. In parts Anderson's lyrics can be eloquent and surreal, in others they border on the banal. In parts, musically, the use of light and shading is impressively effective, while elsewhere there's a total lack of subtlety, almost an overkill. Or worse, predictability. Listening to the album again this week, I felt too that I noticed a certain glibness about the music which I'm sure was never in Ian's head when he composed the piece. Then again there are passages like the poet and painter episode that hit just the right note of purity and poetry. It's on the lyrics, really, though, that *Brick* should be judged. Here, they're not as personalised as on, say, 'Wind-Up' from *Aqualung*, but at the same time they manage to encapsulate most of the feelings Anderson had been hinting at in earlier songs... the way that the life of the common man, whoever he may be — the one 'geared to the average rather than the exceptional' — is merely a tool in the hands of the same elitist group who, on the *Aqualung* set, elected God as the figurehead. Also the same elitist anonymous figures who govern and predestine the life of the common man, and worse still dismiss him with contempt as "thick as a brick", thereby stripping him of feeling."

Seemingly, *Thick As A Brick* offers something to listeners who like a number of things in their music. Within a long song, there are lots of small ideas, many of which have features in common with both classical and popular music; there is a lot of virtuoso musicianship and exploration of complex melody and structure but there is also a lot of repetition both lyrically and melodically. For instance, with a typical pop song lasting usually no more than five minutes and with a structure consisting of no more than six different main sections (an introduction, verses, choruses, a bridge, an instrumental solo, a coda), *Thick As A Brick* breaks convention in that regard because within its forty-three minutes it has a total of over twenty-five different sections of music. However, the use of repetition and there being an almost medley-like quality to the album, presents something that has a lot of variety for listeners to latch onto. It casts its net very wide so to speak.

I'm certainly not saying that when making *Thick As A Brick* a conscious decision was made by the band to plan the album in such way, but certainly, the finished product, intentionally or accidentally, has a lot about it that offers many points of potential interest. Ian Anderson said in an interview on Australian TV in July 1972, "I don't want to get caught up in the commercial aspects of repetition. I don't really like repetition unless it serves a very definite purpose musically within the context of a whole piece. If you look at that record (*Thick As A Brick*) there is some repetition, but not a great deal."

From the mid-sixties, several bands had success with concept albums. Most concept albums from that era are made up of a number of individual songs that tell a story and/or focus on a theme, an example of this being The Who's *Tommy* (1969). Around the same period, other bands such as Deep Purple, The Moody Blues and Emerson, Lake & Palmer incorporated classical music ideas into the rock music they played. In the case of Emerson, Lake & Palmer, their 1971 album was an entire version of the Modest Mussorgsky piece, *Pictures At An Exhibition*. All such bands were predominantly active in writing music that went structurally against what was in place with typical pop music; unpredictable song structure, songs that sometimes lasted the full side of a record (or at least close to it) and virtuoso musicianship.

The creation of large-scale pieces of impressive music that required listeners to keep an open mind certainly wasn't exclusive to Jethro Tull's *Thick As A Brick*. What makes *Thick As A Brick* really stand out is that the song covers the entirety of the record. *Thick As A Brick* contains vocal sections, a few of which repeat content from earlier in the piece. With this, there are many different passages of instrumental music that link the vocal sections together (do take a look at the appendix in this book to see a list that best demonstrates this structure). The point is that although *Thick As A Brick* isn't so radically different stylistically to what other groups were doing at the time, structurally, as a long song, it defies convention. It's a distinctive album because, even if you don't remember every melody upon first hearing it, there's enough going on to make you think, "hang on, this is a bit different!"

It is an intriguingly composed juxtaposition of many musical ideas within one long song. Jethro Tull didn't invent the long song but what they did with the idea was original and innovative. In *Progression Magazine* in 1996, journalist John Covach wrote; "My basic point about the musical structure of *Thick As A Brick* is that this long song is more than a medley or extended jam; the piece hangs together more the way a piece of classical music by Beethoven or Brahms does. And like much classical music, its structure is complicated and rewards repeated and careful listening. Combine this with the lyrics and the packaging, and *Thick As A Brick* becomes fascinating on a number of levels."

Although *Thick As A Brick* was a big step for Jethro Tull, their album before that, *Aqualung*, was certainly suggestive of what the band were capable of. Both the album's title track and 'My God' feature a range of ideas that go beyond typical popular song structure. On BBC Radio in July 1989, Anderson said of *Aqualung*; "Even within the context of an individual song I still like the idea that you can have perhaps a loud riff to start the thing off, and then it goes into a gentle acoustic passage, and then it does some other big stuff and then it changes tempo and feel and goes off into something else, round the houses, a couple of guitar solos, whatever, and back to something else. I like that in music."

On the version of 'By Kind Permission Of' that was recorded on 4th November 1970 live at Carnegie Hall (released on the 1972 album, *Living In The Past*), pianist John Evan plays a long medley of pieces of classical music (Beethoven's 'Pathetique', Debussy's 'Golliwog's Cakewalk' and Rachmaninoff's Prelude in C Sharp Minor op. 3 no. 2) with Ian Anderson improvising on flute. Essentially, the band demonstrated a propensity for playing large scale medleys of music live on stage prior to *Thick As A Brick* coming to be.

Ian Anderson was quoted of *Aqualung* in *Prog* in March 2018; "That's the singer/songwriter side of things, where a lot of the music did come out of me strumming an acoustic guitar with a view to keeping it that way, as opposed to writing that way and turning it electric. That big title track riff came out of an acoustic jam — you've just got to have that imagination to hear that. You have to know that you can make it sing. It went on to sell and sell across the world. It's the album that broke us in countries beyond the UK and US."

A quick note before the next chapter: John Evans went by the name of John Evan. He was quoted in *Jackie* in August 1970 when asked if John Evan was his real name; "Almost — this is the name that just sort of came out. I'd done some session work for the last Jethro Tull LP, and when the sleeve came out there'd been a spelling mistake — and they called me John Evan. My real name is John Evans. But everybody calls me Evan now." Similarly, Jeffery Hammond adopted the name "Hammond-Hammond" as a joke, as both his father's name and mother's maiden name were the same. In such regard, I've transcribed their names as they were written in each original instance.

Also, to address something that often comes up in Jethro Tull fan conversation, there is often debate surrounding whether the band consisted of Ian Anderson plus other musicians or whether it was a group of musicians who contributed equally. The following chapters contain a lot of quotes from Ian Anderson; proportionately a lot more than from any other member of Jethro Tull. This isn't due to the fact that I am saying "Ian Anderson is Jethro Tull and the other musicians' input isn't important" — not at all! It's simply the case that of all the members of Jethro Tull, Ian Anderson has done the vast majority of interviews as the mainstay and founding member of the band and both vintage and recent interviews are reflective of that.

Anderson was quoted of *Thick As A Brick* in *Prog* in August 2016; "I suppose I have to admit that I really imposed the whole idea on the other guys, but for whatever reason they went along with it, and actually warmed to the task once we got stuck into the music." For what it's worth, although Ian Anderson was at the helm of the group in terms of the writing, *Thick As A Brick* was made possible due to the input of everyone who was in Jethro Tull at the time and the following chapters will certainly be reflective of that overall.

Chapter Two

The Making Of Thick As A Brick

Rehearsals for *Thick As A Brick* took place in the Rolling Stones' studio in Bermondsey. It was initially the case that the album wasn't going to be a single continuous piece. The band came up with individual segments and then elected to write short pieces of music to link everything together. Recording began in December 1971 at Morgan Studios in London. With previous Jethro Tull albums, Ian Anderson had generally written the songs in advance but *Thick As A Brick* was much more spontaneous overall.

A lot of *Thick As A Brick* was actually written during the recording sessions. *Thick As A Brick* was built up day by day; Ian Anderson got up early each morning to prepare music for the rest of the band to work on in the afternoon. The lyrics were written first, with the music constructed to fit around them. Anderson was quoted in *Prog* in August 2016 as he said of the area where the Rolling Stones' studio was; "This was based in Bermondsey, a rather dreadful part of South London. The way it worked was that I'd spend the morning in my home in Hampstead — sadly, not the posh part of that North London suburb — and get three or four minutes of music down on a sheet of paper from an exercise book. Then we'd meet as a band and go through not just the new part I'd written, but everything from the beginning. So, gradually we'd build up the piece."

The band recalled the recording process as having been a happy one, with a strong feeling of camaraderie and fun. They were all fans of Monty Python and this style of humour influenced the lyrics and overall concept of *Thick As A Brick*. Guitarist Martin Barre recalled the whole band coming up with ideas for the music. Some sections were recorded in a single take with every member having an input, including significant contributions from keyboard player, John Evan. *Thick As A Brick* was what it was due to many things that *Aqualung* was (and indeed wasn't!) Musically, there are aspects of *Aqualung* that were carried forward (in terms of going against predictable uses of structure, time signature, style and instrumentation). The serious nature of *Aqualung* (in terms of its dark themes and that fact that it wasn't actually a concept album) quite possibly spurred the band on to make *Thick As A Brick* as more of a fun album.

Ian Anderson was quoted in *Jam* in November 1993; "*Thick As A Brick* was the concept album that *Aqualung* wasn't, but some people saw *Aqualung* as a concept album. When it came to doing *Thick As A Brick*, we said 'Hey, let's really give them a concept album here. In fact let's make a little bit of a humorous statement about concept albums. Let's make something that's a bit of fun, not in a nasty way, not to deceive our audience, but just to take the genre and create something larger than life out of it, make a caricature of the concept album, but in a light-hearted way' — The general tone of the album was quite humorous and quite light-hearted. A lot of people didn't see it as a joke. They took it very seriously."

Aqualung was Jethro Tull's fourth album and was released in March 1971. An interesting mixture of folk, jazz and rock, Anderson vocalised all manner of ideas on religion, consumerism and poverty (Anderson was quoted in *New Musical Express* in July 1972 as he described 'My God' as a blues for God, not a condemnation; "A lament for God being a social crutch for so many").

The album did well commercially, and solidified Jethro Tull's reputation in the UK as well as the US. However, when critics began to place the band under the category of prog rock, it went against what Ian Anderson was perhaps aiming for with *Aqualung*. He was quoted of *Aqualung* in *Ultimate Classic Rock* in March 2017; "It was just a bunch of songs, and two or three of them happened to have a link. When I came to do the running order and work on the cover text, as you do when you wrap a Christmas present, you choose nice paper and put a nice bow on it. That process in presenting the album gave it some cohesion. But it was whimsical individual oddities, written in hotel rooms, very often in the US."

Ian Anderson was quoted in *Jam* in November 1993; "The recording of *Aqualung* was not a happy period. We were not having a great time in the studio. It was a difficult album to make, for technical reasons. It also had to do with the fact that we were all pretty homeless and living in hotels and working every day during a long, fairly miserable winter trying to get that album finished. It wasn't a great time. It was an exciting time, but on a day to day basis, we were not really terribly happy. It was a lot of hard work and a lot of things were going wrong. So that doesn't, for me, hold any great memories. And in terms of the touring that surrounded that period of time, it just seemed, well, I don't know — I guess we had some nights that were okay, and some memorable concerts, but it was a hard period that was not as enjoyable perhaps as some of the later periods of Jethro Tull, where tours had kind of settled down into much more enjoyable affairs, both musically and socially. I was trying, with the *Aqualung* album, to first of all deal with some lyrical matter that was a bit more varied in its subject material, what it was about and where it was from. So I was trying to create some variation there, some degrees of depth and dilemma in the lyrics, and in terms of the music, it was a very deliberate attempt to try and integrate some genuinely acoustic performance into Jethro Tull as a rock band. It had happened to some extent on earlier albums, but *Aqualung* was the one where I think I had developed as an acoustic guitar player to the point where I could actually sing and play a song as a more or less solo performance. So that was, for me, what was of greater merit about the album. It kind of stretched out the dynamic range of the group more, marked things out a little bit in terms of saying, 'Hey, we don't have to have drums and bass in everything' and 'we don't have to compete with Led Zeppelin or Mountain or any of our contemporaries at the time. We can go out and be a little bit more varied in our musical instrumentation, our dynamic range and our subject material' — From that point of view, I guess it was a definite move on from what we'd done before. But to me it's just another album."

Anderson was quoted of *Aqualung* in *Guitar World* in September 1999; "*Aqualung* marks the point at which I had the confidence as a songwriter and as a guitarist to actually play the guitar and be at the forefront of the band. It's also the album on which I began to address religious issues in my music, and I think that happened simply because the time was right for it. Addressing religious issues in simplistic pop-rock terms was permissible then. I'd have to disguise some of those sentiments to make them pass muster today. *Aqualung* wasn't a concept album, although a lot of people thought so. The idea came about from a photograph my wife at the time took of a tramp in London. I had feelings of guilt about the homeless, as well as fear and insecurity with people like that who seem a little scary. And I suppose all of that was combined with a slightly romanticised picture of the person who is homeless but yet a free spirit, who either won't or can't join in society's prescribed formats. So from that photograph and those sentiments, I began writing the words to 'Aqualung.' I can remember sitting in a hotel room in LA, working out the chord structure for the verses. It's quite a tortured tangle of chords, but it was meant to really drag you here and there and then set you down into the more gentle acoustic section of the song."

There is a sense that the band felt rushed when it came to making *Aqualung*. Ian Anderson was quoted in *Guitar World* in September 1999; "With 'Locomotive Breath', I knew I wanted a song about a runaway train, where things are going out of control and you can't get off the train. It's safe to say that kind of situation mirrored an aspect of the band's life at the time, what with all the touring we were doing. We actually had to record *Aqualung* in a rather short time between tours, so it was done very quickly. Island Studios had just opened up, and it was a shakedown period for them; there were a lot of technical problems. Plus, the band was having problems recording 'Locomotive Breath'. We just couldn't get the feeling, and I was failing to convey to the band what the song was about and how it should work. So I went out and played high-hat and bass drum for four minutes to lay down a rhythm track; this was in the days before drum machines and sequencers. Then I played an acoustic guitar part and some electric guitar parts, and then we tacked on John Evans' piano intro at the front of it, and the others overdubbed their parts onto mine. So nobody actually played on that track at the same time, but it's not a bad performance whatsoever. That was the only time we ever did anything like that back then."

Martin Barre was quoted of *Aqualung* in *Guitar Legends* in May 1997; "Things were very difficult and very tense, but at the end of the day, this was an important album. I think the songs were so good that it really carried the album through, Ian wrote all of it in as much as he wrote the riff and the verses. The form was just verse-riff and he had the lyrics. We needed a guitar solo, so I said, 'Why don't we just base it on the chords of the verse but break it down into half-time, then do a sort of round sequence to do a solo over?' and it worked well. While I was doing the solo, which was going really well, Jimmy Page walked into the control room and started waving. I thought, 'Should I wave back and mess up the solo or should I just grin

and carry on?' being a professional to the end, I just grinned."
Even before *Thick As A Brick* was released as an album,
there is evidence that the ideas for it were being developed
whilst Jethro Tull were still touring with *Aqualung* as their
latest album. Ian Anderson was quoted of *Thick As A Brick*
in *Guitar Legends* in May 1997; "That was something that
derived from things I was fiddling around with while I was on
tour in the US. I had just purchased my first Martin guitar, and
I played it on the song. A small-bodied guitar lends itself —
because of its wider fret board — to the style of playing that
allows you space between the strings; they are easily picked. A
lot of people sort of assume that it was a finger picking style,
but in fact it was all just played literally as single notes with
a plectrum. The album itself was a response to the critical
assumption that *Aqualung* had been a concept album, which
it was not — although clearly, there were a few songs that did
hang together. *Thick* was a deliberate attempt to come up with
what Saddam Hussein might have referred to as 'the mother
of all concept albums' — it was all delivered tongue-in-cheek,
particularly in terms of its live performance. We delivered it in
a way in which people were clearly not quite sure whether it
was a very serious exercise or whether it was a light comedy.
In truth, it was both of those things."
It wasn't just in hotel rooms that ideas for *Thick As A
Brick* were being developed; they even got an airing on
stage. In November 1971, *Billboard* reported on the band's
performance in New York; "At Madison Square Garden on
October 18th where Jethro Tull appeared, attention focussed
on Ian Anderson, lead vocal and flutist, for his mischievous
antics that were sometimes playful, sometimes demoniac, but
always full of craft and sorcery. The act began with a long song
about evils of society and plastic religion — favourite themes
for this British rock group. They did songs from their latest
album, *Aqualung* (on the Reprise label), and some from one

they plan to release this February, tentatively titled *Thick As A Brick*, British slang for numbskull. Tull's lyrics tend to have a fairy tale quality about them, like medieval British legends. The music also borrowed some of the sounds of that period in their history, especially during John Evan's organ solos, but it was quite evident that the performance and sound was a style all their own."

Of course, there is always a multitude of reasons as to why a record may have been released later than the date initially announced (or indeed assumed) but in the case of *Thick As A Brick*, it is actually plausible that the album was released later than planned in the UK (and therefore America) due to what was going on outside of the band's control. In the UK, the coal miners' strike began on 9th January 1972, and at that time three quarters of the electricity used in the UK was produced by coal-burning power stations. A state of emergency was declared on 9th February, and the miners voted to return to work on 25th February. There was an advert in *New Musical Express* on 26th February 1972 that stated, "*Thick As A Brick* now on sale" but the album was actually released on Friday 3rd March 1972. Essentially, it was the impact of the coal miners' strike that caused a delay in the album's release.

On 18th November 1971, Jethro Tull finished the American leg of the *Aqualung* tour. They set to work on writing and recording *Thick As A Brick* straight away. Across a number of interviews, Ian Anderson has actually stated different time schedules for the making of the album. In one, he stipulated that it took two weeks to arrange and rehearse the music and then up to another two weeks to do all of the recording. In a different interview, he advocated that the whole process took just over six weeks. Whichever account is the most accurate, the fact is that even if it took six weeks to make the whole album, that's a phenomenal achievement considering the scale and ambitiousness of the content. Considering that Jethro Tull came off tour in mid-November and that the album would have most probably came out in February were it not for the UK coal miners' strike at the time, *Thick As A Brick* was a very quickly made album in the grand scheme of things. In addition to this, there was the elaborate design of the album cover that the band was very actively involved with and they began another tour on 6th January 1972.

It comes across that Anderson's approach to writing music has always been fairly relaxed and organic. He was quoted in *Creem* in June 1977; "The academic delving and the subtle sharpness of traditional English music is a relatively sterile intellectual exercise... I believe first and foremost in a folk memory. I'm of particularly mixed origin; my mother is English, my father is Scottish. So you have the peculiar sort of mixture of origins in me. But I do believe in a folk memory or something which is at once Anglo-Saxon and Celtic mixed together from way back a long, long time ago and I believe that we retain something of, certainly not the academic wherewithal to put that type of music together, but something of the emotional response to that music."

I wouldn't want to go so far as to say that there was an extent of naivety in the making of *Thick As A Brick*. I think it would be unfair and arrogant of me to do so. However, it certainly comes across that the band were very experimental in making the album and that they went into the process with an open mind rather than with an end goal in sight. In an interview on Australian TV in 1972, when asked what it was like writing an album that consisted of one long song, Anderson replied, "I really wasn't aware if it had been done before or not. Every day we just went in and a new bit of music came and we said rather than stop there, let's just join it together with that little bit you were playing yesterday, whatever that was. That was a great bit, just to kind of tail out of this and bring us into that. Or we could use that idea we used before and make that a link sequence.

Every day we would add another three or four minutes worth of real time musical arrangement to the stew. The good thing about *Thick As A Brick*, in the making of it, was that it was relatively spontaneous. I would write a piece of music in the morning, go in to rehearsal and we would work on that during the day, tie it into what we had been working on the previous day and then have a run-through of everything to date. So we built up the album day by day. Each day I would come in with a new piece. I was reacting to what I had done before and it was built up in a very organic way."

Anderson was quoted in *Guitar World* in September 1999; "While writing the album, I'd get up every morning and compose a little something, then take it to the band later that morning for rehearsal. We'd work out the parts and perhaps advance the song toward the next stage of its development. We did two weeks of solid rehearsal and then recorded it in about ten days. Some linking sections were created in the studio, but the blood and guts had been worked out well in advance. It wasn't a difficult album to make because all of the material was there and we just had to get it on tape."

Martin Barre was quoted of *Thick As A Brick* in *Guitar Legends* in May 1997; "There were a lot of songs on that album that we just tied together. We would rehearse a song and then do a link which would go to the next song. I remember staying up working on that album until four or five in the morning, getting a few hours of sleep and then starting again. Very often Ian would come in not knowing what the next piece of music was going to be and we'd just sit down and do it. He'd say, 'Got an idea for the next bit?' Other people added ideas and lots of things that John Evan came up with on Hammond organ became classic Tull bits. It was the most difficult music we had played up to that point, as there were lots of odd bars and time signatures."

For the recording of *Thick As A Brick*, a minimum of fifteen different instruments were played by the band. Ergonomically, this exceeded what Jethro Tull had done on their four earlier studio albums and inevitably, it showcased the level of skill within the band by that point.

Fairly enough, the band took credit for their work in the form of a small article, cheekily placed in the St Cleve Chronicle that forms the album's cover art; "Mr Ellis told me that apart from a short orchestral passage, the members of the group played all the instruments themselves. In addition to his usual flute, acoustic guitar and singing roles, Ian Anderson extended his virtuosity to violin, sax and trumpet, while Martin Barre played a few lines on that delightful medieval instrument, the lute, as well as his electric guitar. John Evan played organ, piano and harpsichord, Jeffrey Hammond-Hammond played bass guitar and spoke some words, and new drummer Barriemore Barlow added the timpani and percussion parts."

Due to the instrumentation present on the album, in some ways *Thick As A Brick* is similar to an orchestral concerto; different instruments are given solos throughout a piece that is constantly in motion. There is so much variation in the tone and colour of the music based on the vast range of the way in which instruments are grouped differently on each of the sections (for instance, the instrumental section prior to 'I see you shuffle in the courtroom...').

On the other hand, there are plenty of instances where sections of *Thick As A Brick* sound more like a typical rock band ('see there a son is born...'), or indeed folk group ('really don't mind...'). There is so much texture to the piece and the talent in the band would have certainly been an excellent vehicle with which to facilitate that.

A change from the initial line-up of Jethro Tull was certainly a factor in *Thick As A Brick* coming to be. The recruitment of Martin Barre to the band in December 1968 had expanded the possibilities in terms of instrumentation as well as overall musical style. I feel that it's important to emphasise that it isn't fair to attempt to elevate the status of one musician above the other; everyone has their talents and particular areas of interest. Essentially though, what Barre brought to the table made a significant contribution to *Thick As A Brick*.

Ian Anderson was quoted in *Guitar World* in September 1999; "Mick Abrahams was of the old rock and blues school in the UK. He was a respected guitar player who had a very defined style, and he could play within it convincingly. But outside of it he was a no-hoper: he just couldn't learn anything musically if it didn't fall into the styles he knew."

The journalist continued in the same feature; "In short order, Abrahams, a favourite with Tull's early fans, was fired and Barre recruited in his place. A player of admittedly limited ability, Barre was eager for Anderson's guidance; Anderson, for his part, was only too glad to offer it, directing the young guitarist away from familiar rock and blues rhythms toward complex arpeggiated patterns and unusual time signatures. With Barre holding down electric guitar duties, Anderson added layers of rustic-sounding acoustic guitar, mandolin, balalaika and — his mainstay — flute. The songs that resulted from this menagerie of instruments were unlike anything anyone had heard before. Among the influences of rock, jazz, folk and Eastern music, Anderson injected his songs with images of an England historically depicted in wood-cuts, complete with feasts and fayres, beggars and dandies, minstrels and country squires. Jethro Tull had arrived."

Anderson was quoted in *Rolling Stone* in April 2012; "When I was a teenager, I really didn't like loud rock music. I listened to jazz and blues and folk music. I've always preferred acoustic music. And it was only, I suppose, by the time Jethro Tull was getting underway that we did let the music begin to have a harder edge, in particular with the electric guitar being alongside the flute. Those two instruments and the role of them playing together defined early Jethro Tull."

Ian Anderson advocated that the musical possibilities had expanded from the very point that Martin Barre had joined the band. Anderson was quoted of *Stand Up* in *Guitar World* in September 1999; "This was Martin Barre's first album with us, and it marks the turning point in our music, away from the blues and toward progressive rock. It is a very broad, eclectic album, and the end result is a set of songs that nobody else could have written. I was particularly pleased with the record, and still am, because nobody else was doing that then and the songs are very idiosyncratic in terms of their performance and writing. Looking back on it, it's one of the records that I feel was a really important one."

I've still not said much about the meaning of the lyrics in *Thick As A Brick*. And I'm not going to either, the reason being that it would be pretty feeble to try and do so. Whilst Ian Anderson's lyrics often raise questions, perhaps they don't need to be answered. They are so subjective and that's okay.

Journalist Lester Bangs asked an interesting question about the lyrics of *Thick As A Brick* in *Creem* in May 1973; "(Are they) just a bunch of words that could have as much meaning as you wanted to invest or none at all, and happened to fit the music nicely? Ask a Tull freak and you'll get a blank look; most of them, it seems, have never stopped to analyse it. They just know what they like, which is fine."

Also, whilst it would be easy to think of Anderson's lyrics as being very poetic (*Thick As A Brick* is, after all, based on a poem by Anderson's fictional school boy character, Gerald Bostock), it comes across that he didn't particularly see himself as a writer of poetry. When Anderson was asked if he had any ambitions to, outside of music, write poetry, he was quoted in *Down Beat* in March 1976; "I doubt it would be poetry. I've always had a great suspicion of poetry because the best poetry, I think, falls within a relatively classical style of writing and to work within that area would seem very imitative of style, if not of content. It's rather like saying 'Sit down and write a classical ballet' — One could obviously go out and find a Russian folk theme that has not yet been explored in ballet and one could deal with it in musical terms along the lines of Tchaikovsky and deal with it in choreographic terms along the lines of one of the Russian dance masters of old. And one could arrive at a classical ballet which could, with sufficient money, staging, and stars, be enormously successful. But it would be a sham nonetheless, because it no longer has anything to do with the age that spawned it. It's no longer a product of the romantic glorification of the form and spectacle that is ballet. It's the same with Shakespeare. You have to ham it up — Laurence Olivier it up — in order to be successful. You can't recreate it in a modern style and have it be successful. It merely becomes an amusement, a diversion, an academic exercise, rather than having a real place. So we must necessarily deal with modern technique and style or else go so far back that no-one is forced to make the inevitable comparison. I find, personally, less enjoyment in the modern styles of poetry or prose or dance or serious twentieth century music. I think the visual arts are the only area in which modern technique has really applied itself, if one calls modern art the period from the precursors of the Impressionists on until today. There we obviously already have a tremendously solid and retrospectively valuable collection of art product — a new tradition, if you like, since the 1890s. It may continue to be possible with photography and the visual arts. But that gets us back to the question of repetition. It's something which horrifies me, because it's very hard to do."

Ultimately, Anderson himself has often advocated strongly against over analysing his music. He was quoted in *Down Beat* in March 1976; "As soon as I begin to analyse my approach to playing music on stage, it then becomes a very deliberate and conscious dissemination of what I'm doing. And as soon as it becomes that, it immediately goes against the grain of the music I write and play. I don't sit down and say today I'm going to write a song that's going to be about this or that and then calculate a means of arriving at that end. Whatever I write — a forty second piece or a forty-minute one — has always begun its life as a pure emotional feeling or observation. The act of building that into a finished recording is, of course, to a large extent, contrived, in as much as it's a conscious effort to derive a relationship between life and music and lyrics and put it into a sort of professionally embodied package and then sell it to the consumer and make money. All of that is a very conscious thing. I'm aware of all that, but I don't want to start getting any of that mixed up with the essence of what music is all about and the essence of what being a performer of music is all about."

In the same feature, Anderson was quoted of his musical influences. It comes across that he was advocating for again, not getting too into the study of the music and to just go with the feel of it; "I'm interested in music in general and I've listened to all sorts of music a little bit, but I've never been moved by anything on a continuing basis, other than a very limited selection of some Negro blues, which I find now is still as moving to me as it ever was. And I find that some of the indigenous folk forms of England and Scotland also continue to move me. But I think perhaps because of the comparisons that have been made between what I write and the folky, traditional stuff, that I tend not to listen to any of that music at all. I certainly don't want to be a student of that kind of music; so if there's a similarity, it must remain really coincidental. It's something that I have only a passing awareness of. Since I was brought up in Edinburgh, Scotland, and I heard the bagpipes from an early age, it's a sound that rings in my ears. It becomes almost a folk memory of certain sounds and relationships of notes — a motive stirring of the blood."

With particular regard to *Thick As A Brick*, it is possible that Ian Anderson actively wanted people to make their own mind up about what the album, the lyrics and their meaning(s) were. The *Melbourne Sun* reported in July 1972; "Anderson is leader of the English rock group Jethro Tull, in Melbourne for two concerts at Festival Hall. The group has become one of the most influential and respected forces in modern music since its formation four years ago. Noted for zany stage antics, Anderson and other group members, Jeffrey Hammond-Hammond, John Evan, Martin Barre and Barriemore Barlow, arrived at yesterday's press conference in white trench coats and peaked caps. Anderson said the group was on tour for about five months of a year. He wrote most of his songs in his hotel room while on tour. He would not give any explanation or interpretations of his music."

The reason for this was a pretty sensible one though. Anderson was quoted in the same feature; "Everyone's interpretation of what I write is as valid as mine. If I explained what a song is about people would be forced to reject their own interpretations and would stop thinking about the music. My whole intention is to make people think — to ask questions. I won't give any answers because I probably don't know them myself — and the questions are far more important than the answers."

Phenomenally perhaps, a lot of the fascination surrounding *Thick As A Brick* may be that for every person who has ever tried to analyse it from a music theory perspective, they could certainly be making links that aren't in line with what Jethro Tull were aiming for when working on it. As a stunning piece of music, I can certainly see why looking at *Thick As A Brick* from a music theory perspective could be interesting and enjoyable but equally, to aspire to an entire understanding of the compositional process might not be realistic.

Ian Anderson was quoted in *Down Beat* in March 1976 as he commented on the fact that he hadn't had any music training;

"I obviously know a little bit about it, but not in a formal sense. I don't read music. Actually, the music that we play before the concert begins is some music that I wrote for orchestra which has never, and will never, be released, because it's an amateurish attempt. It sounds good, but it ain't. I know that it isn't actually good music. But I'm dealing with something that immediately sounds like classical music. Therefore, I'm not about to expose myself to ridicule or — even worse — acclaim for it. It's the first time I sat down to just write some music and see how it turns out and get some other people to play it. I did that really as an experiment in 1974, just because I wanted to see if it was fulfilling. It was actually extraordinarily fulfilling. I collaborated with my good friend David Palmer, who's worked with us over the years on strings or whatever else we have on record that we didn't play ourselves."

I'm not saying that without conventional music training, a person is incapable of analysing their own work, not at all! What I'm saying is that Ian Anderson's approach to music, whatever that might have been when making *Thick As A Brick*, resulted in a masterpiece being made and it seems that a lot of the thought process behind it was perhaps very laid back and certainly not academically intensive. And rightly so too! It didn't need to be.

Whilst Ian Anderson has often encouraged people not to over analyse his music, that's not to say that there is an absence of intention when it comes to him creating imagery with it. He was quoted in *Acoustic Guitar* in November 2000; "I like singing songs that put people in a landscape. I have a picture in my head for each song that I write, and it's a framed, still image. My early training as a painter and drafter, I think, produced in me a way of writing music and lyrics that illustrate visual ideas. I try to bring some maturity to the thing I've been doing for most of my career, writing songs that tell people a story, not in the temporal sense, but a story they make up to fit the picture I suggest to them. It's like sending people a postcard." The lyrics from *Thick As A Brick* about "the cattle quietly grazing..." spring to mind here.

Cash Box reviewed *Thick As A Brick* in May 1972; "The long awaited Jethro Tull album has finally arrived. Unlike the group's previous efforts, this time around, Ian Anderson has written an epic poem, if you will — so in actuality, *Thick As A Brick* contains a single song. Basically, the LP demonstrates the band's versatility as musicians capable of changing moods and timings in a moment's notice. Needless to say, this effort will follow *Aqualung* into the gold vaults."

Billboard reviewed it in the same month; "Ian Anderson and friends have a penchant for creating albums that delight, amaze and thoroughly entertain, *Thick As A Brick* being no exception. It is a suitable successor to the genius that was *Aqualung*, the wildly enigmatic imagery producing a spellbinding fascination. There are no individual songs as such, simply side one and two with no separation between the grooves."

If you want to get really geeky about it, it's actually pretty mind blowing that the record is a 12" album with no groove separations in it; physically it looks more like a 12" single!

It comes across that the line-up behind *Thick As A Brick* were working happily together. Ian Anderson was quoted in *New Musical Express* in March 1973; "I'm the only original member left, but we are very much together as a group. When a group has existed a few years, one learns to tolerate other people. I don't believe in the Who's we-hate-each-other gimmick which they used in the beginning. I really think they are as together as a group as we are. The other members of the band aren't just musicians — they are friends."

Equally, perhaps based on the success of *Thick As A Brick*, the plan at the time was to continue making music in the vein of long songs. When asked if he could envisage "a time when Jethro might return to albums built not on a theme but as a collection of songs in the old tradition", Ian Anderson was quoted in the same feature; "I don't think so. We're very satisfied with what we're doing now. Of course, we play music lasting for three to five minutes. But today it's phrases within the whole work."

Of course, after *A Passion Play* in 1973, Jethro Tull went back to doing songs of a shorter length, as was the case on their 1974 album, *War Child* (on which there is no song that exceeds six minutes in length). But at the time, the impact of *Thick As A Brick*, both musically and in terms of what it did for the band commercially, was such that the intention was to do long songs for the foreseeable.

Long song or shorter and more structurally conventional song, Jethro Tull's music was always made with the scope for repeated play in mind. Ian Anderson was quoted in *Down Beat* in March 1976; "Music is the prime abstract art. Not my music, I'm not saying that. But music, in its finest form, is the abstract, and literature is the verbal reality, almost on a conversational level. Film, since the talkies, has been the totally accessible, very immediate, art form. It works immediately. It has to, because conventionally it's employed as a one act experience — you go to the movie, see it, and go home, whereas with music, one has access to repeated performances, either live or through recordings. Music stands repetition. One gets more into it as a result of repetition if the music is worth anything at all. Particularly in England now, we've arrived at a media situation where the music is so instant — where it's designed to appeal only once. And I might not like it the first time. I would hope to be involved with music that will withstand repetition. I'm into repetition, and the musical formats that we deal with employ repetition."

Whilst Anderson was talking in general terms in the context of this quote, the replay value of *Thick As A Brick* is certainly there, so much so that to listen to it just once would be to do it a disservice.

Chapter Three

Thick As A Brick Live

T*hick As A Brick* lent itself to a style of live performance that could be theatrical, creative and unusual. Anderson was quoted in *Prog* in March 2018; "After *Aqualung*, I felt we had to take a big step forward. Many writers wrote about *Aqualung* as a concept album, and I kept saying, 'Maybe two or three songs in the same area, but not a concept' — In the wake of all of that, I thought, 'Right, let's show them what a concept album is' and it seemed like an amusing idea to go down that route in this Pythonesque way and to try to use surreal humour. It clicked in America, which was a surprise, and it was our first real foray in that sort of theatrical presentation."

Charisma and eccentricity would have certainly been key ingredients in doing *Thick As A Brick* live. Ian Anderson was quoted in *New Musical Express* in March 1973 as he advocated of his act onstage; "I'm just acting because I'm living the music; it makes me act. I'd be bored to death if I sat in the audience and had to listen to a group playing for hours, with no movement... It's just humour. Neither is it a satire on other singers. I don't even think Mick Jagger takes himself too seriously when he's doing his sexy stage act. Talking about Jagger, I still think the Rolling Stones are the world's greatest rock 'n' roll band. Maybe they're not the best musicians. They've got charisma, though. And good ideas."

In May 1972, *Cash Box* reviewed a performance that took place at New York's Nassau Coliseum; "Jethro Tull provided one of the most outrageous stage shows ever witnessed for about 30,000 people during two shows at the new arena — it was the last stop on their current tour. They had the audience with them all the way and eventually left amidst thunderous applause. With the PA system suspended from the ceiling so as to provide a better side view, the quintet first performed their Reprise LP, *Thick As A Brick*. The rendition included added instrumental detours as well as a reading of the news by Jeffrey Hammond-Hammond. This featured the group dressed in assorted costumes such as a rabbit and gorilla and provided for a short humorous break near the end of the song. To single out Ian Anderson's flute solo might be somewhat unfair as each member played exceptionally well, but he was simply incredible. Anderson is the only original member left but Jethro Tull exhibited why they are one of the best groups around. After *Brick*, and assorted duck calls and antics, 'Cross-Eyed Mary' followed and was a smashing success. The group also made effective use of tape to launch 'New Day Yesterday' and immediately afterwards, 'Aqualung'. Tull had now been on stage for two incredibly packed hours of fun and music. They left with the audience simply amazed yet calling for more. Obliging, 'Wind-Up' eventually did close the show. All that can be said is that Jethro Tull were simply unbelievable."

When considering the wild stage antics of the live shows, it would be easy to assume that there was perhaps a sense of chaos behind them. There probably wasn't though. Ian Anderson gave a bit of the game away when he was quoted in *Billboard* in December 1978; "Most of the things I used to do onstage went against these accepted rules of showbiz... I would keep doing things that were in a sense amusing and were certainly contradictory to the accepted rules, but Terry (Ellis) and Chris (Wright) (management at Chrysalis) certainly saw the validity of that sort of approach and would encourage me to do more. I tried a number of things that they suggested, some of them worked, some of them didn't, but they gave me the encouragement to try more. They would also confirm what I thought was working in terms of audience reaction — you know, that song works, that idea works. They would help me or whoever the artist was to exploit himself, to put across whatever was inside, whatever innate talent you possessed. They were wise enough to see that and that was their forte as managers. It's something to be very grateful for. I'm sure most managers would have tried to coerce me or Jethro Tull to try things a certain way whereas Terry and Chris always allowed us to use our head."

It seems that there was certainly method in the madness, even in so far as, Ian Anderson and Jethro Tull perhaps had the space to go a bit wild with the comedy sketches onstage not because it was exclusively carefree or because it was manufactured, but because their management gave them the space to create.

In March 1972, *New Musical Express* reported on Jethro Tull's tour plans; "In case you didn't know already, Jethro Tull are big business. About to undertake their biggest-ever British tour, the group have just returned from Europe, where they broke house records in Berlin, Frankfurt and Rome — the records having been previously held by the Stones and Zeppelin. The tour, which starts today (Thursday) and goes on until March 28th, will also be the first British gig for new Tullman, drummer Barrie Barlow. Barlow, who replaced Clive Bunker, has already done a couple of Jethro tours in America, where the band is now among the top half dozen rock attractions. On the British tour, Jethro will be playing almost every day, and the sell-out reports have already started rolling in. Portsmouth, Bristol, Birmingham, Newcastle, Norwich, Oxford, Manchester and Sheffield have all sold out at least two weeks in advance. The Albert Hall reports that it will be sold out within a day or so — the only tickets they have left are those for 60p. To tie in with the tour, Jethro this week release their cleverly advertised and much-awaited new album *Thick As A Brick*. Support group for the tour is the Irish folk duo Tir Na Nog, who played some of their earliest British dates on a Jethro tour. Since then they've added experience to their skill and have carved themselves a nice little reputation."

As *Melody Maker* reported in March 1972; "Jethro Tull open their biggest ever British tour tonight at the Portsmouth Guildhall and already sell out signs are up outside halls up and down the country. Tickets for the twenty-three venues went on sale a week ago and already sold out are dates at Portsmouth, Bristol, Birmingham, Newcastle, Sheffield, Norwich, Oxford and Manchester. This week also sees the release of Jethro's new album *Thick As A Brick*. It was due out last week but the power strike delayed production of the covers for one week."

New Musical Express reviewed the opening performance of the UK tour in March 1972; "Portsmouth Guildhall was packed to capacity on the opening night (Thursday) of Jethro Tull's current tour. With one or two minor reservations, the audience got its money's worth. The tour, Jethro's biggest ever in the UK, is also the first British tour for new drummer Barriemore Barlow, who replaced Clive Bunker shortly before the last US tour. Jethro are enormous in the US, of course, and the mistakes were the result of lack of acclimatisation with British audiences. US concerts are larger, seat more people, and therefore require more obvious stage presentation. English audiences are more subtle and on a couple of occasions Jethro seemed to have forgotten that. The show was fast, furious, skilful and colourful though. Anderson spreads the spotlight more than he used to, and each member of the group got a section — either musical or humorous — all to himself. 'A new Jethro', commented photographer Robert Ellis. Tull arrived onstage in peculiar fashion and proceeded to launch their new sociological/scatological epic, *Thick As A Brick*. A review of this appears on page ten this week, suffice for me to add the live performance is fast, technically perfect and even the hardest Tullheads in the front stalls were delighted and confused at the same time. Ian Anderson, dressed in black knee breeches and chequered coat tails, still catfoots around the stage like a combination of Max Wall and Mephisto. Almost vaudeville and almost high camp, but most of all pure Anderson (yes, he still stands on one leg). Martin Barre, dressed in a baggy suit of appalling hound's tooth, contributed careful guitar work with his usual diffidence, Jeffrey Hammond-Hammond, attired in revolting lime green tails, moved well with a curious jerky dancing motion, and played precision bass work throughout. Barlow drummed solidly and crisply, and his solo, which took place in the second half of the concert, was very fast and skilful — rather after the manner of Carl Palmer. John Evan, looning from piano (stage left) to organ (stage right) resembled a dissolute planter, with his crumpled white suit and his wild hair and beard and all. His looning was itself a put-on of Anderson's own unique movements, and on one occasion it got out of hand — so much so that Ian had to forcefully lead the raving Evan back to the organ stool and seat him upon it. There was a curious interlude between *Thick As A Brick* and the closing pieces. It was, I think, "humour", and it took the form of a comic dialogue between Hammond and Evan. It was well intentioned, but I personally didn't think it very funny. It didn't last long. Anderson was soon back, and he launched into 'Cross-Eyed Mary', which was received deliriously by the Tullheads. 'New Day Yesterday' followed, and finally 'Wind-Up'. All of these pieces were skilfully linked by taped voices, discussing the act, and the timing of these tapes, like the immaculate timing of the music itself plus other "effects", was a revelation. Off they went, and came back for the statutory encore. And this, in my opinion, was one place that Tull miscalculated. Prior to the last number, legions of fans had rushed the stage, obviously peaking in excitement. But the encore proved too long and too dynamically slow to retain this mass high. Martin Barre played a long and slightly un-worked-out guitar solo which left me cold (in contrast to his fine work earlier in the performance) and the whole thing was allowed to droop unnecessarily. But it was the first night of the tour, Jethro Tull are a highly professional and original band, and no doubt things will be adjusted."

On tour, *Thick As A Brick* was a large scale performance. It was often played in its entirety. Solos and comedy sketches were added. A lot of skill and thought clearly went into the whole thing. So much so that with the earlier shows on the tour, Martin Barre recalled them as being a "terrible experience" due to the complexity of the music and the changes in time signatures. As with many other prog rock bands, it is plausible that Jethro Tull thought of their songs as composed pieces of music to be presented accurately when played live. That is to say, take any live performance of *Thick As A Brick* that was recorded and there isn't really much in the way of improvisation or variation on the specific sections as they present on the LP. It *does* happen, but not with such a tremendous frequency that it drifts, overall, that far from what is on the studio album.

For instance, a bootleg exists of just the audio from Toronto on 4th June 1972. There is just so much of the performance that is faithful to the musical content on the original album — for instance, the intricate rhythms in the drum fills prior to the "where the hell..." section of the lyrics, and the emphasis that Anderson places on his phrasing of the lyrics. However, the solos that *did* exist in the live shows between the content that is faithful to the record, made each live performance of *Thick As A Brick* unique in its own way. Notably, in the reviews of shows from the 1972 tour of the album, different lengths are stated regarding how long each show lasted. This suggests that whilst the content from the record was played faithfully, the sections added in between were likely to have been more spontaneous. In all honesty, it's actually quite hard to tell how spontaneous the added solo sections really were because in every available recording of Jethro Tull playing *Thick As A Brick* live, the band always sound so tight and together. The musical diversity present on the LP is such that it arguably lent itself tremendously to providing the scope for very theatrical live performances. *Thick As A Brick* was reviewed in *New Musical Express* in March 1972 under the fascinating title, "Brick — Is This Jethro's Tommy?"; "Ian Anderson's ultimate epic; with lyrics, allegedly, by one Gerald Bostock. And it's on lyrics that *Thick As A Brick* stands or falls. Personally it took me several listenings before I was able to make up my mind. I've finally decided I like it. Encased in a fine and well-designed sleeve (resembling a banal local newspaper), *Thick As A Brick* is an assault on the mediocrity and harshness of lower middle class existence in seventies Britain. The set opens with a quiet acoustic guitar passage from Anderson in alternating 3/4 and 4/4 time. Anderson sings the main refrain in couplets while the piece slowly builds with piano flourishes and the occasional powerful stab from the rest of the band. A clean guitar phrase from Barre leads into a short organ solo from John Evan. Building all the time, several machine gun riffs lead into the second major theme, preceded by a short flute break. 'The Poet And The Painter', although majestic, suffers a little from banal lyrics. A long, slightly rambling guitar solo follows and then guitar and organ swap phrases before leading into a long instrumental passage in which Evan has the spotlight all to himself. His organ work flaps a little and resembles Sandy McPherson at times — no doubt intentionally. The piece turns into a 2/4 march — still building — in which organ states and flute answers. The final section of the first side is musically a folky jingle which develops into downright carnival music. At this point the whole *Brick* piece starts to get a little less strong lyrically but stronger musically. Side one ends with a three-beat pulse that is repeated, gradually mixing in echo, until the only thing left is the echo response. Side two opens in a similar way, then drops into an amazingly fast 6/8 passage, slightly reminiscent of ELP on 'Bitches Crystal'. This feeling is enhanced when new drummer Barriemore Barlow takes a solo that, for all its warmer production, resembles Carl Palmer's work. He finishes with overdubbed timpani. The drum solo introduces a free-blowing passage, interspersed by spoken words from Jeffrey Hammond-Hammond. Cacophonous, but it's probably intended to be. From now on the album degenerates. Lyrics and music get a bit boring, and the earlier inspiration seems to have died — although the arrangements and link-passages are still as exacting as ever. Shortly before the end an orchestra has about eight bars' worth of track then it's back to the original theme — both musically and lyrically — for the wind-up. Throughout the album Jethro play extremely well and very tightly, and it's obviously intended to be Jethro Tull's own stand-or-fall epic after the lines of *Tommy*. To Tullheads it will, of course, succeed; personally, I have some doubts."

The review pretty much hits the nail on the head in terms of how it describes the music technically. It's a good assessment of the variety present on *Thick As A Brick*. In the days before Youtube and considering the limited scope for radio play that the long song had, I advocate that the reviewer's description of what is going on musically is at least, to an extent, a helpful pointer for the record buying public. Helpful as in, it gives them a reasonable idea of what they might be able to expect (or indeed, not expect in comparison to conventional pop songs) from *Thick As A Brick*.

The comparison to the rock opera by The Who was also alluded to in *Melody Maker*'s review of a performance of *Thick As A Brick* in March 1972 under the title of "Tull's *Tommy*?"; "One-legged pop flautist Ian Anderson caused a storm in the press world this week when he refused to comment on his latest "pop" recording, *Thick As A Brick*, or his recent concert at

Portsmouth Guildhall described in many quarters as 'obscene', 'disgusting' and 'deafening'. From a telephone box, somewhere in Beckenham, his representative told a *Melody Maker* reporter on Sunday night: 'Ian doesn't want to talk about his concerts or the album until he has read the reviews' — Whitehall experts, China watchers and spokesmen said early this morning: 'This latest development will be viewed with some concern. Does it mean the end of the entente cordiale or is it a subterfuge to throw the Western alliance into confusion? These are the questions informed sources will be asking themselves — tomorrow afternoon. News At Ten, Catford, Monday.' So Jethro Tull won't talk eh? Never mind, this is nothing new in the "pop business". In 1932 the Canadian pop singer George Smith refused to speak to local radio stations for many weeks until he received an official apology for being described as 'that awful singer' during a broadcast discussion. Again, in the late fifties, rock balladeer Brian Barnes was notorious for his refusal to comment on his rare performances. But it remains a disquieting moment when the clamp-down of silence comes and we are left to blindly form our own opinions. Stumbling through the morass of conflicting evidence, I can only say that *Thick As A Brick* is a work that will receive as much acclaim as *Tommy*, and cause the trans-oceanic cables to hum with an excited chatter. The album work forms a major part of the new Tull stage act and is based on an impressive poem by one Gerald Bostock. It's one of those poems that fixes one with a penetrating gaze and snaps somewhat bitterly: 'I may make you feel but I can't make you think.' It goes on to say: 'I've come down from the upper class to mend your rotten ways.' Well you'll just have to read the poem, and fortunately it's all included in a massive sleeve note to the album, produced to read and look like a local newspaper. Whatever the interpretations placed upon Mr Bostock's lyrical flight, it has certainly inspired the men of Tull to new heights."

The feature continued; "The opening night of their first

British tour in a year, at Portsmouth, was the best rehearsed and most cleverly executed show staged by a rock band. Their performance came somewhere between the musical excellence of Yes and the inventive audacity of the Mothers Of Invention. Many groups have tried a little stage "business", but few have succeeded in pulling it off so well. Even if their humour is not always hilarious in its written aspect, the natural humour of any Ian Anderson performance, and the perfect support he receives from Jeffrey Hammond-Hammond and John Evan, produces an impact that is quite unique. Their timing is superb and their ability to virtually play with an audience is quite fascinating. Near my seat in the back of the Guildhall, there were a few lads ready to shout the odd comment in their rustic simplicity. But even they were slightly stunned by the barrage of pre-recorded tapes, startling use of stage props, lights, and dynamics that in turn baffled, amused and finally delighted a crowd who responded by roaring great cheers of approval. My first impressions of the album (described elsewhere in this issue), were not enough to gain a full appreciation of *Brick*. And I still would prefer to hear them playing this massive work "live". At the concert they opened with a complete version of the *Brick* saga which lasted some forty-five minutes, with barely a pause. In fact Jethro were so ready to give us a mass of music, Ian was moved to apologise for the discomfort caused to patrons glued to their seats for a show that eventually lasted nearly three hours. 'It's a bit like Ben Hur,' he admitted solicitously. Despite the security clamp down, word has filtered through that the Tull men would prefer us not to reveal all the little dodges they get up to during the show, and as it would be rather like yelling 'Tony Perkins dun it', at a second house queue for *Psycho*, I shall merely say that I enjoyed the telephone, the tent and the men in white coats. And the playing was pretty good as well. New drummer (to Britain at any rate), Barriemore Barlow, proved a fast, accurate and hard-hitting percussionist, who played a dynamite solo and snap-locked on to the arrangements with great tenacity. The interplay between Ian and John Evan's educated piano and organ work was a source of great satisfaction, and stalwart Tullian, Martin Barre, while not a great soloist, lent just the right form of attack or subtlety, where needed. John's organ sometimes tended to be a bit over-loud, as did the whole band during their heavier moments."

Still from the same feature; "Still a wondrous sight in this age of modern marvels is that of Ian Anderson, dancing about the stage like some mad Austrian music master. He once told me his brother had ballet lessons and some of it rubbed off. I can well believe this when watching Mr Tull arch his body backwards, hair cascading over narrow shoulders, while his legs splay in many directions. He conducts his fellow musicians with mocking absurdity, and one of the funniest moments in the show came when John Evan, himself a strange gallumphing figure, like the male lead in a Chekhov comedy, began a berserk imitation of his leader, only to be led gently back to the organ and put firmly in his place. Amidst the clowning, as good as any vaudeville act in northern cabaret, Ian also plays a mean flute. It seemed to me his technique has been much improved, and that a considerable amount of practice has been put in. His melodic tone and ability to blow hard and soft on a difficult instrument has always been there. But some notably fast runs came through and some beautifully constructed phrasing that shows Ian ain't always fooling when it comes to fluting. It will be interesting to see the show again after a few days on the road have elapsed. Will they be able to sustain the comic interludes? Will they tighten up the "encore" which ran on too long at Portsmouth and gave us a surfeit of goodies? *Thick As A Brick* was a lot of music to take for an audience that had never heard any of it before. Its success was self-evident. The cheers were for all the effort the band had put into writing and playing the stuff, and not, as is often the case, for instantly recognisable material, easy to assimilate. The premiere of such a piece of craftsmanship is not an everyday occurrence, and Jethro Tull can be proud of their contribution to the arts and sciences of rock."

A good point there from the reviewer in terms of how, was *Thick As A Brick* asking too much of a concert-going audience? A show full of entirely new material rather than old favourites is probably always going to be a risk but equally, there was perhaps an element of "you're damned if you do and you're damned if you don't."

In May 1972, *Billboard* reviewed a performance that took place at New York's Nassau Coliseum; "Both shows (Jethro Tull and Wild Turkey) at the Coliseum had been sold out in six hours, and one might have reasonably expected no small measure of tension in a crowd of those dimensions, particularly in view of the near-riot Jethro Tull had inspired at the Garden during their last tour. Yet Sunday's performance was marked by extraordinary courtesy on the part of the audience. The band didn't put them to sleep. Mixing music with pre-recorded tape and anarchic vaudeville, their set began with an hour and twenty minutes of *Thick As A Brick*, their latest and easily most ambitious Reprise album — which showed off the band's last year of development. The loose grouping of basic themes which forms the album was further expanded here, yet the band sustained an awesome intensity throughout the performance. There were customary extended solos, but it was clearly the ensemble playing that offered the most exciting music."

In December 1972, *Billboard* reviewed a performance at New York's Madison Square Garden; "Chrysalis Records' Jethro Tull conquered the inhabitants of the Garden in a performance excelling in music, comedy and drama. More than a mere rock group, Tull has fashioned itself into a totally absorbing theatrical rock experience. Drawing essentially from the music of *Aqualung* and *Thick As A Brick*, the UK group wove a web of delicate acoustical stylings with hard gut-grabbing rock and beautiful English folk melodies, as each "movement" of their extended works was greeted with hearty waves of recognition. Lead vocalist, writer and musician, Ian Anderson, impresses as a whirling dervish. The man's energy output is simply startling. Dressed in something out of a stray Dickens novel, Anderson lurched, lunged and minced about the stage, coddling his fellow players like a concerned mother hen brandishing his omnipresent flute as a majorette gone mad might. In fact, there is an intensity and interaction between each member of the fivesome, sparked by Anderson, that keeps the show flowing, dead centre tight, always alive and never boring. Near the end of the more than two hour set, the Garden became the home of an English Music Hall Revue featuring the "Jethro Tull Players" in a series of sketches bordering on burlesque. The finale finds the five men suddenly disappearing in a burst of billowing white smoke filling the entire coliseum."

In November 1972, *Record World* reported on Jethro Tull's performance at the Garden in New York; "Headlining the bill was the ever so phenomenal Jethro Tull! For myself, and many others there that evening, this was most definitely the concert of the year! For more than two hours of total stupification, Ian Anderson and company leaped around the stage in a frenzy of wild antics putting together, musically and theatrically, one of the most entertaining shows to be seen anywhere in a long time. Act one of this brilliant performance was *Thick As A Brick*, to be followed by 'Aqualung' more than an hour and a half later. The audience was ecstatically captivated. The group was extremely appreciative and gracious. Beautiful rapport. An evening to be remembered."

The rapport and joking with the audience as part of the sketches probably varied quite a bit from one night to the next. In July 1972, *Cash Box* reported on a performance that took place at the Forum in LA; "Jethro Tull, as always, was an exciting, original and inventive group to both watch and hear. Tull's only contrast is the basic framework of its act and music. They have probably never performed a set the same way twice. Without ever resorting to the vulgar idiocies or negative machinations other groups thrive on, Tull manages to hold its audience visually captive with rather zany antics. The first piece Tull performed was *Thick As A Brick*. Ian Anderson was at his elfin best in this number, bounding all over and using his enchanted flute to emit sounds of its own. The group completed its set with four of its recognisable songs and were then forced into two encores. They are still one of the best."

It seems that *Thick As A Brick* as an album, provided excellent scope for delivering a theatrical performance onstage. More so perhaps than Jethro Tull's previous albums. In December 1972, *Cash Box* reviewed the performance that took place in New York's Madison Square Garden; "Ian Anderson and company, affectionately known as Jethro Tull, returned to Madison Square Garden last week to destroy another one of their sell-out crowds with their fine music and zany stage antics. Performing *Thick As A Brick* in its entirety is a feat unto itself, but that was just for openers. Twirling his silver flute while leading his group through starts, stops and solos, Anderson proved once again that he is one of the most inventive showmen in the business. That's show business! Tull provides the audience with looking and listening pleasure, but the entire group pitches in, adding to the overall success of a concert that we could have watched all evening. Performing for almost two solid hours, Jethro Tull pulled material from all of their albums — and if the arrangements were the same as on their previous tour, the theatrics weren't. More and more groups are learning to combine theatre with music. But Jethro Tull, who have been leaders in the field since the very conception of the band, proved that they are master of both."

Ian Anderson's delivery on stage was (and still is)

distinctive and unique. The sardonic humour he puts across is perhaps close to that of the social commentary of a court jester, as is very apparent on *Thick As A Brick*. Anderson is surely keen on delivering a performance that is musically sound and technically tight; clearly a lot of thought went into the live gigs when touring *Thick As A Brick*. The comedy sketches and banter with the audience added something almost surreal to performances of *Thick As A Brick*. As much as the music from the album was played faithfully to what was on the LP, there was a lot of spontaneity in the humour that was put across in between those parts. Anderson comes across as being aware of the juxtaposition between the silly and the serious, the accurate and the spontaneous. He was quoted of performing *Thick As A Brick* in *Jethro Tull 25th Complete Lyrics* in 1996; "There was a time in my life when I got very upset with the audiences, back in around 1972, when we were performing *Thick As A Brick*. The difficulty then was trying to play the acoustic music that we didn't have to play when we were doing the heavy rock music of the *Aqualung* album. The audience was just about able to cope with the acoustic section in 'Aqualung', or in 'Wind-Up' or 'My God', knowing that they were going to get the big rock 'n' roll riff any minute. With *Thick As A Brick*, suddenly there was a lot more music that was really stretched out. The audiences, particularly in America, were not sympathetic to the concert atmosphere that it was necessary to maintain: that they had to be quiet in the quiet places, and could react and jump up and down in the loud bits. In 1992 in almost every country in the world the people have now learned how to respond to that song. Today, as soon as I start playing *Thick As A Brick* there's a great wave of recognition, but then immediately people go quiet."

In April 1972, *Record Mirror* reviewed a performance that took place at the Royal Albert Hall; "It's nearly time for Jethro Tull's set on a dimly lit stage on Tuesday (21st March), and there are these five roadies all dressed in neat white Bogart macs and tartan caps, doing the last-minute adjustments. Or could it be Jethro Tull? Confusion builds as similarly hairy individuals in identical garb slowly filter out from the various stage entrances until there are a round dozen on stage. The situation is resolved at length when seven of them fade back into the wings and the genuine Jethros hang their uniforms on a hat stand and launch straight into *Thick As A Brick*. Jethro Tull really don't miss a trick — even such mundanities, as their arrival on stage is handled with style, imagination and wit. They kept up the standard right through almost two hours of non-stop music interrupted only by some brief interludes of some Pythonesque Tull humour. While *Thick As A Brick* is slightly disappointing on record, it comes alive in the extended stage version, aided by Ian Anderson's masterly use of the stage and lightning switches from comedy to drama and back. Despite personnel changes over the years, Jethro Tull has always played superbly as a unit. But as usual, it was Anderson who stole the show musically as well as visually. His flute pumps along fiercely like none in pop did before him and his two solos during the new work were excellent: the first hovered and fluttered round the Albert Hall like a giant bird, the second was perfectly punctuated train rhythm. For good measure, the new theme was followed by 'A New Day Yesterday', an early Tull classic, and most of *Aqualung*. The latter particularly shows that if Anderson had not decided to lead a rock band, he could have made it as a solo acoustic singer-songwriter. Tull's absence from this country has prevented the group from attaining quite the reputation it deserves. Hopefully, their current month-long tour will change that. Obviously, the group still enjoys playing here, and Anderson admitted, 'This is the only country where we'd dare to try something new' — They get my vote for Best Concert of '72 so far, by a short head from Randy Newman."

Melody Maker also reviewed the same performance; "For

some time, there have been threats by prominent groups that they will bring circus effects to their shows: clowns, elephants, jugglers and the Big Top. It's reassuring to find showbiz is alive in rock and that theatricality is never far away — but Jethro Tull prove that such excesses are totally unnecessary for them. Their own circus is all-human, totally man-made and all the better for that. The general misconception of the group as being one man in check pants standing on one leg playing a flute is quickly being wiped out, and musically they are coming up fast and strong as one of our most biting, creative units with a penchant for well-written, extended works. Ian Anderson is, of course, still cavorting around brilliantly, playing the Pied Piper, and Martin Barre still plays the fall guy in their unfunny attempts to be funny. But at London's Albert Hall last Tuesday, Anderson demonstrated again why Jethro's popularity is still building and why they are jamming concert halls with the converted throughout Britain. It's because they are a perfect blend of rock and showbiz. From the moment they came out disguised in white raincoats and flat caps and wandered about the stage, unrecognised by the audience, until they left two and a half hours later, very few eyes could have stopped focusing on their magnetic presence, their overwhelming drive. Their new album, *Thick As A Brick*, is attempting to become the tour de force that once was *Aqualung* alone. Ian is an underrated acoustic guitarist who opened the show in style, and his flute playing flows cleanly. Yet he should beware of over-long solos and of waiting for too long for the dynamics of guitars to bring back the pace. When the guitars do return, the boiling, fierce, peculiarly Tullian sound is remarkable — but several times, rather long flute solos could have been chopped down with effect. It was strange to find them ending with an *Aqualung* sequence. They run the risk of allowing that master work to eclipse other inventions, and it was odd that the forceful Anderson hadn't confidence to wind up with *Thick As A Brick*.

He might regret not projecting his new work as a finale: ask Pete Townshend. But nothing can obscure the fact that Jethro Tull's creative energy is like a breath of air. Unpretentious and fun-loving, yet always playing extremely well, they have that rare ability to laugh at themselves. That alone is therapeutic for both musicians and audience."

Sounds' take on the same performance was also reviewed soon after the gig; "There was a due sense of occasion at the Royal Albert Hall when Jethro Tull played their monster piece *Thick As A Brick* last Tuesday (21st March). It was a full house, which is a tribute to the pulling power of a band which by now must rate pretty highly on the credit side of Britain's balance of payments. So it is with some sorrow and a little trepidation that I have to report that Jethro bored me rigid. From Ian Anderson's opening chords on acoustic guitar, a black cloud of depression lowered itself over the press box and did not lift until the end of the *Thick As A Brick* set, over an hour later. A quiet and restrained American gentleman, not noted for extreme or unfair judgements, shook his head doubtfully and muttered, 'very weird music'; a brash blonde lady exclaimed, less tactfully, 'utter crap!'; but from the floor and from the vast circular gallery above, the audience rose to its feet to cheer as one man. Even Ian Anderson himself, who must find standing ovations a bit old hat by now, was moved to a little speech as the applause finally died away through the sprouting mushrooms of the Albert's lofty dome: 'This is the only country where we could do a new piece like this straight off. In America they would jump all over us' — Now jump all over Jethro I don't want to do. It's pretty pointless when a lot of people have had a lot of fun. An Albert Hall-full of fans can't be wrong. I suspect that the audience loved them for the very same things I found excruciating: the precision of all the instrumental work, the control over light and shade in the texture of the music, the smartly-rehearsed ad-libbing and the slapstick gags, above all

Ian Anderson's jabbering flute and prancing antics. I admired the perfectly-drilled changes when the band suddenly swoops from one section to the next, admired Barriemore Barlow's relentlessly paced drumming, Martin Barre's gutsy guitar work, John Evan's swelling, churchy organ piece. I marvelled at Ian Anderson's agility and the curious warbly sounds he conjured from the flute, raised a faint smile for the routine with the telephone, frowned at the rather tasteless parody of a television news bulletin (with the lightest of hearts, Vietnam still isn't funny). No, the real give-away happened when Martin Barre (it was actually Jeffrey Hammond!) stepped forward to the mic to make another announcement-link and described exactly how Tull were going to reach the next 'final orgasmic conclusion' — sorry mate, but the joke's on you; if you want to show everyone exactly how the music is put together, either you're guilty of demystification or of cynicism. You can't go around exposing how the machine works. That's what Tull came across as — a music machine, well-oiled and in perfect working order. The original inspiration — impossible to deny that it's there — has been gradually drained away in the search to perfect the show, just as happened to Townshend's *Tommy*. And the heaviest criticism is that, with all the perfectly rehearsed different sections, *Thick As A Brick* ended up sounding all alike."

Jeffrey Hammond's speech referred to in the above review was, "Ian is playing a rhythmic link sequence consisting of alternating bars of C minor suspended 4th and F Major. This very quiet and pleasant interlude precedes an entry by John's organ which then unites with the guitar to provide a textural overlay rich in percussive counter-rhythms. Young Gerald Bostock's poem is then taken up once more, sung of course by Mr Anderson, and then after a further ten bars the guitarist, the drummer, and I myself blend and aspire towards eager participation in anticipation of the orgasmic sensation to follow."

I think it's brilliant how Hammond doesn't hold back from sharing a bit of music theory with the audience. His comment about the "alternating bars of C minor suspended 4th and F Major" applies to the first section of *Thick As A Brick* (the one that opens with the lyrics, "really don't mind").

There is much value in having three different reviews of the same performance because it serves to provide a strong example of the way in which any art form, but particularly Jethro Tull and *Thick As A Brick*, got through (or indeed didn't!) to different people in very different ways. Jethro Tull have always been one of those bands responsible for music that people usually aren't on the fence about; they seem to either love it or hate it.

Melody Maker reported in November 1972; "Although the American press has never treated Ian Anderson and his boys very well, Jethro Tull managed to sell out the huge Madison Square Garden once again, and played for an astounding two-and-a-half hours to an ecstatic crowd. They began their set with 'a rather long number' from their last LP, *Thick As A Brick*, which lasted ninety minutes (sic) and was laced with extended soloing and rather bizarre dramatics. Mr Anderson introduced the second tune in his usual way, and Jethro Tull launched into a pastiche of hot hits from previous discs, including 'Locomotive Breath', 'Bourée' and 'Wind-Up'. Surprisingly enough, the band performed several numbers which have not yet been put on disc; they seemed to be quite diverse in nature, ranging from the very complicated melodic and rhythmic transitions which we've been used to from Tull to rather simple, three-chord riffs lifted straight out of The Who's repertoire. Their set was, for the most part, extremely tight and well-arranged, with notes always right in place even when Ian performed some unnatural acts upon the person of the guitarist, a gimmick which reeked of Bowieness. The rest of Jethro Tull is not to be overlooked, as they're fairly interesting characters as well. Jeffrey Hammond-

Hammond is the only member of the band lacking a beard, and his stage manner also has much of the Don Van Vliet (Beefheart) to it, even to the bass playing. Whenever John Evan got out from behind his piano he acted like a mimic of Anderson, twirling around his hands and doing what has come to be known as the Ian Strut. Drummer Barrie Barlow played a twenty-minute solo which owed too much to Clive Bunker and Ginger Baker, in addition to being extraordinarily boring; his drumming during the rest of the show was flawless, so this tasteless display was a bit of a surprise. Martin Lancelot Barre (whose birthday it was the very day of the concert) played a fine rhythm guitar but fell apart during his half-hour solo, which consisted of techniques ripped-off of various modern masters (Pete Townshend, Jimmy Page, and Eric Clapton)."

By the point that *Thick As A Brick* was being toured, Jethro Tull had come a long way. Ian Anderson was quoted in *Down Beat* in March 1976; "It took the music press in England some little while to wake up to the fact that we were actually around. We played for six or eight months all over the clubs in England and were one of the major-drawing underground groups of the time — by underground, I mean we received no national or music paper publicity at all. Then we played at a summer festival in England to about 80,000 people — the Sunbury Jazz festival in 1968. Having played to lots of little audiences in small clubs, it all ended up at the festival. All those people had seen us play at one time or another, and we were, even if I say it myself, the hit of the festival. The only other act that had a similar reception at the three-day event was a surprise jam by Eric Clapton and Ginger Baker. But we received absolutely zero press coverage on that occasion for one simple reason: the press were all in the press tent drinking free beer. It's the gospel truth. I've always been wary of the press. Let's say that derives from a mutual suspicion, because any member of the press finds my personality and bearing at once at odds with what I appear to be on stage. But I say that what I appear to be on stage is me. When I go home tonight, there's no Jekyll-and-Hyde transformation. There's no alteration on my attitude towards people or music — except that another part of my character becomes a little more prevalent than the part you're seeing now. I become more in evidence physically and emotionally sometimes. But it's the same me. Nevertheless, I'm prepared to believe that it doesn't look like me. So obviously the problem that any journalist has is deciding which one of these two Ian Andersons he's seen is an act."

Chapter Four

Humour

Ian Anderson was quoted in *Classic Rock* in December 2016; "When I wrote *Thick As A Brick* I tried to approach it in a humorous and satirical way. The whole idea happened very quickly. It was done in a fast and furious period of time. I'd just turn up at rehearsal every lunchtime with what I'd written that morning. Then the guys would dutifully grapple with it and we'd try to recap on what we did yesterday and the day before. By the end of ten days we'd rehearsed to a performance level all the elements of *Thick As A Brick*. And we went in and recorded it, literally in a few days. The album cover actually took us longer than the music itself."

In July 1972, *Billboard* reviewed a performance that took place at the Forum in LA; "Combining theatrics with music is nothing new in rock, but it's always a pleasant surprise when it comes off as well as it did during Jethro Tull's return to LA. Dressed in trenchcoats and caps, the same outfits as their roadies, the group wandered on stage unannounced and launched into a ninety-minute version of *Thick As A Brick*, their current album. Expanding on the instrumental content of the album, lead singer Ian Anderson added a ten-minute flute solo. Organist John Evan, guitarist Martin Barre and drummer Barrie Barlow also played long solo spots whilst bassist Jeffery Hammond-Hammond punctuated the music with readings from the newspaper cover of the LP. Anderson, in leotards and bathrobe, was, as always, the centre of the act, using his flute as a baton for twirling and conducting the band. Band members also changed clothes onstage, ran through Marx Brothers type chase scenes and appeared in various animal costumes. The 'Aqualung' encore seemed almost anticlimactic but was welcome from the crowd."

In an interview on the 1997 re-mastered CD of *Thick As A Brick*, Ian Anderson said that the album "came about primarily because the thing we had done a year before, which was the *Aqualung* album, had generally been perceived as a concept album, whereas to me it was just a bunch of songs, as I've always said. So the first thing about *Thick As A Brick* was, let's come up with something which is the mother of all concept albums, and really is a mind-boggler in terms of what was then relatively complex music, and also lyrically was complex, confusing, and above all a bit of a spoof. It was quite deliberately, but in a nice way, tongue-in-cheek, and meant to send up ourselves, the music critics and the audience perhaps, but not necessarily in that order! This was the period of *Monty Python's Flying Circus* and a very British kind of humour, which was not terribly well understood by the Japanese or the Americans when we finally went out to perform *Thick As A Brick* in concert. But they sat politely if a little confused through the whole thing and came back next time for more so it can't have gone too far amiss."

I suppose what the band were ultimately saying, albeit in a very light hearted way, was, "Okay, if you want a concept album, we'll give you one!" There is also an element of irony perhaps in terms of how despite the consideration that maybe America doesn't "get" the style of humour in *Thick As A Brick*, the album did very well there commercially (as did Monty Python in their heyday for what it's worth — it's that kind of humour, isn't it, where people either really love it, or they can't stand it because it goes over their head. Python, Tull, it's probably all a bit of a Marmite thing when you get right down to it).

Ian Anderson was quoted in *Ultimate Classic Rock* in

March 2017; "That humour works, but it's not just about rib-tickling, wisecracking humour. It's got to have some substance. It's got to be making a point. Monty Python, at its best, made those points. Sometimes it degenerated and it wasn't always good, which I'm sure the Pythons themselves would be second to recognise. Sometimes, there were a lot of duds in there."

Anderson was quoted in *Prog* in August 2016; "Monty Python lampooned the British way of life, yet did it in such a way that made us all laugh while celebrating it. To me, that's what we as a band did on *Thick As A Brick*. We were spoofing the idea of the concept album, but in a fun way that didn't totally mock it."

There is also (potentially!) a connection between *Spinal Tap* and *Thick As A Brick*. The St Cleve Chronicle mentions a made-up person's name; Derek Smalls. Anderson was quoted in *Prog* in August 2016; "I was convinced that Harry Shearer (the actor who played the character of Derek Smalls in the film) must have gotten the name from *Thick As A Brick*, especially as the Smalls in the film smoked a Peterson pipe — and the only three people I know in rock 'n' roll who smoke such a pipe were all members of Jethro Tull! But, when I got the chance to interview Harry for a US TV show, he denied ever hearing *Thick As A Brick*. I find that somewhat hard to believe."

Melody Maker reported in July 1972, under the headline of "Bewildered By Jethro's Gorilla"; "Jethro Tull climaxed their world tour with a tremendous performance of *Thick As A Brick* in Tokyo last week. Despite an exhausting schedule of concerts that took them all the way from America to Australia, Tull sounded as fresh and committed as they did when *Brick* was premiered in England two months ago. Their humour and timing was just as sharp although guitarist Martin Barre later confirmed that the unexpected sound of English laughter from the audience had spurred them on. Most Tull fans will now be familiar with their opening routine. The group shuffle on stage in white raincoats and fumble with the equipment like plain clothes detectives. When the coats are thrown off, a roar of recognition goes up. Unfortunately at the Koselnemkin Hall, the sultry heat had put Martin's guitar out of tune, and some forty minutes of fumbling elapsed, while a hapless Jeffery Hammond-Hammond was forced to prolong stage antics scheduled to last only a few moments. It threatened to spoil the show, but when Ian Anderson appeared and murmured, 'So sorry we're late' all was forgiven. The theatre was ideal for Tull's presentation, in which good lighting and acoustics are vital. All tickets had sold out three weeks previously and the hip Japanese teenagers were obviously familiar with the music, although their general behaviour was polite and reserved. Rather like Dutch rock fans. The only shouts and oaths came from the contingent of American young people who live or are on vacation in Japan. The band seem to have tightened up considerably and playing particularly well were drummer Barriemore Barlow and Mr Barre on guitar. Their forte is the use of dynamics, and they are experts at contrasting volume levels between Ian's flute and acoustic guitar, and more violent organ and guitar sections. The arrangements were flawless, but a weak point seemed a tendency to repeat certain unison phrases over too many choruses. John Evan's organ tones were occasionally lacking in colour. But these are only minor criticisms of a beautifully conceived show that has few peers in rock. Apart from the lengthy *Brick* saga, other favourites include the powerful main title from *Aqualung*, and John Evan's bravura reading of the weather forecast. Guest appearances by various roadies in rabbit and gorilla suits made me laugh, even if the Japanese were slightly bewildered. Best moment — when the gorilla, who walked on after *Brick*, began taking flash photographs of the audience. Ian's facility on flute is now being matched by his increasingly enjoyable acoustic guitar work. He is still the central pivot of the band, but each player has a defined role, and

Tull seem much more of a cohesive unit. Barry's drum solo was a highlight, featuring his fast, attacking style. And he showed a sense of humour too with a comic finale involving a specially rigged choke cymbal up front. When struck, after a great deal of posing in red underwear by Mr Barlow, it was mysteriously answered from the wings. Within seconds the rest of the group came dancing on stage in a lunatic ballet, bathed in flickering strobe light beating cymbals. It was pure pantomime that drew amazed cheers. Ian is now working on Tull's next album, and an entirely new stage act is being planned for next year. Jethro Tull are a band that never stop working to perfect and improve their show. And it explains why a band once resident at a Soho club can now tour the planet and delight fans from Los Angeles to Melbourne and Tokyo."

From the point at which the band arrived in Japan, their sense of humour was pretty much on the table straight away. *New Musical Express* reported in July 1972; "Jethro Tull's arrival in Tokyo was marked by an entertaining press reception in the Red Pearl Room of the Tokyo Hotel and an even better performance a day later at the Koseinemkin Hall, where the band played to an enthusiastic capacity house. Tull's reception was in a large conference room, dotted with tables behind which sat the inscrutable Japanese press, and a long table behind which sat the inestimable band, sheltered beneath pith helmets, yachting caps and straw head gear. It was an amusing affair. Although manager Terry Ellis seemed disconcerted at the presence of such unexpected faces as that of *NME* photographer Bob Ellis, Ian Anderson was handling things with his usual aplomb and good humour. The questions from the floor were pleasant, polite and predictable, answered with good humour. Someone wanted to know what Ian thought of Japanese audiences. 'You sir, have won a prize,' cried Anderson, leaping to his feet and awarding the bewildered gent his lighter, 'It has always bewildered me as to why any nation should concern itself as to what another thought of them!' His next victim was a young man enquiring about his peculiarity of playing on one leg. This was answered graphically — 'rude — it's rude,' shouted Anderson in mock indignation, 'when I was very young,' he elaborated, 'I was often left at home on my own with a little puppy dog who also used to play the flute. I just copied him' — He suited action to these words by cocking a leg against a convenient wall to illustrate the point. The audience seemed to enjoy the joke. A question regarding musical categorisation was dealt with more succinctly. 'It is not for me to categorise my music,' said Ian, 'that is a function of the press, and you must judge for yourselves.' — Next a question regarding Mr Anderson's suggestive hand movements — 'bloody weird isn't it,' suggested Mr A through his interpreter, 'The truth is that it is a decadent way of conducting the group. No, the truth is that I have these injections in my hand (he waves the offending article). No the truth is — if she enjoyed it so did I' — Will the gentleman bearing a passing resemblance to Cat Stevens stand up? He certainly will, and asks: 'What stories were you interested in and influenced by as a child? I understand from your lyrics that you were much under the inspiration of the fairy stories, and how much were you taking...' 'The answer's twice a day,' says Ian emphatically. At this point in the proceedings he suddenly notices a cement face ornamented by moustache — which is me. 'It's Keith Thingy,' he suggests to Martin Barre, 'From Thingy' — Meanwhile, back at the question? — 'The truth is that I was never exposed to fairy stories,' says Anderson, 'the first thing my parents gave me to read was Mickey Spillane' — And why, we ask ourselves, did the album *Living In The Past*, contain so many old singles which they had previously told us would not be issued — 'Because of the rest of the world,' said Ian, 'they were some old songs which many countries outside the UK had not heard, and some of them were not bad' — There followed an amazing diatribe about "Gerald", star of *Thick As A Brick*.

At this point came a ceremonial presentation of a bamboo pipe ('the type I cannot play') and the man himself falls into various poses, blowing and grinning. Ian expressed the opinion that he is happy to be in a land where everybody is so polite, because everybody in England is dirty and hairy."

New Musical Express also reported in July 1972; "Jethro Tull, with Ian Anderson in his world-famous role as the Catweazle of rock and roll, slammed out musical fun and games to a capacity crowd at the Tokyo date of their Japanese tour. The band opened with a lengthy selection from *Thick As A Brick*, designed to have you 'shifting about restlessly from buttock to buttock' — I had not heard the band for over a year, and having not been put in very favourable frame of mind prior to the performance (more amazing revelations on that later), was prepared to be ultra-critical of the new act. But to Tull's great credit they completely won me over. After the first few minutes of *Brick* there came an amplified phone call, which Ian took on top of the piano. He announced it was for a 'Mr Mike Nelson' and that 'there appears to be a Dover sole on the line' — Enter stage right a gent clad from mask to flipper in frogman's gear, with an oxygen cylinder strapped to his back and dripping wet, to answer the phone. Anderson, back at the music, is flinging himself about in gay abandon. Faultlessly in time with the music he gyrates, simulates innumerable phallic poses with his flute, spits, leers and generally makes himself a figure of obnoxious attraction. He also has the ability to turn it off just at the right moment and get into the music — his flute work is considerably improved and the band are much tighter all round. Guitarist Martin Barre plays some extremely listenable "sneakies" in the middle of a jam, and should get more credit than he does for his solo work, which, if not inspired, certainly veers to the exceptional rather than the average. Organist Jon Evan tends to become over-concerned with extracting sounds from his machine rather than blending in with the general funk, but fits perfectly when he transfers to piano. During the selection from *Aqualung* — more rock-filth folks — two female fans' voices were suddenly heard upon the air discussing the relative merits of the group's work and apparently being picked up by the amplifiers. The action was all heavily camped up by the group, who looked around in apparent bewilderment. I'm not sure that the audience understood the humour of this, but they certainly understood Tull's master stroke of providing Japanese sub-titles to Ian's farmyard impressions. Somehow his cows all came out sounding like birds, and his giraffe's "necking" as motor horns. Good for anyone with a sense of the ridiculous. Barriemore Barlow's drum solo proved he is a force to be reckoned with, although somehow I felt he should have climaxed the piece before he went into his comedy routine with the cymbal which he punctuated by saying 'good evening' in Japanese at every opportunity. John Evan contributed his own weird touch with a piano solo which stated off sounding like 'The Moonlight Sonata' and ended up in a frantic jam which brought the house down. To sum up, Tull are brilliant entertainers who with a little more tightening up have the most amusing act on the scene and some intriguing music to boot. Ian Anderson is extraordinary. The band are now something not to be missed."

After reviewing the gig, the journalist added, "One sour note was brought about by a confrontation with manager Terry Ellis, who refused to allow me to talk to Ian, who had previously seemed most amenable to the idea. Ellis thinks the band are misrepresented by the press. He also claimed that they were embarrassed to find themselves in the middle of the ELP visit to Japan. There are to be no interviews with Tull for the UK at present. Mr Ellis also made it quite clear that he objected to the presence of Mr R Ellis at the Hilton reception, where *NME*'s photographer was merely kneeling among the other invited press representatives. Strange, very strange."

Ian Anderson was quoted in *Ultimate Classic Rock* in

March 2017; "I had a rule of thumb when we went out and did concerts. My assumption was that fifty percent of them got it, fifty percent of them didn't. But one hundred percent of them didn't ask for their money back. I think it worked as a musical package. Whether people got what was going on was a moot point when you got to countries where English wasn't even a second language. It wasn't the international language it is today. People didn't understand what was going on, but that didn't stop us from doing well. The Japanese just stared at us blankly, despite our manager Terry Ellis going out on stage with huge signs written in Japanese, explaining the quirky oddities — and apparently naked, although he had underpants on that couldn't be seen behind the placards. It was a surprise that it got across in Scotland. My Edinburgh tones had long gone, and as a Scot going back to play something that seemed worryingly English, I felt a little self-conscious. It was a welcome relief that it didn't antagonise the Scots."

Clearly, the humour in *Thick As A Brick* (both intended and perceived) didn't gel with everyone but essentially, it is of central importance to the character of the album because it is so prominent throughout. It informed the very basis on which the album was built, and indeed, the cover art and the comedy sketches in the live shows. Without the humour, there would possibly not even be *Thick As A Brick*. Anderson was quoted in *The Arizona Republic* in July 2013; "the album was a spoof to the albums of Yes and Emerson, Lake & Palmer, much like what the movie *Airplane!* had been to *Airport.*"

His angle on the whole thing was, as he was quoted in Scott Allen Nollen's 2002 book *Jethro Tull: A History Of The Band, 1968–2001*, "a bit of a satire about the whole concept of grand rock-based concept albums." *Thick As A Brick* pokes fun at progressive rock itself. Anderson held the belief that by the early seventies, the music had gone a bit too far up its own backside and *Thick As A Brick* was somewhat intended as an antidote to that. Anderson was quoted in *Prog* in August 2016; "When progressive rock started out, it was all about bands such as ourselves moving beyond merely being influenced by American blues. We stopped trying to be the next Fleetwood Mac or Chicken Shack — in other words, derivative of Elmore James — and began to take on board so many diverse musical ideas. It was exciting and dynamic. But, by the time the 1970s had begun, bands like ELP were a little up their own arses. Everything was too serious and overblown. So, we set out with *Thick As A Brick* to show up this side of the genre."

Anderson was quoted in *Ultimate Classic Rock* in March 2017; "It was a spoof of what was happening in the world, with particularly British bands like Yes, ELP and Genesis and so on, I was going to out-prog them, really."

Anderson was quoted in *Prog* in August 2016; "I must admit to being a little surprised that we got to the top of the charts over there but everything had been building for us. *Aqualung* sold steadily, so either *Thick As A Brick* was going to take off, or we'd just sink. However, I'm not sure our American fans understood the humour behind our live performance on the subsequent tour. We decided to bring all the characters mentioned on the album and in the cover newspaper to life, and it was quirky, very British. We weren't trying to be comedians, just to enhance the concept. The rest of the band got the chance to step outside of their dapper personae. It was funny because we had a laugh. But in the US, well, all I can say is that I'm none too certain they understood what we were doing. I recall a few years later when the film *Monty Python And The Holy Grail* was released... I'd help to finance it, and saw a preview in New York. The audience laughed in all the wrong places, which was what happened with *Thick As A Brick* live. Progressive rock is a purely British phenomenon. And these days all of us — and I include the likes of ELP here — know that there was a sense of fun about it. Privately, we all saw the silly side, we were like

John Cleese in a bowler hat lampooning the bureaucrats, while revelling in it. It is hard sometimes to differentiate between what's serious and what's a send-up. But, for me, that's the beauty of true prog rock — it must have both."

The *Sydney Morning Herald* reported in July 1972; "Rock fans will doubtless be aghast to learn that, as far as Jethro Tull is concerned, they just don't rate. The shaggy men who comprise the top British pop group flew into Sydney yesterday and solemnly pronounced: 'We don't care about the audience — as long as they don't interfere.' Ian Anderson, flautist, and the group's leader, went on: 'We've had people dancing and singing in the aisles. It means nothing to us. We get up there and just play for ourselves.' — The group consists of Jeffrey Hammond-Hammond, Martin Barre, Ian Anderson, John Evan and Barrymore Barlowe (sic). They will perform in Melbourne, Adelaide and Sydney next Tuesday, Wednesday and Thursday nights. With them came seventy-two pieces of equipment weighing more than 5000lbs and insured for $45,000. Said Anderson, 'I don't know about pop or rock. We are who we are, and we do what we do'."

It was perhaps this element of not pandering to audiences that empowered Jethro Tull to create without the fear of what people might think of their work. Such attitude could have easily facilitated the band in feeling comfortable to put their humour into their work. To create something comical probably requires an element of being uninhibited. Interestingly, it would be possible to read the *Sydney Morning Herald*'s account as being somewhat derogatory to Jethro Tull; it comes across that it presents the band as a group of people who don't care about their audience. It's a subjectively worded article in all fairness. But whatever, Ian Anderson's philosophy to the whole thing is ultimately what made *Thick As A Brick* what it is.

Besides, it was in the following week that the *Sydney Morning Herald* reported positively of Jethro Tull's live performance;

"Leering, sneering, ranting, raving flautist Ian Anderson led his group, Jethro Tull, through a brilliantly sustained and successful rock concert at the Hordern Pavilion last night. Like a crazy Scottish rake, he conducted a madhouse of superb musical and theatrical performers. Anderson sometimes blew a fiendish flute. At other times he strummed a restful balladist's guitar. When he was not playing, he danced about the stage, conducting his four assistants with his twirling flute. He never let up, even though the group played continuously for two and a half hours. His right-hand man, Jeffrey Hammond-Hammond, played bass as if he was a cunning French baron. At the sudden increases in volume he would stride and strut, trailing his guitar lead. On odd occasions he turned into a pukka BBC radio announcer. Storming at intervals about the arena was John Evan, playing the part of a demented English aristocrat. When seated at his organ, or at the piano, he flailed his arms in wild response to Anderson. The whirlwind drummer, Barriemore Barlowe (sic), kept cool in the garb of a neck-to-knee swimming champion. And the end of his solo, he led the group in a hilarious chorus of crash-cymbals. The lead guitarist, Martin Barre, sought no greater status amid his peer-group than that of a pink-cheeked yeoman. Jethro Tull were superb musically. Their numbers were beautifully controlled, despite frenzied spurts of adrenalin. Their riffs were almost classical in origin. But above all, Jethro Tull were superb theatrically. Their decadent dramatics dragged their evil electronics to great heights. Jethro Tull's performance derived from the theatre of the absurd, with frogmen and apes making unexpected entrances. The group took the foppish drama of The Who and the insane music of the early Pink Floyd to their logical conclusions. The audience obviously appreciated every delicate note, every sinister beat. They kept a stunned silence throughout the first number — a seventy minute recital of *Thick As A Brick* — and were knocked out by the collection of older songs. Jethro Tull can be seen and heard at the Hordern Pavilion again tonight and tomorrow night — if there are any tickets left."

The very first review of *Thick As A Brick* gave a warning to people that they might find it a bit weird; "One doubts at times the validity of what appears to be an expanding theme throughout the two continuous sides of this record but the result is at worst entertaining and at least aesthetically palatable. Poor, or perhaps naïve taste is responsible for some of the ugly changes of time signature and banal instrumental passages linking the main sections but ability in this direction should come with maturity." And where was this review from?... Not *Melody Maker* or *Sounds* but from the St Cleve Chronicle of course! As if to playfully beat the press at their own game, Ian Anderson wrote the review himself. Such was the scope that the St Cleve Chronicle, the mock newspaper that packaged the original LP, provided.

Anderson was quoted of the review he wrote in the St Cleve Chronicle in *Classic Rock* in December 2016; "It's okay for me to say those things about my own work but I don't think it's too cool if somebody else tries to do it, because I'm already well aware of it. There's every scope to say that this is noodly, extreme, anal, pompous, bombastic, arrogant — all of those words are applicable to prog rock and definitely applicable to *Thick As A Brick* — but they're there on purpose. And if you don't get the joke, fuck off! Don't start telling me something that I know full well, because I wrote it to be like that. That's the point!"

A ballsy comment indeed! It would be so easy to read this and think of Ian Anderson and Co as being both a bit defenceless and arrogant. I don't think that is the case at all though. I would argue that Jethro Tull was (and still is!) a group of professionals who were confident in what they wanted to create without being uncaring about it.

Australia's *Sun* reported in July 1972; "Jethro Chased The

Baby Away!... Who said Jethro Tull didn't give a damn about their audiences! At the Hordern on Tuesday night, Ian Anderson spotted a young mother holding her baby — seated in the front row. Just before the band started playing, Anderson told her she was 'mad to bring a small baby in here — you'll destroy his ears!' The young wife and baby and husband got up and moved — or left the hall... Tull went on to give one of the most professional visual and musical performances ever seen here — their antics and gestures on stage left the Pavilion breaking up. And satisfied. Whatever their real attitudes to their audiences ('don't interfere'/'we just play music for business'/'don't care about audience participation'), they certainly know how to give out the money's worth in a show. If you missed the Monday and Tuesday shows, you just *might* be able to catch them tonight. Try."

Additionally, there was arguably a lot of authenticity and honesty in Ian Anderson's approach to his creativity. He was quoted in *Down Beat* in March 1976; "I have to do what I want to do. Otherwise, we have no possible excuse for getting together, me and the audience. We have no reason under the sun to even breathe the same air, unless it's the result of me saying I'm playing what I want to play because I actually have to cope with this and say it for whatever obscure or selfish set of personal reasons. So there exists a coincidence where other people derive some enjoyment or some emotional sort of reward from that. That's all it amounts to really, a coincidence, because I'm not terribly responsible when it comes to catering to what people want."

The depth and extent of the authenticity that Anderson was perhaps aiming for certainly seemed to be very candid. He was quoted in the same feature; "We're not performers or actors in the sense that we're "showbiz". We're not your David Bowie or Elton John. I'm not into that at all. I'm into being me. If I feel bad, I'm going to tell the audience. If in the last week I've had diarrhoea, I'm likely to speak about that. That's what ideally it should be. Personal truth. It may be entirely irrelevant to the audience, but by dint of personality it becomes not just a personal exclusive truth, but relatable to other people. It becomes entertainment for other people as a by-product of what we're doing. That's what makes it work for them, and it may be an entirely different level than how it works for me."

The complexity of the album cover was such that Ian Anderson had to persuade Chrysalis to go with the idea. From the record company's point of view, it was feared that the cover art would be too expensive to produce. But, as ambitious about the record's packaging as he was about the music, Anderson stubbornly reasoned that if a real newspaper could be so easily mass produced then making a parody of one would be no less practical. He was quoted in *Billboard* in December 1978; "There have been times when I've pushed Terry (Ellis — management at Chrysalis) against his wishes on things, you know. Album covers like the *Thick As A Brick* one, which he wasn't keen on at all. I really had to insist on that one but ultimately it came out, I thought, rather well and was instrumental in the identity and selling power of that album. Likewise there have been things which I haven't particularly wanted to do but I've gone along with Terry and he's been proven right. I think Terry would be the first to admit that he's learnt a few things from me as much as I've learnt a few things from him."

It comes across that Ian and Terry had a fascinating working dynamic in the sense that they were both creative but naturally, had different loyalties and responsibilities within any given project. Anderson was quoted in the same feature; "Certainly Terry and I have had a lot of rows, you know, real screamers. We haven't had one for a long time now but I can remember the last one in a dressing room somewhere about five years ago. It was a real corker and about half way through we were both hoarse from shouting, everybody else had cleared out, had fled, both Terry's lot and my lot, and I said to him, 'It's pointless having these arguments because you know I always win, Terry' — I don't know why I said it but it was a good bluff, it worked and he gave up. I didn't always win though, I should tell you."

Fair enough I suppose. Nothing wrong with being blunt if it gets things done. Ellis was quoted in *Billboard* in June 1977; "I can't have cosmetic conversation with people. I like to be direct and take care of business right away. For that reason I don't have too many formalised meetings. Why have an hour meeting when I can deal with something in ten minutes over the phone? For that reason I don't have too many formal lunches unless it's purely social or to relax. Actually, my hobbies are food and wine and I really enjoy them when I have the time. I'd rather work to ensure a better wine in a better restaurant." On balance, there are numerous interviews in which Anderson spoke highly of Terry Ellis and his approach to business.

One of the most beautiful things about humour perhaps, is that it often walks such a fine line between hilarity and darkness. The lyrics in *Thick As A Brick* are certainly symptomatic of that. The album is just as funny as it is serious at times. Although the lyrics of *Thick As A Brick* deal with some difficult subjects, they are presented with fun as if they were a poem written by Gerald "Little Milton" Bostock, a fictional eight year old school boy created by Ian Anderson who said on BBC Radio in March 1979; "He's the little figure that I'm sort of saying is me as a little lad, who was supposed to have everything going for him, a really quite precocious little lad, very bright, very clever — read books, and knew a lot of things at an early age, but was well into opting out of that and making his own way... a sort of exaggerated version of me as a similarly-aged child."

For all of its eccentric qualities, Jethro Tull's music has openly explored the cynical aspect of human nature. It is possibly the case as a result of Ian Anderson's philosophical wonderings as well as a reluctance to indulge in the hedonism that existed in abundance during the early seventies, when sex, drugs and rock and roll were adopted (if only in part!) by virtually most rock bands.

Anderson was quoted in *Rolling Stone* in April 2012; "When the show was done, we would go back to our hotel rooms and watch TV or read a book and have a pretty quiet and calm kind of life. We knew how to get up at 8:00 in the morning, or even earlier, to travel to the next place. So we were quite pragmatic in our approach towards the lifestyle of being on the road."

He was quoted in *Guitar World* in September 1999; "I wasn't into the drug culture and party culture of the times. It always offended me that people assumed I was on amphetamines, or something. We were Led Zeppelin's support act on a rather lengthy arena tour. And although they were party animals and certainly lived life to the excess, we got on fine with them. But Robert Plant didn't like the idea that I wasn't playing the game. I suspect he found that irritating about me, and I think that's part of the reason he and I never hit it off... No one likes folks who appear to be bucking the trend."

It was advocated in the same feature; "Half of *Aqualung* is devoted to songs in which Anderson indulges his personal grudge against religious hypocrisy, while *Thick As A Brick* is a tirade against society's tendency to encourage social decorum and financial success at the expense of personal expression and individuality."

Anderson was quoted in the same feature; "Most of my subjects have come out of that confusing emotional, spiritual and psychological period of time when you're going through puberty. All of that stuff is still fermenting in me like a very old wine. I can uncork that bottle now when I'm writing a song and identify with that earlier version of me. That's why I maintain that I feel very much the same person I was when I was fourteen or fifteen years old. I just really feel like I'm the same guy."

Upon opening the gatefold of the LP and unfolding the bottom section, hey presto, you're suddenly holding a full size twelve page newspaper. It contains fictional stories and adverts that range from the mundane to the farcical. As well as the lyrics (Bostock's poem) and mock album review, there's a crossword puzzle, and a naughty dot to dot puzzle. *Thick As A Brick*'s album artwork was just as creative and off the wall as the music contained within.

The album artwork was also noteworthy due to the extent that the band themselves were active in the creation of it, with all band members making a contribution to the newspaper. Ian Anderson said of it on BBC Radio in March 1979; "All of that album cover, and I've said this before and it's absolutely true, took longer to put together than the album. I'm not suggesting it's any more important, but it took a long time to write all of that. I did, I suppose, more than half of it — Jeffrey (Hammond) did quite a lot and John Evan did a bit, and it was put together, put into columns and laid out, by Royston Eldridge at Chrysalis."

On the 1997 re-mastered version of *Thick As A Brick*, Jeffrey Hammond said; "I just remember doing a lot of recording into a Dictaphone, or a small tape recorder, and tapes got sent off to various secretaries to type up. But most of it was giggling, I think, and laughing at some of the more immature sections of it."

Royston Eldridge's experience from a job he did prior to working for Chrysalis Records came in handy tremendously; He had worked as a rock music journalist for *Melody Maker* and *Sounds* as well as for a small town newspaper. In 2008 in the documentary produced and directed by Jon Brewer, *Jethro Tull — Classic Artists: Their Fully Authorised Story*, Eldridge gave an account of designing the cover for *Thick As A Brick*; "When the group had the idea to do it like a newspaper, I was the obvious mug to help them put it together. It was a pretty complex thing, actually. I'd hate to try to do it now. I don't think you could do it nowadays. There were enormous problems with how you put it together to keep the record safe, who was going to print it. Some of the paper was too thin and tore too easily. We had problems with retailers making sure it fit into the racks. Everything in the paper, the whole twelve pages from births, deaths, marriages, sport reports (the weirdest sports you even heard of), it was all written by the group. Every photograph features either friends of the group, members of the road crew, even a review of the album inside. Terry Ellis, for instance, he's featured in a photograph. Robin Black (the album's producer) is the roller skating champion. Every small ad had some relevance."

Even if it was logistically something of a pain to do the album artwork as it was, it is certainly a very memorable feature of *Thick As A Brick*. I would imagine that a lot of fans are glad that it was made; it's just so iconic and adds insight into the type of humour that the band was going for. Anderson was quoted in *Ultimate Classic Rock* in March 2017; "It was very carefully studied. I amassed a pile of papers and drew inspiration from the really silly stories that people would write about because there wasn't anything else to write about. That was part of the fun, and definitely made it a concept album."

Of course, Jethro Tull haven't been the only band to use the idea of making an album cover look like a newspaper. It was done in the fifties with albums by Elvis Presley and also, The Dave Brubeck Quartet. In the sixties, the idea was utilised by Jefferson Airplane. In the eighties, Guns n' Roses did something similar on one of their albums. So were Jethro Tull the original innovators of such idea? Of course not. But was their use of the newspaper idea the most expansive and the most in depth? Absolutely! Anderson was quoted of John Lennon's use of newspaper related imagery for album art in *Ultimate Classic Rock* in March 2017; "He had his album *Some Time In New York City* in the works. He'd used *The New York Times* as the

cover. *Thick As A Brick* came out a few weeks before his —
he had a single page, whereas the St Cleve Chronicle was an
altogether more ambitious affair, which luckily made it to the
record store before his."

When *Rolling Stone* reviewed *Thick As A Brick* in June
1972, there was much attention paid to the newspaper (the
comments regarding the album not being in the shops correlates
with the American release date on the Reprise record label);
"Although not in the shops yet, I was able to acquire a "white
label" pressing of the current Jethro Tull winner *Thick As A
Brick* from their London agents, Chrysalis Artists. Written
around a poem by St Cleve child prodigy Gerald Bostock, their
music spins a delicate web of sensitive sounds: sometimes
lilting, sometimes soaring to form a brilliant backdrop for
the meaningful lyrics and improvisational techniques... ('One
doubts at times the validity of what appears to be an expanding
theme throughout the two continuous sides of this record but
the result is at worst entertaining and at least aesthetically
palatable') — Ian Anderson (a.k.a. Julian Stone-Mason BA)
has not only slyly reviewed his own album, he's also supplied
the newspaper which contains it. Like so much flounder,
Thick As A Brick comes wrapped in the St Cleve's Chronicle,
an apocryphal yet typical daily of Anderson's design. Played
across the front page is the Gerald "Little Milton" Bostock
scandal (the epithet refers to the author of *Paradise Lost*, not the
soul singer). Eight-year-old Gerald is adjudged unfit to accept
first prize from The Society for Literary Advancement and
Gestation (SLAG) by virtue of the questionable contents of his
epic poem, *Thick As A Brick*. Gerald is one of Ian Anderson's
incarnations and ruses. Besides lyricist and impersonator,
Anderson is also composer, arranger, singer, flutist, acoustic
guitarist, violinist, saxophonist, trumpeter, satirist and overall
composer. His adeptness at most of these functions, in particular,
his ability to balance and fuse them, has created one of rock's

most sophisticated and ground breaking products. Most of the Chronicle's features display a dry, fatuous, very English sense of humour. Under the 'Deaths' column, there is the late Charles Stiff; and stories have titles along the lines of 'Mongrel Dog Soils Actor's Foot' and 'Non-Rabbit Missing' — Characters in, say, a page two story will turn up again on page five in equally ludicrous circumstances. It is all very clever, yet at first seemingly irrelevant. Page seven carries the words to *Thick As A Brick*. The writing is very dense and enigmatic, and the unidentified shifts in narrative voice compound the difficulty. The poem, as best I can make out, is a sweeping social critique, as pessimistic about poets, painters and the generally virtuous as it is condemnatory of politicians and other figures of authority. And what more perfectly encompasses or embodies the world Anderson aims to criticise than a daily newspaper? The paper in turn encompasses the poem. Furthermore, there are names in the poem which refer back to items in the newspaper. The poem "reviews" the newspaper, just as Stone-Mason reviewed the record. The entire package operates with the allusiveness of a Nabokov novel."

The St Cleve Chronicle is pretty sizeable by local newspaper standards; it contains many articles, a horoscope, puzzles, television and radio listings, advertisements, and comic strips. The articles consist of local news stories, advice columns and sports reports. All such items showcase the band's sense of humour. Whilst a lot of the headlines are daft and fun ("Mongrel Dog Soils Actor's Foot"; and "Magistrate Fines Himself"), there are also a number of them that convey a less light-hearted side. For instance, "Do Not See Me Rabbit" is about a pilot who was shot down over London during the second world war. Numerous articles are about the controversy surrounding Gerald Bostock and Jethro Tull's musical interpretation of his poem. On the front page, under the headline of "Judges Disqualify "Little Milton" in Last Minute

Rumpus", it is reported that the BBC received angry protests from viewers who were offended by Bostock's poem due to it containing an "extremely unwholesome attitude towards life, his God and country".

There really is a strong mix of the poignant and the silly throughout the St Cleve Chronicle. The headline, "Major Beat Group Records Gerald's Poem" reports that "one-legged pop flautist Ian Anderson... was so enthused by (Bostock's poem) that he wrote forty-five minutes of pop music to go with it". In the classified section, there is an advert for, "Brick urgently required. Must be thick and well kept."

The St Cleve Chronicle could best be described as spoof or parody but all the same, some people thought that Gerald Bostock was real. *Record World* reviewed the album in May 1972; "Ian Anderson and Co have based their latest concept album on a poem written by young St Cleve lad Gerald Bostock. Highly informative package tells controversial story. Group's progressive movements tell story just as well. Gold for sure."

Anderson elaborated as he was quoted in *Prog* in August 2016; "Yes, there's an autobiographical element in what I wrote. As a child, I was a bit of a rebel. Most of my peers aspired to going to grammar school, getting eight O Levels and three A Levels, then becoming part of conventional society. That never appealed to me. I was the sort of child who loved spending time collecting pond life and then analysing it. I also loved science fiction stories of the era (the 1950s), because they told of a different, exciting future. So, I stood apart from others of my age, and drew on this for the character of Gerald Bostock. But he himself is a fiction. We put together a lot of silly stories and also used lyrics from the album itself. We also got the road crew, label people and girlfriends to pose for photos."

The humour behind *Thick As A Brick* was clearly lost on people who weren't aware of the fact that Bostock was fictional. Anderson was quoted in *Classic Rock* in December 2016; "I drew upon my own childhood and my own early experiences for ideas for sections within the overall work. But I was also drawing very much on the world of the eight-year-old Gerald Bostock. It was part of the absurdity... (*Thick As A Brick*) was written very much as I went along, and was a very natural, organically evolving piece of music. There was an almost Monty Pythonesque idea in my head of this pastiche approach to creating this idea — 'the mother of all concept albums', as I've come to call it. It was presenting such a preposterous notion that an eight-year-old boy had written this saga in some poetry competition. Of course, you can then suspend disbelief and just go with it. But there were a lot of countries where they just didn't get the joke. They thought it was a real story, that this precocious schoolboy had written this stuff and somehow I turned it into an album. You have to preserve the fiction to some extent, because that's your starting point — the absurdity of precocious youth and complex ideas; that somehow *Thick As A Brick* is an album about what this youth might become and the distortion of his ideas as a prepubescent child. Essentially it's setting out future scenarios of what might happen."

Anderson was quoted in *Guitar World* in September 1999; "Since people thought *Aqualung* was a concept album, we decided to give them one. *Thick As A Brick* was tongue in cheek, what with the album's pretence that the lyrics had been written by a school boy named Gerald Bostock. Monty Python had just come to prominence, and people were in tune with that slightly surreal type of British humour. And at the same time, the album expressed some serious sentiments about English society, as well as some rather serious music writing. But it was also meant to be a bit of fun."

There are also daft references to stuffed penguins, rabbits, and non-rabbits throughout. Much like some of the comedy costumes used in the live shows. As was reported in *New Musical Express* in November 1972; "Jethro Tull sold out

Madison Square Garden. They appeared with Gentle Giant, who were unbearably gigantic, but certainly not gentle. Tull took forty minutes to set up, finally opening with forty minutes' worth of *Thick As A Brick*. We wanted to see them do 'Sympathy For The Devil' — or have Mott The Hoople come out and beat them up with a little ultraviolence. Drummer Barrie Barlow is a bit too repetitive on the high hats, mustering a lot of drill figures and exercises, not very exciting. He hangs onto a beat long enough to pull in his audience, and then, when he finally has them, changes to another tack. He did come out in his red longjohns in an incredible change-clothes strip, flashing about like a dog in heat with a hydrant, soon followed by keyboard man, John Evan, attired first as a gorilla, and then as a big white rabbit. Bass player Jeffrey Hammond served as a BBC-type moderator, reading off the news from *Thick As A Brick*. Ian Anderson provided some flashy phallic flutings, and proved that he is, as ever, master of Jethro's destiny. The crazed audience couldn't get enough."

The audience might have enjoyed the music and humour more than the reviewer. And Barlow's drumming repetitive? It's certainly complex and complementary of the music on the *Thick As A Brick* album! Either he was having an extremely bad night or simply, the reviewer just wasn't a fan. Barlow's drumming speaks for itself.

Drumming disagreements aside, the humour in the live shows continued much in the same lexicon, as was reported in *Creem* in May 1973; "Tull concerts now are a real experience, and a unique one, for better or worse. Make no mistake: in terms of sheer professionalism, Jethro Tull are without peer. They stand out by never failing to deliver a full-scale show, complete with everything they know any kid would gladly pay his money to see: music, volume, costumes, theatrics, flashy solos, long sets, two encores. Jethro Tull are slick and disciplined; they work hard and they deliver. What they deliver is one of the most curious melanges on any stage. If their lyrics generally take a moralistic bent, the band themselves come on like total goofballs, and the contrast works nicely. All of them dress to the teeth, usually in Victorian waistcoats and tight pants, and from the instant Ian Anderson hits the stage he works the audience with all the masterful puppeteer mojo of the Merlin he often poses as. He whirls and whips in total spastic grace, creating a maelstrom around himself, flinging his fingers in the air as if hurling arcane incantations at the balcony. His eyes take on a satyr's gleam, get wild and pop from his head. He very effectively passes himself off as a madman reeling in riptide gales from unimaginable places. He exploits his flute exhaustively: baton, wand, sword, gun, phallus, club, virtuoso's magic axe. He twirls it like a cheerleader and stirs the audience to a frothing frenzy with it, then raises the ladle to his chops and puts the audience in a trance with an extended melodramatic solo. Jethro Tull are such solid entertainers that even if you can't stand the music, they're usually providing something for you to gawk at. A lot of it is real vaudeville: Barlow walks up to the mic during a pause, holds up a toy cymbal, raises a drumstick and hits it with an extravagant flourish. As he does so he rises on left tiptoes and arches his right leg out behind him like a cartoon Nureyev, rolling his eyes at the audience and mugging shamelessly. He gets cheers and an echoing cymbal shot which seems to come from nowhere and puts him into similarly exaggerated perplexity. He looks around, scratches his head and hits the cymbals again. Again the echo. Getting really worked up, he hits the cymbal again and again, faster and faster, the echoes coming at the same pace, and suddenly the rest of the band converges on him, each of them holding identical cymbal and stick and wildly bashing away."

The feature continued, "The audience eats it up. Costumes are utilised too, in a manner that's too calculated and too successful to be off the cuff. But what would you think if you saw a band stop an extended song in the middle to: Read a bogus "weather report", run through a bit where a band member walks to the microphone and begins to gesticulate and address the audience, while another member dressed as a gorilla stands behind him aping his every move, hop around the stage dressed as bunny rabbits, stop the music again, the silence broken by the ringing of a prop phone onstage which one band member answers: 'Hello? Oh yes, I'll see if he's here', then he turns to the audience, 'There's a call here for a Mr Mike Nelson.' So a roadie or somebody, dressed in full diving gear complete with fins, mask and aqualung, flaps on from stage left, picks up the phone, wordlessly mimics a brief conversation, then flaps back as the band tears into a particularly wild passage from *Brick* to wild cheers from the gallery. If that's your idea of entertainment, scarf up a ticket the next time Jethro Tull hit town. If you can get one, that is. It's a long way from my idea of rock 'n' roll, but then maybe that idea is dated. Or maybe this isn't rock 'n' roll, and doesn't need to apologise for being something else either. Jethro Tull are going to be around for a while, will undoubtedly get even bigger than they are now, and their musical productions will become even more."

It was advocated in *New Musical Express* in July 1972; "As a music producing unit, Jethro Tull have always been one of the most misunderstood and underrated of bands — although their credentials as a dynamic stage act have rarely been called into question. That very charismatic quality on stage is, in fact, the crux of the dilemma; the reason why, as far back as 1969, Jethro were recognising the difficulty of persuading critics and public not to regard them dismissively as — to quote Martin Barre — 'a joke band'. This kind of attitude tends to run thus: a band turns in a good, entertaining show, then from this particular process of thought it follows that the show must be an act. An act needs rehearsing. If it's rehearsed then it's mechanical. And if the show is mechanical, then the music must be too

— to follow things to their (il)logical conclusion. While Ian Anderson's stage theatricals are in one respect Jethro's greatest asset, in a musical context they could also be said to be the band's greatest liability. All that to one side, truth is that Jethro Tull have always been a conscientious and dedicated band in the studio. They started with little enough knowledge of recording techniques, or of music too for that matter, relatively speaking, but set about mastering the arts of both aspects with a relentlessly inquisitive zeal."

I find this to be a fascinating observation as both onstage and on their albums, Jethro Tull were both humorous and serious. It is this very characteristic of the band that is very much at the fore with *Thick As A Brick*. There are elements of the album that fall into both categories. The way it has been perceived is demonstrative of that and even Anderson himself has commented on both the humour and some of the darker themes on the album.

It is often said that *Thick As A Brick* was in line with a *Monty Python* style of humour in terms of how they both play on the audience's willingness to accept the surreal. As part of that though, another commonality with such style of humour is that typically, some people totally get it whilst it leaves others completely baffled. The following review is, I would suggest, certainly reflective of that:

Under the headline of "Tull Disappoints", *Record World* reported in July 1972; "Appearing at the Forum (in LA), Jethro Tull played to capacity crowds with a show that came close to becoming a circus. What happened to Ian Anderson the perfectionist? Instead of the near brilliant, tightly finished show we used to get from Tull, we were given a very disjointed set broken up in the oddest places by comedy sketches that can only be described as dull and amateurish. Why this was done defies the imagination but whatever the reason, the outcome only detracted from what could have been a decent concert. The opening number, *Thick As A Brick*, lasted for well over an hour, was involved and intricate, sometimes boring, sometimes great, and broken up by those absurd "comedy" sketches. Fortunately though, Ian Anderson saved the day. A superb showman and the core of the group, he leapt and cavorted around stage looking like a frantic Fagan but with the grace and precision of a ballet dancer. Alternating between acoustic guitar and flute, Anderson kept the show alive and the audience yelling for more. All in all, the show was disappointing and Anderson's magical quality of being able to mesmerise and mould his audience was lost in such a vast arena as the Forum. Instead, Jethro Tull have become superstars, relying too much on their reputation and not enough on the fact that they *can* play good music."

What the review seems to be getting at, essentially, is "stop playing for laughs and get back to the music". Fair point if the sketches in *Thick As A Brick* didn't crack you up. But would *Thick As A Brick* be what it was without the quirky style of humour that was liberally injected into it by Jethro Tull? Probably not.

UK original album sleeve

UK first press label design.

US original

US reissue

Jethro Tull was already building a strong following in America before the release of *Thick As A Brick*. In keeping with the previous albums Chrysalis had licensed them to Reprise, the label created in 1960 by Frank Sinatra. However the deal soon ended and Chrysalis switched US releases to its own imprint the following year.

The complexity of the album artwork that folded out into a full newspaper was arguably the most ambitious ever undertaken. Every single aspect of it was created from the band members' own input. Although clearly all the articles were spoofs, today it might be considered fake news!

Due to the nature of the artwork there wasn't really any variations around the world. However, some South American countries did include the album title in Spanish as illustrated here with this version from Uruguay.

The Japanese released it with the ubiquitous obi strip. The green one is a first pressing and the red a later reissue.

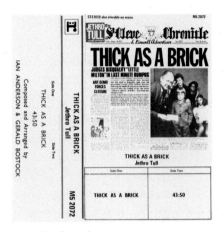

Australia, first release

Australia reissue

India

Canada reissue

Fans who chose to buy the album on cassette missed out on the newspaper but as the pictures here show there wasn't the same global uniformity in the way the cover was presented.

Original Reprise reel release.

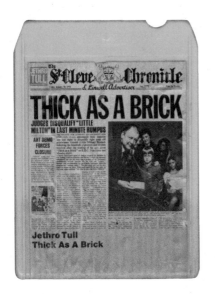
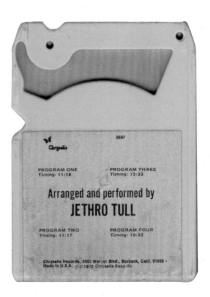

UK

Italy

The album was also released on 8-track cartridge. A particularly popular format in the States, despite the fact that it meant the album was split into 4 parts.

8-tracks were less popular elsewhere but the album was also released in that format in the UK and Italy.

A variety of label variations on Reprise.
Clockwise: Argentina, New Zealand, Mexico and the rare
Japanese promo version.

Thick As A Brick has proven to be a continual seller, decades on from its original release, as these later variations of the label designs testify.

The advent of CD only helped to add to the increased sales. In 1988 a remastered version was released. The CD format also allowed for additional material to be added to an album. The 1998 CD release added a live version of part of the album as well as an interview with Anderson, Barre and Hammond-Hammond. The artwork was cleverly changed to reflect the difference.

Chapter Five

The Legend Lives On

T*hick As A Brick* was noteworthy when the album came out because the music went against the grain; whilst employing a number of features in common with other progressive rock at the time, *Brick* also had so much uniqueness to it that it grabbed the record buying public's attention in a big way and, as part of that, propelled Jethro Tull to new heights as a band who were still, on reflection, in the relative infancy of their tenure. With a range of short but memorable melodies, the entire piece offers so many points of interest and showcases the talent within the band. Many of the instrumental passages are less than two minutes long but they are always ambitious in terms of melody, time signature, subject matter and indeed, the musical virtuosity required to produce them.

In November 1978, *Cash Box* asserted of a performance that took place at the Forum in LA: "Perhaps the group's most serious problem onstage is selecting which songs to perform, whether to rely on the critically acclaimed earlier material from *Aqualung* or concentrate on the newer, more familiar works such as *Songs From The Wood*. As on the live LP, Tull takes the middle road, mixing such old favourites as 'Cross-Eyed Mary' and 'Locomotive Breath' with more recent efforts. Of course, there was a whirlwind rendition of *Thick As A Brick*, although newer hits, 'Bungle In The Jungle' and 'Skating Away On The Thin Ice Of A New Day' were noticeably absent, but with a catalogue like Jethro Tull's, some omissions are inevitable."

Being spoilt for choice of material to do live is probably not a bad position for any group to be in. Such was the popularity of *Thick As A Brick* that, as part of Jethro Tull's older material by that point, it survived being culled from the setlist. Impressive really considering the size of the menu by that point in the band's career.

A lot of Jethro Tull's albums could be regarded as concept ones in how every track is based on a theme. For instance; *Too Old To Rock 'N' Roll: Too Young To Die* (an ageing rock musician), *Songs From The Wood* (nature and folklore) and *Heavy Horses* (farming and rural life). However, even where some Jethro Tull albums have been considered as concept albums, Ian Anderson has been keen to assert that they are not. Even years after *Aqualung* was made and Anderson had stipulated that it wasn't a concept album, it wasn't uncommon for it still to be discussed as such.

It was advocated in *Down Beat* in March 1976; "Jethro Tull's first concept album, *Aqualung*, was an early entry in the soon-to-be crowded rock opera race. Anderson's LP side of related songs about the title character — a wheezing down-and-outer in London — catapulted the troupe to superstar status. The release of *Thick As A Brick*, an album-long ballad, solidified the group's reputation and allowed Anderson room to display his lyrical talents by sketching childhood impressions of comic heroes and vaguely ominous father-son confrontations, recounted in mock-epic style. Later in the same year, *Living In The Past*, a two record collection of live performances and early songs unreleased in America, brought the group to top ten radio status via its title single."

Discussion surrounding which of Jethro Tull's albums are and aren't concept ones seems to be one of those grey areas whereby, no matter how eloquently Ian Anderson states which is which, there is perhaps always going to be room for debate. That's not to say that Ian Anderson isn't the ultimate reliable source of information (of course he is!) but even with *Thick As*

A Brick being stipulated as a concept album by the man himself, the ambiguity of the lyrics could perhaps lend themselves to disagreement over whether they all stay close to a particular theme.

Anderson was quoted in *Down Beat* in March 1976 as he addressed the question of how the conception for *Thick As A Brick* began; "It wasn't a conception really, just the act of writing a song thinking about what I might have been, what I began life as being, what kind of childhood images moved me — dealt with in a very oblique fashion, because I'm not setting out to create a threadbare tale of emotional woe or to even delineate emotional happenings. I'm just creating a background lyrical summation of a lot of things I feel about being a contemporary child in this age and the problems that one has — the problems of being precocious beyond one's age or having interests beyond one's age, and to some extent being ruled in a kind of heavy-handed, unexplained fashion by the father figures you describe."

There seems to be a very strong attitude of rebellion against various father figures, such as parents, the church, school, in a number of Jethro Tull albums. Ian Anderson was quoted in the same feature; "I suppose my childhood was basically very normal — a normalcy which I've occasionally, ineptly, let come across in some of my lyrics. Possibly that's what appeals to other people. It's certainly not an unusual phenomenon to be in one's parents' bad graces during adolescence. The songs verbalise for people, thoughts that they clearly have difficulty in verbalising for themselves in the lucid way that the lyricist has, if he's a good one — or a popular one, I should say."

Ultimately, Anderson's lyrics cover a number of specific themes in *Thick As A Brick* and there is often such an amount of ambiguity in them anyway. Many tangents are explored and there is not necessarily a linear plotline present. But that's okay. That's certainly not problematic and is arguably what a lot of the appeal of a lot of Jethro Tull's music is. Anderson has often spoken keenly in interviews with regards to encouraging people not to take his words too seriously. Again, it's perhaps in line with that whole absurd type of humour present in Monty Python, as in, take it as it is and don't over think it.

A strong theme in the lyrics of *Thick As A Brick* is the importance of being a free thinking individual; someone who doesn't let themselves be steamrolled by a dominant majority in society. As Ian Anderson put it in an interview on Australian TV in July 1972; "In the case of *Thick As A Brick*, it started off from one line. The concept, or concepts, expressed in the music, or in the lyrics, is that everyone's right. And the necessity, I think, should be apparent for everyone to decide, to make their own judgment on things in their own way, regardless of age or experience, or even intelligence. We have at one end of the scale, the intellectual society, who are necessarily making judgments on people on the other end of the scale who may be thick as a brick — 'Your wise men don't know how it feels to be thick as a brick' — How the hell can they decide for the man in the street what he should want."

Anderson was quoted in *Ultimate Classic Rock* in March 2017; "I was subjected as a schoolboy to the nationalistic and unpleasant boys' magazines, which were not the best way of grooming young minds for the sixties and seventies. There was a radical change in society, most notable in the US. We weren't prepared for that in schoolboy literature. It was that stereotyping that I was lampooning, pretending the album had been written by someone writing adult themes through the distorted mind of a schoolboy. It was relatively easy to do. It was a tall order to have it accepted."

I could be wrong in this association but the lyrics about the "paperback edition of the boy scout manual" spring to mind here.

Testament to an album being a landmark for a band is often

when they are faced with the worry of how they're going to follow up the same level of success with their next album. A double-edged sword of a situation perhaps; on the one hand, *Thick As A Brick* propelled Jethro Tull to new heights of recognition and thus, popularity but on the other hand, such success was always going to be a hard act to follow, regardless of what their next project was to be. Ian Anderson was quoted in *Jam* in November 1993:

"I guess when it came to doing *A Passion Play*, we suddenly realised we created a bit of a monster in the fact that we had done the concept album and it had been taken seriously. Our big mistake was then to go and move on to release an album that was a concept album, but without the humour, without the self-deprecating approach that *Thick As A Brick* had. Although *Passion Play* is these days one of those albums that a lot of people, a definite group of people, hold up as being their all-time favourite Jethro Tull album, it isn't one of my favourite Jethro Tull albums — but it has some good moments in it."

He was quoted of *A Passion Play* in *Prog* in March 2018; "The 'step too far' album. We decamped to the Château d'Hérouville in France where Elton had recorded, and had a rotten time: technical issues, gastric bugs… we just wanted to go home. So we did, and had a frantic few weeks of writing a new album. Two pieces made it on to the *War Child* album and one or two morphed into something more sophisticated, but they never came to light on that album. Steve Harris (of Iron Maiden) loves *A Passion Play*. I'm glad someone liked it!"

It was reported in *New Musical Express* in March 1973; "Although their current 1973 schedule allows for only two concerts in Britain this year, there are no signs of a let up in Jethro Tull's apparent ambition to take the title of The World's Most Travelled Rock Band. In between sessions at North London's Morgan Studios on the upcoming *Passion Play* album, Jethro recently completed a European tour playing to capacity houses all along the line. In Copenhagen they opened a new concert hall, and drew a sell-out crowd of 5,000 — the major part of their set, approximately 1½ hours, consisted of an improvised *Thick As A Brick*."

Ian Anderson was quoted in the same feature; "I can't remember when I had my last day off. It must be well over one year ago. This year we're going to play three American tours — each one lasting four weeks. We're in the middle of a European tour, and we're going to the Far East and Down Under. So far we're not as big in Japan as we are in England and the States, but we got a very good reception in Japan the first time we played there, and we're going back this year. Anyway, I'm not interested in the markets, only in the music. Besides this hard programme, we have recording plans. We've already taped numbers for one and a half LPs to come after *Passion Play*, but I'm not sure whether we'll use this material. *Passion Play* was also recorded almost a year ago — but the music changed a lot after we taped it. So, after a few months, we decided to do the whole thing again. Thank God we're in a financial position where we are able to re-record, in spite of the high costs. That's why *Passion Play* has been a long time on the way."

It seems that the pressure was on. With the hectic touring of *Thick As A Brick* and the need to follow it up with another good album, it is very possible that there was an extent of burnout going on. It was reported in *Sounds* on 28th April 1973 under the headline, "Jethro Cancel Wembley Gigs (Doctor orders Ian to rest)"; "Jethro Tull have been forced to cancel both their Wembley concerts this weekend (April 28th and 29th). Chrysalis announced this week that Ian Anderson was suffering from nervous exhaustion and is under orders from his doctor to rest for at least two weeks. Tull have rescheduled both Wembley concerts and will now appear on Friday, June 22nd, and Saturday, June 23rd. Ticket holders for this Saturday's concert will now have their tickets honoured at the June 22nd concert, and holders for this Sunday will be able to get in on June 23rd. Ticket money will, however, be refunded if they are returned to whence they came. A spokesman from Chrysalis told *Sounds* that Tull had not taken a holiday for a year — they have been appearing continuously in countries all over the world, and in addition to live appearances they have been recording. In March the band finished their European tour, and since then they have been rehearsing their *Passion Play* stage show and recording a five-minute film which will be shown during the *Passion Play* stage show. Tull are scheduled to go to America at the beginning of May but they may miss the beginning of the tour unless Anderson has recovered. The band had hoped to take a holiday during June but they will now play Wembley instead."

Even before *A Passion Play* was premiered, Jethro Tull had more than likely reached the point at which they needed a rest. Ian Anderson was quoted in *New Musical Express* in March 1973; "In 1974 we won't be touring as much as this year. We need a rest — a rest to create a new show totally different to most other presentations nowadays… I'm working almost twenty-four hours a day in Jethro Tull, so I don't have much time to go and see other groups. I wouldn't slam David Bowie — but his music does nothing to me. Alice Cooper is an interesting fellow. I don't think he takes himself too seriously. He just creates a shocking effect — that's what it's about. David Cassidy has a good voice, but awful material. He's the typical American showbiz teenybopper, created by some smart people who probably earn a lot more than he does. I think he's a pretty lonely boy at the top. At least, the Osmond Brothers have each other to lean on, while Cassidy is on his own. He's a typical industrial product… I couldn't go on night after night just to entertain without saying a meaningful word. It's my personal philosophy that you have to put a mirror in front of yourself each night to see what you've done that day. In a way, you have to analyse yourself."

Back on the road in May, the good reviews for performances of *Thick As A Brick* kept coming. In May 1973, *The Evansville Press* reviewed Jethro Tull's performance at Roberts Stadium under the headline of "Rock Concert Packs Stadium"; "Flute-playing Ian Anderson and Jethro Tull, writhing in an abundance of rock music, captivated an overflow audience last night at Roberts Stadium. The frisbees floated free and the marijuana smoke wafted in the coloured lights as the English group, in its first US concert for 1973, exploded onto the stage and began their brutal rendition of *Thick As A Brick*. It took nearly forty-five minutes for the sounds to finally die off from the title song of one of the group's albums. As expected, Anderson — with shoulder length curly hair and almost insane facial expressions — was the star of the show, with his flute wailing to the beat of the drums and the pounding of the two guitars. Anderson, dressed spryly in a pair of tight blue tights, knee boots, a silver belt and a plaid coat, used the flute as a baton to direct the band and skimmed over the stage as the music played. There was no doubt that he was in control and the degree of professionalism of the entire show — which is sometimes lacking in other performances here — made the high-ticket price seem worthwhile. The sound system for the concert was excellent and the timing of the lights precise. This was the second time that the Jethro Tull group has been in Evansville. The group was here nearly two years ago when its popularity was limited to a smaller, underground audience. Also appearing with Jethro Tull last night were Brewer & Shipley, who would have been enjoyable to hear in concert by themselves. Their mellow harmony on such songs as 'Tarkio Road' and 'One Toke Over the Line' provided a good down-home mood which was soon shattered by the driving sound of Jethro Tull."

Such was the success and impact of *Thick As A Brick* that it must have really put the pressure on the band when it came to making their next album. In such regard, it is perhaps plausible that no matter what they did next, the project that followed *Thick As A Brick* would have inevitably been in the firing line. As it happened, it was *Passion Play*.

In June 1973, it was reported in *Melody Maker* under the title of "Crime Of Passion"; "One and a half hours of solid good music by Jethro Tull at the Empire Pool, Wembley, would have been sufficient to send home many more contented fans. Instead, an over-long over-produced marathon seriously impaired their impact — and their reputation. The *Passion Play* which constituted the first part of the concert, and is the basis of their next album, was a disappointment. And time-wasting tactical errors like the back-projection spun out proceedings to such length that final items like 'My God' and 'Locomotive Breath' became a test of endurance for those glued by duty to the hard seating of the Pool, instead of a rewarding musical experience. As a fan of Jethro Tull, I had hoped not to fall into the general clamour of critical abuse that has been heaped on them in recent months. Tull are a band who always set themselves high levels of achievement. They spend such long hours in perfecting stage presentation, great chunks of arranged music, and volumes of words, that it seems almost churlish to raise a voice of protest and criticism. I'm sure Ian Anderson feels that too. During his greetings to the large and ecstatic audience, he bowed elaborately to the VIP enclosure (in which I was seated), and said, 'How are yer? Panel of judges. You always win in the end' — Come, come Ian, let's not squabble. Any band can over-reach itself, make mistakes, err or commit acts of folly. Let it first be understood that my comments are made purely in the spirit of constructive criticism, and are no way intended as personal slights, insults or wrong-headed prejudiced, jaundiced, short-sighted, purblind, one-sided, superficial, illiberal, intolerant, warped, dogmatic hyper-criticism. Instead I come as Solomon would among the squabbling wives, and 'midst a clap of thunder and sheet lightning cry: 'Enough!' First of all it must be positively stated that the concert last Friday was a success as far as the vast majority of the audience was concerned. Long and loud were the cheers. Fans to the left and right of me were beating time with their hands, heads down and feet stomping. It was the first time they had seen Tull in well over a year, and they were determined to enjoy all that came before them."

The feature continued; "Reviewers of Tull concerts seem to spend a lot of time glancing at their watches, and I found myself checking out the time at frequent intervals. According to my Accurist (twenty-one jewels, anti-magnetic), it was 9pm when the screen came down and the dot started pulsating. But later I found my watch was fast, and after brief calculations, ascertained that it was in fact 9pm when the first bout of slow-hand clapping broke out, five minutes before the first flight of paper darts were stacked up and circling over the arena waiting for clearance. At 9pm the tone changed to a higher pitch, and quite a few people looked up at the screen to notice the dot had got larger. It occurred to me that this was one of Ian Anderson's little games with audiences, and it could have been more effective if the sequence had been shortened and if the house lights had been turned out. In a place as brightly lit and vast as the Empire Pool, attention cannot be focused on a distant grey screen for long. But it was a good time for meditation and a pause in the hurly-burly of life... But where are we — sitting on an intolerably hard seat waiting for Jethro Tull. Come on, lads, get it together for Chrissake. But lo — what was this? The dot was replaced by a frozen shot of a ballerina. Brilliantly this came to life, slowly, and gathering momentum, until the young lady leapt through a mirror. A stunning shot, and well worth the wait. By this time all the delay had been forgiven, and another brilliant stroke — Martin o' the guitar leapt on stage in a flash and puff of smoke followed by the rest of the band. Settle down chaps — it's all happening now — I thought. The

Passion Play was about to be unleashed. The music seemed fast and powerful, Ian swapping 'midst that Tullian expertise at the lighting controls, from flute-with-band to acoustic guitar-unaccompanied out front. A new innovation — Ian played soprano sax with an attachment, with considerable facility, which added a new tonal dimension to the band sound. Jeffery Hammond-Hammond, their bass player, charged around the stage in suit and panama hat, in a kind of Monty Python-ish silly walk that seemed a parody of the natural movements of a musician inspired by his music. The piece continued unabated and bearing in mind we haven't heard the album yet, seemed to take a considerable time to show any signs of cohesion. The structure had a kind of Elizabethan mode, with a plethora of changes that did not resolve into any satisfying or logical direction. The drums had to pound home each change and accent in pursuit of the main line and resulted in the group sounding like a circus band following the actions of a juggler. Hup — two, three, four! It began to occur to me that this was very poor music indeed. It was not that the complexity was daunting, simply that the musical structure was no longer a vehicle for self-expression. It was cold and unemotional. Not once during the evening did the music catch me in the pit of the stomach or cause hair to rise on the neck. Perhaps I was seeing Tull too soon after witnessing the glories of the Mahavishnu Orchestra."

Still from the same feature; "The lyrics or story of the *Passion Play* did not communicate one whit. At the end of the evening I had absolutely no idea what it was about. And I have sat and watched the Kabuki Theatre in Japan, where the actors howl and grunt in long-dead dialects, and their timeless plays of real passion shine with simplicity, that only the thickest brick could fail to understand. Part of the play was taken up with a movie, filmed in colour featuring members of the group and a ballet company. This fell flat at first, greeted with yells of 'no substitute', with which I was bound to agree, although a colleague who thought the whole show terrible, said the film was the best part, which at least shows how opinions can differ. It was beautifully photographed, but what did it mean, and what was the relevance to the play? My feeling was if I had known we were about to attend a movie show, I would have chosen to see *Soylent Green* at the Empire, Leicester Square. The film portrayed various bees and newts prancing in some kind of provincial pantomime about a rabbit who had lost his spectacles. It was actually more pointless than Frank Zappa's *2000 Motels*. Thence we returned to Ian singing endless baffling lyrics, and a singular lack of good improvisation or real melody from the band. The ballerina popped back out of the mirror and the audience cheered in the baffling way that audiences cheer when their critical faculties are numbed by misplaced loyalty. At last now the *Passion Play* was out of the way, perhaps the band could afford to relax and start blowing. And Ian came on strongly with announcements that always entertain with their dry wit. To a heckler he touched his forelock and said: 'Yes sir, right away sir, what is it you want? *Thick As A Brick*? Right!' He told the audience they were looking really well and later said it was a pleasure to be back in Blackpool. When pianist John Evan did a run for the piano, featuring a neat forward roll on the way, Ian made me laugh aloud when he said: 'It's hard to believe he does this nearly every night' — Now the real Jethro Tull was going to stand up, and at 10:15pm came the first enjoyable moment. A brilliant flute solo by Ian on *Thick As A Brick*, as full of life, invention and joy as the *Passion Play* had been drear and lifeless. Ian's playing was pure quicksilver. A unison passage with bells was sheer delight. And the band rightly received an ovation for a drop of good playing. 'I really must apologise to the fellow who said "get on with it"', said Ian, harking back to his previous put-down. It seemed a new spirit of instrumental creativity was infiltrating the group and then came the next highlight of Barriemore Barlow's exciting and entertaining drum solo. It followed a fairly predictable pattern in terms of construction, but he played a beautifully fast snare drum and the double bass drums thundered in the grand manner. The by-play with a choke cymbal at the front of the stage was funny, and the final freak out with every member of the group hitting cymbals and dancing in a strobe light was a knock out. Barrie finished his solo wreathed in smoke and next the band launched into 'Aqualung', notable for more excellent fills by Barrie, swirling round the kit and ending with a crack on the snare."

The feature concluded; "The band left the stage, to return for an encore, Ian introducing Martin as 'balding and diminutive', cueing him in for his guitar solo, not to mention a piano feature by the strangely strange John Evan. In his white suit and red tie he presents the appearance of a clumsy beach deckchair attendant, and plays curiously cold piano in a kind of perverse, classically-trained style, where the occasional introduction of "blue" or jazz notes sound almost quaint. There was more stage "business", with the famed telephone, which refused to ring, until the band had left the stage for good, when it rang twice and was symbolically unanswered. It was the signal for more yells and applause — but the house lights came up and the show was over. After the show I felt uncomfortable and filled with inner torment. The combination of hard planks and hot dogs can play havoc with the nether extremities. Also the music could take some of the blame. Arguments will rage long and loud over the merits of the show, but my final conclusion was that it should have been sub-edited and presented in a proper theatre for maximum effect and greater satisfaction. Before Jethro Tull jump through their next mirror — they should stop, and take a long cool look at themselves. The answer, my friends, is blowing in the flute."

I have quoted the majority of the article from June 1973's

Melody Maker and the reason for doing so is that there are a lot of key points made by the reviewer that are tremendously relevant to *Thick As A Brick*. First of all, the fact that Jethro Tull had some big shoes to fill after *Thick As A Brick* very much comes across in the review and it could be considered that *A Passion Play* was, at least somewhat doomed based on that very fact alone. However, as the review alluded to, it may have been the case that *A Passion Play* demanded more from an audience; it required them to engage with complex music featuring minimal use of immediately memorable melodies, all of which were presented through the expansive lens of multimedia.

By any stretch of the imagination, it could be argued that *A Passion Play* was a risk in its own right, regardless of the fact that (*Living In The Past* accounted for) it was the album that happened to follow *Thick As A Brick*. From the review, there is also a sense that the audience were hungry for some music that they actually recognised, hence perhaps, the "get on with it" comment. I do actually think it is genuinely sad that as ever, Jethro Tull probably put their all into *A Passion Play* and yet were so explicitly heckled during their performance of the piece. That can't have been a nice feeling. It comes across that at the time of working on *A Passion Play*, Jethro Tull had faith in the project. It was reported in *Sounds* in September 1973; "The band's manager, Terry Ellis, said in last week's statement that the group considered *A Passion Play* to be the best thing they had done yet, and added that 'the abuse heaped upon the show by the critics has been bitterly disappointing to the group', who have therefore found it 'increasingly difficult to go on stage without worrying whether the audience are enjoying what they are playing'."

The heckling must have felt like particularly fickle behaviour from the audience considering the positive response to *Thick As A Brick*. After *A Passion Play*, the fact that *Thick*

As A Brick was described as "the first enjoyable moment", well, that says it all really doesn't it; it comes across that the audience just about tolerated *A Passion Play* whilst anxiously waiting for some Jethro Tull material that they were more familiar with.

However, *Thick As A Brick* would have also have taken some getting used to as a long song when that was first toured in 1972. Still though, *Thick As A Brick* was presented on stage with a lot of humour and *A Passion Play* was perhaps also risky in terms of how thematically, it was in a much darker vein. Ian Anderson was quoted in *Guitar World* in September 1999; "*Stand Up* is sort of an "up" album, followed by *Benefit*, which is sort of a "down", dark album. Likewise with *Thick As A Brick* and *A Passion Play*. When you're making an album every year, I think you do tend to oscillate between having feelings of cheerfulness followed by feelings of introspection."

Perhaps though, the humour wasn't completely absent from *A Passion Play* when it was performed live. Ian Anderson was quoted in *New Musical Express* in March 1973; "It's (*A Passion Play*) a piece I wrote about life and death. But it's not limited to that subject. *Thick As A Brick* isn't the same to me as when I wrote it. People can put into it what they want. As long as they like the music."

In the same feature, the journalist stipulated, "Anderson denies that *Brick* is a religious piece, but agrees that it's possibly about a human being searching for a higher meaning in life. It sometimes appears that Jethro has a schizoid identity — serious on records, but the essence of humour on stage."

To which Anderson replied; "I can't see the paradox. Our stage act is both funny and serious. Serious because life is serious, and funny because the audience would be bored if they got more than two hours of seriousness."

The *Melody Maker* review of *A Passion Play* wasn't exceptional. The same performance was reviewed in *New Musical Express* in June 1973 under the headline of "Jethro

Tull, Where's The Passion Now?" and predominantly, the same complaints were expressed; "'God, they've changed a helluva lot,' I thought, sitting in the Wembley Stadium. But Ian Anderson was never content to stand still. Whatever comes out of his bag tonight there'd be no denying Tull's importance to rock music. They were the first underground outfit to make it, also playing an important part in building an image for Island Records. Right down to the final detail of their album sleeves Tull had been innovators. *Passion Play* started with a circle of white light projected onto a screen suspended behind the stage. As the circle grew larger, so did the volume of heartbeat which preceded the light. Strange eerie noises came out of the speakers, including what sounded like an Italian opera singer taking his morning gargle, and the circle finally enveloped the screen — at which point a lifeless ballerina appeared in its place. After a few minutes the ballerina was given motion and did a little dance before disappearing through a mirror. Enter one Jethro Tull amid smoke bombs and flashing lights. Anderson followed brandishing flute and the show had begun. What followed is difficult to describe because it's difficult to remember. Not one piece of music from *Passion Play* stayed in my head longer than a second after it was played. And this is the real criticism. It was just too much to take in one hearing, especially when one's concentration on the music was interrupted by another film sequence. This time there were two ballerinas and a whole lot of *Alice In Wonderland* animals. The story, I think, had something vaguely to do with the hare losing his spectacles. During the piece Anderson played flute, soprano sax, a sopranino and an acoustic guitar. He also whistled and sang. Much as I admire Tull for not repeating old material — and as much as I can marvel at the band's professionalism in delivering *Passion Play* — it didn't make much sense on one hearing. However, the audience, apart from one young man in front of me, who described the piece as 'rubbish', received

Passion Play warmly."

The feature continued; "*Thick As A Brick* — the middle bit starting with the organ riff — made much more sense and showed Tull can reproduce their live sound onstage with no trouble. Yes, this was the madcap Anderson, dressed in tartan frock coat and knee-high boots. Okay — so his flute technique wouldn't stand up alongside Roland Kirk or Herbie Mann, but Anderson is communicating to a lot of people. He talks and barks like a dog into the flute. There's a hint of Bach and just a slice of 'Bourée'. Hammond-Hammond attempted that fabulous flowing bass line which Glenn Cornick played on the original but it didn't quite come off. Anderson cavorted like a demented leper, conducting the band with his foot, as *Thick As A Brick* came to its conclusion the audience sang along with him. The next song, which began with a brief acoustic passage before developing into some real thunder and lightning, was presumably a new number not included on *Passion Play*. Martin Barre, who had previously hung back in the shadows of his speaker cabinets, started to move. He jumped around as if trying to deaden a fire. Barlow is left onstage for a drum solo. It was okay but, like the smoke bombs that followed, unnecessary. Jethro Tull don't need to resort to such clichés of modern day rock. No introduction is needed as the band break loose into 'Aqualung'. All of a sudden — what timing — the band stopped playing and crept over to a white telephone which has sat on stage all night. They cringed away from it and continue 'Aqualung'. But haven't we seen this before, Ian? The encore of 'Wind-Up'/'Locomotive Breath' is the best piece of the night. Evan started to loon, almost a parody of Anderson himself, and only just short of him in the eccentricity stakes. Anderson's voice is crystal clear and his spitting onto the stage when he comes to the line about school teachers grooming him for success conveys the bitterness which is such an essential part of his writing. Evan played beautiful piano and is clearly

Tull's finest musician. Barre's solo was distorted and self-indulgent. Tull left the stage and the telephone started ringing again. Anderson returned to answer it and, after a few seconds' conversation, told the audience the call was for them. Truly a Tullian touch. So this was Tull's first British gig in over a year. For me, *Passion Play* failed musically and visually. What was that film about — other than just a surreal trick of its maker? Maybe the film and music will make more sense with the album's release. It would be nice to see Anderson writing an album of songs, rather than of extended pieces — in rock they rarely work. The stage patter was there but didn't seem so funny as it was a couple of years ago and Anderson's movements were a mite contrived. But it was good to see these five eccentrics back on home territory — personally though, I can't help but long for the days when Anderson flirted with Go-Go dancers and the thought of Jethro Tull getting into mixed media seemed laughable. Still, Ian Anderson couldn't really stand still."

The reviewer made a good point about the fact that due to *A Passion Play* not having been released as an album prior to the live performance, this could have been prohibitive to audience engagement. This is one logistical problem that *Thick As A Brick* couldn't have fallen by as it was released before the vast majority of live performances of it took place. Whether it was based on the success of *Thick As A Brick* in America or purely a matter of taste, *Passion Play* was seemingly met with a better reception in there.

In June 1973, *RPM* reviewed a performance that took place in Toronto on 30th May; "Once again, Toronto had the pleasure of being host to one of Britain's finest super groups. The pleasure was in the likeness of The Jethro Tull Show, a complete audio/visual sensorium that comes this way but once a year. The opening act happened to be Brewer & Shipley, although by the time the concert was over it was hard to remember that they were really there. They did, however, get a roar of approval on their famous 'One Toke Over The Line'. Jethro Tull (an English agriculturalist/inventor who lived in the 1700s) comes in the form of five concert musicians, each member a star in his own right. Band leader and heartbeat of the quintet is singer, flautist, writer, dancer and genius extraordinaire, Ian Anderson, along with lead guitarist, Martin "Lancelot" Barre, who comprise the only two originals of the band. John Evan is Tull's keyboard man, applying his expertise to piano, organ and the new field of synthesised sound, all at a time when keyboards are becoming an integral part of many bands, especially British. Jeffery Hammond-Hammond plays an amazing bass guitar and Barriemore Barlow makes up his fifth in the percussion department. This five-man line-up combines all its individual energies into one explosive power unit. With hundreds of watts of electricity hissing through the suspended speakers, the crowd was ready to be freaked out. After a hypnotic opening to the *Passion Play*, a fantasy movie took those who wanted to go, into the fourth dimension. Unfortunately though, there were technical difficulties in the Toronto show and the second movie had to be canned, so some of the effect of the *Play* was lost. But in Ottawa (where general admission tickets caused nothing but aggravation for the young crowd), the show was complete and the audience received Tull's message more clearly: we're all part of the *Passion Play*. The *Passion Play* actually dominated the show as this is Jethro Tull's newest work following their previous composition, *Thick As A Brick*. *Passion* complements *Thick* as the second concept album to come from the group and supplies us with the answers to the queries we had about how Tull would top *Thick*. Both sides of the album were performed and at this point, avid fans are impatiently awaiting the release of the *Passion Play* album (on the Chrysalis label). The show supplied its own stage and technical apparatus including suspended lights that bathed the stage in colour and accented the band's colourful costumes.

Sound equipment was excellent, simultaneously creating ear shattering but crystal clear sounds. Barre, playing his pet Gibson Les Paul, cranked out a powerful sound with no fancy attachments, while Barlow's three-part drum solo was really unbeatable. He moved at super speed and pulled off a set that combined hard work and guts. Every member did his respective solo with great finesse. For their second number, an unexpected excerpt from *Thick As A Brick* led the way for a medley of other Tull favourites. The audience was enthralled but dismayed to find that 'Aqualung' would bring the show to an end. However, the band came back, and although the encore was pre-planned it probably wouldn't have been effective otherwise. Tull had by this time wound everyone up to such a state that 'Locomotive Breath', which incorporated into 'Wind-Up', blew the audience out totally. But then, Ian Anderson regretfully strummed his last chords and said goodbye, amid little applause and much sighing."

Notably the reviewer got a vital fact wrong in terms of how Martin Barre joined Jethro Tull after the band's first album, *This Was*. This is suggestive that the reviewer might not have been the biggest fan of Jethro Tull and it is interesting to consider how that may have informed how he assessed the performance. Still though, the technical complexity of performing *A Passion Play* on stage must have come with an element of risk as in, where do you go with it if there's a technical problem with the very content that has been designed to be a key part of the performance? This is possibly symptomatic of how *Passion Play* was perhaps overtly ambitious and maybe, just maybe, the pressure of having to follow up *Thick As A Brick* may have informed that, at least to a point.

In September 1973, *Record World* reported on Jethro Tull's performance; "New York — Madison Square Garden, jam packed with adoring fans, was treated once again this week to the brilliant theatrics and music of Jethro Tull. This New York appearance was contained in the third and last section of their American tour. The group recently announced an indefinite retirement from concert appearances, which according to their manager Terry Ellis, was partly due to the bad reviews on their show, *A Passion Play*. If true, there was absolutely nothing to confirm that in the reaction of the New York audience. *A Passion Play* is beyond the shadow of the doubt the group's best work to date. Ian Anderson has added abstract ballet movements to his own repertoire of antics and dance which he does throughout the rest of the show. And, one might add, with excellent results. The performance takes on an air of sophistication and grace with the addition of the visual medium created by the film and light show. Also performed were parts of last year's success, *Thick As A Brick* (minus the top hat and hare's costume). And previous to the fantastic and well-deserved encore, was the even earlier, 'Aqualung', which had the audience on their feet from the start."

After the release of *Living In The Past*, a compilation album of the group's songs, *A Passion Play* followed *Thick As A Brick* as Jethro Tull's next studio album. Whilst technically, musically and creatively it is a worthwhile piece in its own right, in some ways, it would have been bound to struggle, at least to a point, as the album that happened to follow *Thick As A Brick*. Whilst the reviews of the live performances of *A Passion Play* received a mixed reception, the album itself was still met with generally positive acclaim. *Billboard* reviewed *A Passion Play* in July 1973; "One of this summer's more widespread pastimes for record buyers will undoubtedly be to try deciphering what the Tull passion play is all about. The LP gives every sign of becoming the most mysteriously worded gold album since *Sgt. Pepper*. Format of the album is a single disc with no separate cuts. But basically the sound is a little changed from *Thick As A Brick* and the songs can be easily lifted from the clever instrumental connecting sections. There's also a spoken fairy tale with musical fills that work a lot better than the usual such efforts. Double fold jacket features more mystery — a dead ballerina and a fold in program showing the group as the cast of a provincial British theatre. The group are currently touring and their entire show is the stage version of this album."

It's great to see that *A Passion Play* wasn't completely panned. People who liked it, really liked it. It was true then and it's probably still the case now. But the thing about *A Passion Play* being panned to an extent that it caused the group to commit themselves to indefinite retirement from live shows, well that was simply a rumour that got out of hand. It was reported in *Down Beat* in March 1976; "Tull's most ambitious project to date has been *Passion Play*, an extended composition which Ian integrated into live performances with a film that he wrote and directed. But despite healthy sales and sold-out concerts, both the tour and the album were panned by a majority of critics as being contrived and confusing. Rumour spread that the sensitive Anderson was disbanding the group and had cancelled the remainder of their tour."

Ian Anderson was keen to shed some light on the matter. When asked to address the rumour that he had cancelled the second half of the tour because of the critical reaction to *A Passion Play*, he was quoted in *Down Beat* in March 1976; "No, that's not true. The gentleman who works for the *New York Times* overheard that in a bar. I don't mean to be facetious. I personally researched the reasons for the appearance of that rumour. He overheard gossip that, due to the negative reaction to the stage performance of Jethro Tull's new album, Jethro Tull had broken a tour halfway through and fled back to England — with all the implications of returned tickets and promoters' money out of pocket. I won't say it was a lie, because I'm sure that the gentleman was just unprofessionally incorrect. He made no attempt to check it out with agency management, record company, or anyone else officially representing us. Jethro Tull have never cancelled our part of a tour, let alone half a tour... The only dates that have been cancelled have been when I'm ill. If one of the other guys is ill, I think we'd still probably make it on stage one way or another. But if it's me, it's unfair to go out to the audience and play without me. In fact, the *Passion Play* tour was as good as any other tour and better than the ones before. Seen retrospectively, it was probably more theatrically oriented a performance than what we're doing now, which is trying to get away from any tag."

Historically, Ian Anderson has perhaps put across mixed feelings about *A Passion Play*. On the one hand, he stands by the music he puts out there but is sometimes equally candid about what, with hindsight, he might have preferred to do differently. He was quoted of *A Passion Play* in *Guitar World* in September 1999; "With *Thick As A Brick*, we took the idea of the concept album and had some fun with it. Now we thought it was time to do something a bit more serious and make an album that wasn't a spoof and wasn't meant to be fun. We ended up going to record the album at Château d'Hérouville, in France, where people like Elton John and Cat Stevens had made records. Our original plan was not to make another concept album. The project started off as a collection of songs, including two that ended up going onto our next album, *War Child*: 'Bungle In The Jungle' and 'Skating Away On The Thin Ice Of The New Day'. A certain theme had begun to emerge among the songs — how the animal life is mirrored in the dog-eat-dog world of human society — but the project just wasn't working out. So we abandoned what we'd done and went back to England. Back home, I ended up almost completely rewriting all of the material we'd worked on in France, and this became *A Passion Play*. The concept grew out of wondering about the possible choices one might face after death. It was a dark album, just as we had intended, but it was missing some of the fun and variety that was in *Thick As A Brick*. The critics savaged us. Chris Welch of *Melody Maker* and Bob Hilburn at the *Los Angeles Times* wrote really negative reviews that everybody jumped on and reprinted or based their own reviews on. It really snowballed from there, and we got a fair old pasting for that one. On reflection, the album is a bit one-dimensional. It's certainly not one of my favourites, although it has become something of a cult album with some fans." (Material — that survived — from the abandoned sessions was put together on the double CD released in 1993, *Nightcap*).

Anderson was quoted in *Down Beat* in March 1976; "All I ever wanted to be was just a professional musician. It was never important to be a success, which after all, is a very relative thing. Success is only what you're doing today compared to what you were doing yesterday. I also get a lot of tears and personal heartbreak out of it as well. You take a week of seven concerts and three of them are going to be bad, at least in my mind. I'm going to come off the stage near to tears for one reason or another. There's many times I get into the studio and it just doesn't happen. Something I believed would be a good result just fails to materialise. I have to throw away the tape."

In the same feature, the interviewer threw quite the brutal question to Anderson; "Have you ever wished you'd thrown away *Passion Play*, considering some of the negative response it received?" To which Anderson replied; "No. Obviously, if it didn't satisfy my musical intent, *Passion Play* would never have been released."

Arguably an inquisitive and very intelligent individual, Ian Anderson was quoted in *Down Beat* in March 1976 as he directed to the interviewer; "I think you possibly feel that the group is stale, that I'm necessarily becoming bored with it and thinking about some other possibilities. That *Passion Play* or *Thick As A Brick* has somehow been a blundering attempt to get away from the real creative ability that might have shown in our earlier music." To which the interviewer replied, "No, I'm sorry if that's come across. I think *Thick As A Brick* was a fantastic, really surprising album for the group to do. I'm not that familiar with *Passion Play*. I've heard it once and haven't really formed any strong opinion about it."

Anderson continued, "Well, between those two records there was actually a double album recorded of new material. It wasn't released and the tapes were burned, apart from one which emerged on *War Child* as the sole survivor of a year trying to do something different than *Thick As A Brick*. That double album consisted of individual songs ranging from a minute and a half long to eight or ten minutes. They were all related, in a sense. We recorded three sides of that double album, and I, rather than the group, felt dissatisfied with what seemed to me to be a conscious attempt to be doing something different than *Thick As A Brick*, without really having any reason for doing so. Because what I really wanted to do was something like *Thick As A Brick*, only better and more intense. So finally we went back and recorded *Passion Play*, which was written and recorded in a very short space of time, but under great emotional intensity. I can understand that it would be difficult for other people to relate to it, because they would just say, 'What's all this going on? I don't need this. Let me get back to my Cream's Greatest Hits' — one can expect that things like that will happen, but I've got to be prepared to take risks musically to satisfy myself and the other members of the group first, before I start thinking about satisfying an audience."

A lot of the appeal of Jethro Tull's music is in the fact that, according to Ian Anderson, it was never created to pander to any specific commercial whims or trends. He was quoted in *Guitar World* in September 1999; "We've never been a hit band that appeared regularly on television or in the pop charts. We don't have record sales that are driven by singles, by radio play, by MTV videos or whatever. In fact, most of our fifty million or so album sales have occurred in dribs and drabs over a long period of time and in a lot of countries all over the world. This kind of operation isn't based on how good or bad your latest record or tour might be but on the commitment and loyalty of the fans. Because they will forgive you a lot."

In the same feature, the interviewer added, "Jethro Tull has needed a pardon on more than one occasion. Back in 1973, for example, when the group released *A Passion Play*, a critically reviled concept album that was excessive even by prog rock standards. But along with the bad, much good has come too. *Aqualung* and *Thick As A Brick* today rank among the best-selling and most influential albums of the seventies, while *Stand Up* (1969), *War Child* (1974) and *Songs From The Wood* (1977) remain strong favourites among even casual fans of the group."

Even as a compilation album released not long after *Thick As A Brick*, *Living In The Past* was reviewed predominantly in comparison to the former. Again, it demonstrates the extent to which many people perhaps regarded *Thick As A Brick* as being the definitive Jethro Tull sound by that point.

In February 1973, *Rolling Stone* reviewed *Living In The Past*. It's interesting to see the comparisons that were made between the band responsible for *Thick As A Brick* and the earlier line-up of Jethro Tull, as was featured on *Living In The Past;* "Who/what is (a) Jethro Tull? Like a pollster in an asylum, you'll probably get every conceivable answer, since Ian Anderson has yet to put the same cast of characters on two successive LPs. Although *Living In The Past* is no more than a hodgepodge of old English-only singles, EP sides, album tracks and a couple of live cuts, it answers the question fairly well, effectively telling the story of a band that's had as many faces and sounds as Medusa had snakes. When Anderson, Mick Abrahams, Glenn Cornick and Clive Bunker formed Jethro Tull in 1968, they were an extremely crude outfit that occasionally came on like an amplified Salvation Army band. *This Was*, though an uneven first release, was lit by frequent flashes of brilliance from Abrahams' guitar and Bunker's drums. 'A Song For Jeffrey' and 'Love Story' represent that segment of Tull's past here, and leave little doubt why the band was once the darling of the American underground. But though their combination of earthy, Muddy Waters-ish street blues and psychedelic pyrotechnics was the order of the day in the immediate post-Cream period, it didn't sit well with purist Abrahams; when the issue of musical direction finally came to a head, he was soon on his way to forming Blodwyn Pig. The addition of Martin Lancelot Barre plunged Tull deep into heavy rockdom, but hardly into the pit of directionless plodding inhabited by wah-wah wonders who shall remain nameless. Tull's songs became logically constructed, the playing was remarkably tight, and the lyrics were far more than words between jam sessions. They may have relied heavily on repeated riffs, but they were intricate, groin-rattling licks. The magnificent *Stand Up* was recorded with this Tull alignment, as were numbers like 'Driving Song' and 'Singing All Day'. The latter showcased the band's mellow side — not the contrived introspectiveness of an 'I'm Your Captain', but a touching expression of life's inner joys and sorrows. But Anderson, ever the perfectionist, felt the band's alignment was too restrictive, preventing the flute and the guitar from exploring their outermost capabilities. So enter an old school chum, John Evan, for the *Benefit* sessions, which worked out so well that Tull number three soon became a reality with his permanent addition. His rollicking piano and calliope-like organ fit in perfectly, allowing the band far more experimentation and versatility than ever before. Tull switched from soft, swaying ballads like 'Just Trying To Be' and 'Wond'ring Again' to hard rockers like 'Teacher' with an ease that defines imagination."

The *Rolling Stone* review continued; "*Living In The*

Past's two live cuts further demonstrate Tull number three's complexity and power. Evan showcases his virtuosity on 'By Kind Permission Of', weaving in and out of various classical, blues and neo-jazz themes, paced ever so gently by Anderson's haunting flute. 'Dharma For One' may be slightly restructured ('...which means it's a wee bit louder'), but it rocks out even more raucously than the original. Frequently, Anderson and Barre fly off on separate, simultaneous sorties, using the thumping, pounding backing of their fellows as an explosive launching pad. Was it any wonder why these guys were voted most promising new talent in a 1970 musician's poll? But for all its potential, the band was in deep trouble, a schism rapidly forming within its ranks. Bunker and Cornick wanted to stick with solid riff-rock, while Evan and Anderson were dead set on a lighter, airier, less substantial sound. Cornick was the first to go, being replaced by another Anderson crony, Jeffrey Hammond-Hammond. The change affected Tull's sound drastically; *Aqualung*'s release saw the band's spirit and drive replaced by plodding efficiency and ho-hum competence. For many the album was a bitter disappointment: though it was Tull's first gold LP, it was frequently filed away after only a few listenings. Bunker's replacement by Barriemore Barlow completed Anderson's coup — he had handpicked his own group of sidemen, proficient but hardly a threat to his control over material. Their output (an EP and the epic *Thick As A Brick*) has been little more than amplified folkiedom and moralistic pop-rock — a pale shadow of their early work. Where once was a powerful English rock band appeared a pseudo-Socratic troubadour with an eclectic band of thespian yes-men. While it's an admittedly personal preference, I'd much rather have the dynamic 'Back To The Family' than a piece of heinous shlock like 'Up The Pool' or a work as emotionally vapid as *Thick As A Brick*. In his haste to avoid tuneless heaviness, Anderson seems to have forgotten that a little amplified talent was never a crime. Tull once had the talent; this new bunch I'm not so sure about. It sure hurts to lose an old friend, and if Tull doesn't get back on the right track soon. there's gonna be a lot more disappointed folks living in the past."

An interesting review and one that was clearly peppered with strong opinions. Where the reviewer considered *Thick As A Brick* to be "emotionally vapid" then well, where do you really go from there? Personally I would suggest that when you consider the humorous elements of *Thick As A Brick*, it is worth noting that humour isn't synonymous with an absence of emotional intelligence. Still though, that's just one review; just one person's opinion. But it does raise an interesting question in terms of "I wonder if some people were perhaps a bit quick to negate the merits of *Thick As A Brick* purely on the basis that they equated its jovial nature (at least on the surface of things) as being a bit superficial?"

Anderson was quoted in *Guitar World* in September 1999; "*Living In The Past* was simply done to compile our singles onto one album. We had released a number of singles up to this point — 'Living In The Past,' 'Teacher,' 'The Witch's Promise' — and they were all contrived for a very specific reason. Once we started touring in the USA, we used the singles as a way of keeping the water warm back in the UK, so as not to risk losing our audience there. The singles were never songs that were left over from album sessions; in fact, they were completely divorced from the album recording process. 'Living In The Past' was written and recorded during our first US tour, in '69. It was written in Boston, the backing track was recorded in New York and the vocals in San Francisco or Los Angeles. It was mixed and the tape sent back to the UK, where it was released while we were still on tour."

Thick As A Brick signified a strong stylistic change for Jethro Tull. Whilst their album prior to it, *Aqualung*, certainly hinted at what was to become possible in *Thick As A Brick*, the band's music prior to that was arguably more typical of what other bands were doing at the time. For instance, the structure and lyrical content of *Thick As A Brick* is somewhat beyond classification, being so wide ranging, whereas Jethro Tull's earlier work was, for want of better term perhaps, more on trend with other popular music at the time. In the late sixties, it was common for rock music to address contemporary issues. One such issue was the Vietnam War and the single released in 1969, 'Living In The Past', certainly features lyrics that could be associated with such subject matter. Still though, from their very first album, Jethro Tull lyrics have always dealt with, to some extent, social critique, examples being in 'Sossity; You're A Woman' from *Benefit* in 1970 and certainly most tracks on *Aqualung*.

On 'My Sunday Feeling', the first song on Jethro Tull's debut album *This Was*, the use of call and response verse form is present (whereby the singer sings a line, then a response follows it; the pattern is very predictable). Whilst the opening section of *Thick As A Brick* could be regarded as having an element of call and response ("really don't mind..." followed by a flute response to this line of lyric) overall, the blues influence has all but vanished.

Equally, regarding flute technique, Anderson often sang through the flute on Jethro Tull's blues-influenced songs on the band's earlier albums. Such technique lends itself to giving the instrument more of a thick, almost guitar-like timbre. On *Thick As A Brick* though, Anderson plays the flute in a way that creates a clearer timbre. Expansion of instrumental repertoire was very much a key ingredient that made *Thick As A Brick* possible. On *This Was*, Anderson contributed vocals, flute, harmonica and piano.

By the time of *Stand Up*, Anderson added acoustic guitar, balalaika, bouzouki, and mandolin to his recording repertoire. *New Musical Express* explained of Anderson's musicianship in

July 1972; "First off, he taught himself flute, albeit borrowing a lot from Roland Kirk — Kirk's 'Serenade To A Cuckoo' is on the *This Was* LP and was the first flute piece Anderson picked up — but, since then, Ian's own feel and inventiveness have made him a power on the instrument in his own right. Each successive album has seen Anderson adding new instruments to his playing credits. Up to date, his abilities now stretch to flute, acoustic/electric guitar, organ, harmonica, mandolin, balalaika, violin, sax and trumpet." Such expansion of instrumental repertoire continued after *Thick As A Brick*. For example, on *Songs From The Wood*, Martin Barre played the lute and Barriemore Barlow played marimba, glockenspiel, bells, tabor and nakers.

Anderson was quoted in *Ultimate Classic Rock* in March 2017; "*Stand Up* was the first album that wasn't just pastiche twelve bar blues, so it's always going to be close to my heart. *Aqualung* was a singer-songwriter album, and it marked a difference for me because I was in the studio with an acoustic guitar, performing songs on which the other band members would join in. *Thick As A Brick* was a landmark, then we jump ahead to *Songs From The Wood*, being more of a folk-rock album; then *Crest Of A Knave*, which did really well in America but not so well elsewhere. You can toss *Heavy Horses* into that, and I'd guess most people would agree with four or five of my choices."

As much as *Thick As A Brick* solidified Jethro Tull's reputation as a band who were certainly capable of delivering long songs that could achieve both musical acclaim and commercial success, it didn't determine they would stick to such approach in their later albums.

As was reported in *Down Beat* in March 1976; "On *War Child*, Anderson returned to the conventional song lengths; another single, the bouncy 'Bungle In The Jungle', soared to the top of the charts last year. *Minstrel In The Gallery* appeared next, seemingly something of a compromise between the commercial and the more experimental sides to Anderson's ambitions. Along with shorter, catchy songs like 'Cold Wind To Valhalla', the album includes 'Baker Street Muse', a typically cryptic but somewhat bitter saga of sexual and musical tribulation."

Anderson was quoted in the same feature; "My big private goal, my actual composing ideal, is just to write a thirty second piece that just totally evokes something. Everyone will say, 'I know just what he means' — that's my sort of private thing. I don't get caught up in that too often, just once in a while." (By the time of this interview, Anderson had certainly got close to that goal; the track, 'Grace' on the 1975 album, *Minstrel In The Gallery*, is forty seconds long).

Anderson was quoted in *Ultimate Classic Rock* in April 2012; "If someone had suggested that I might release a prog-concept album in the year 2012, I would have thought him seriously, dangerously even, off his trolley. But that is precisely what happened."

In 2012, he announced plans for the album, *Thick As A Brick 2: Whatever Happened To Gerald Bostock?* According to the Jethro Tull website, the album was planned as "a full-length progressive rock "concept" album worthy of its predecessor. Boy to man and beyond, it looks at what might have befallen the child poet Gerald Bostock in later life. Or, perhaps, any of us."

Thick As A Brick 2 was released in April 2012, albeit as an Ian Anderson album. It describes five different potential scenarios for Gerald Bostock's life, where he potentially becomes a greedy investment banker, a homeless homosexual man, a soldier in the Afghan War, a sanctimonious evangelist preacher, and a most ordinary man who runs a corner store and is married and childless. *Thick As A Brick 2* lists seventeen separate songs merged into thirteen distinct tracks (some are labelled as medleys). They do though, flow together much like a single song.

To do a sequel to *Thick As A Brick* was a risky idea. Any kind of follow up to the original would have had big shoes to fill and essentially, sequels can often be met with scepticism owing to the very nature of them. That said, by 2012, Ian Anderson and indeed Jethro Tull had largely been out of the public eye for a number of decades, in which case, why not revisit one of their most successful albums and draw inspiration from their heyday.

Regardless of how anyone feels about sequels and whether or not they are a good idea, *Thick As A Brick* is one of those albums that needs to be heard to be believed, appreciated and assessed. Objectively, all I'll say on the matter is draw your own conclusions. *Thick As A Brick 2* is certainly not a threat to the legacy of the original 1972 album and it does offer a lot of points of interest, regardless of how it may or may not compare overall.

In terms of its content, *Thick As A Brick 2* faithfully recreates the musical variety and energy of the original album, without being a complete reprise of it. There is a good balance of old and new ideas and the lyrical satire certainly isn't absent. Whilst the original *Thick As A Brick* was an expression of cynicism well beyond Gerald's years, Anderson's lyrical approach is possibly more literal in its narrative on *Thick As A Brick 2*. Throughout the album, ideas regarding what could have happened to Gerald since 1972 are explored. As ever, Anderson's penchant for tongue in cheek wordplay and social satire are present.

Billboard reviewed *Thick As A Brick 2* in April 2012; "Jethro Tull's audaciously ambitious 1972 concept album, *Thick As A Brick*, made prog rock history. For the album's 40th anniversary, frontman, Ian Anderson — sans Tull — has crafted a sequel that's just as ambitious as its predecessor. Like the original, *Thick As A Brick 2* comprises of one continuous, album length suite with a linear lyrical narrative but multiple shifts in feel. Wisely, Anderson eschewed overt musical modernisation in favour of a style that's more in keeping with the folk/rock/classical amalgam of Tull's '72 prog milestone. Anderson's melodic motifs are constantly compelling, and his trademark sardonic wit remains sharp as he examines the possible paths taken by Gerald Bostock (the fictional child around whom the original album's concept revolved), who would now be forty-eight years old. Trying to follow in the footsteps of such a classic rock staple could easily have been disastrous, but Anderson triumphs against the odds. Even without his Tull mates, he convincingly picks up where he left off four decades earlier, proving that there are still vital sonic statements to be made within the old-school prog rock realm."

Although *Thick As A Brick 2* is labelled as an Ian Anderson album and not a Jethro Tull one, it very much has the qualities of a Jethro Tull album in the interplay between virtuoso musicians. A rose by any other name and all that. When asked to address the fact that *Thick As A Brick 2* was credited to him as a solo artist when in fact, he was the only constant member of Jethro Tull anyway, Anderson was quoted in *Rolling Stone* in April 2012; "I can follow the argument. Jethro Tull has been a bit of a revolving door for a lot of musicians over the years. There's been, by my reckoning, about twenty-two or twenty-three members of Jethro Tull, if we count a member as someone who's either performed on a number of tours or performed as a member of the band on at least one album. And I quite like the idea of this sort of extended family over a period of time that, to me, are all folks that have all imparted something very positive to the band and who've at some point helped shape the music. But by the same token, the music is virtually all written by me and the lyrics are one hundred percent written by me. In a way, I do feel a sense of ownership that nobody else can really feel.

I felt that it was better to have this (*Thick As A Brick 2*) be, at least in part, under my own name since it's not likely to meet with a great deal of commercial success anyway. I suppose an obvious comparison would be to Roger Waters going out and saying 'Hey, I'm the guy who wrote *The Wall*. It's my baby and I've got every right to go out there and perform it with whoever I choose' — I don't think anyone could argue against that. In some rather parallel way, I suppose that's the position for me — albeit I wouldn't be going out and doing *Thick As A Brick* this year if I didn't have what I thought was an honourable sequel to that."

As with the original *Thick As A Brick*, many musical passages in *Thick As A Brick 2* are self-contained, and there is isn't a sense of there being one overriding melodic idea across the album. It's not trying to be the original *Thick As A Brick* but characteristically, it is a viable medium through which Gerald Bostock's coming of age can be explored. A lot of the charm of *Thick As A Brick 2* is in how it deals with the idea of all the different paths that a person could potentially take in life.

Whilst the album is centred around the character of Gerald Bostock, the general idea of life's paths being so diverse in their possibilities was probably at least inspired by something autobiographical and philosophical. Anderson was quoted in *Rolling Stone* in April 2012; "When I was in my teenage years, I went to sign up as a cadet entrant to the police force but was at the very last moment rejected, just as I was about to sign my name on the dotted line. I won't get into why that happened, but it was a moment where it could've been predetermined then that I was off to become a policeman. I certainly was very serious about it at the time. I also was quite serious about becoming a journalist, and so I tried to enrol as an office boy/gofer in the local newspaper. They didn't want me either, so that didn't happen. I was quite keen on silviculture, the growing of trees, and that was something I gave a lot of thought to. Maybe I could've gone in that direction. But it just so happened that while I was trying to make up my mind, I enrolled in art school and there I began to develop my interest in music, parallel with my interest in the visual arts. I also worked in the lowly stages selling magazines and newspapers in a shop. I kind of like the idea of living a rather ordinary life as a shopkeeper, and I examine that possibility as one of the outcomes of the young Gerald Bostock growing older."

Prog reviewed *Thick As A Brick 2* in April 2012; "Now, Anderson could have easily been a victim of his own success with this project, constrained by expectations which will always be associated with *Thick As A Brick*. He could have simply fallen into the trap of making this sound too much like the original record, or conversely removing it so far that he'd have been accused of cashing in on the cachet of that iconic record. But he has avoided both of these dilemmas. Instead, he has allowed himself a considerable musical and lyrical freedom, while also remaining true to the spirit of 1972. The story itself gave a huge opportunity for imagination and plotline creativity, because it isn't tied to anything in the past. This is Anderson's interpretation of the possible ways Bostock's life could have unfolded. And he's also used the character as an allegory to look at the way the world in general has changed and shifted over the past forty years. It's a tribute to Anderson's intelligence, pragmatism and innate sense of theatricality that you actually get caught up in the lyrics, and start to realise some of the criticisms aimed at the way we've chosen to let others dictate how we pattern our lives. Religion, politics and social indifferences are all addressed here. But not in the world-weary way of someone who feels everything was so much better in the seventies. No, he chooses to be satirical yet objective, while never losing sight of the fact this has to be focused on Gerald Bostock's turbulent story. None of this would really matter if the music was a disappointment. But, thankfully, this is never even close to being the case. Given Anderson's acute respect for his own past, it was obvious he'd set out to do something that was mindful of what had gone before, while also steering clear of repetition or mimicry. The result is a satisfying, robust musical journey. In effect one fifty-three minute long piece that's split into movements, this serves as the soundtrack to Bostock's tale, while also standing alone. The ambience here does bring to mind the original *Thick As A Brick*, because much of this was recorded live and also because it has the same instrumentation as was used back then. There's also cunning use of recurring themes, to ensure that you realise everything is linked. The performances of the musicians are of the highest calibre. John O'Hara on keyboards and Florian Opahle on guitar both have their chances to shine, which they take advantage of wholeheartedly. And inevitably, there are flourishes of flute that colour the soundscape at pertinent moments. Because this entire album is intended to be taken as one single track, it's the overall ebb and flow that matters rather than any individual peaks. But the dramatic punctuations serve to take the atmosphere across the emotional spectrum, from melancholy to wit, and a sense of worth. Some might suggest that Anderson's voice has lost a little of its timbre over the years. But this is surely to be expected at his time of life. Besides, he still makes every note and line sound clear and convincing. Very much the driving force of the whole project, you feel the man's zest and vitality pulsing throughout the album. Of all people, he is aware of the reverence with which *Thick As A Brick* is regarded, and has ensured that its heritage is never damaged here."

Thick As A Brick 2 was reviewed in *Ultimate Classic Rock* in April 2012; "Gerald Bostock is now fifty years old and, as Ian Anderson himself explains on his website, this sequel will 'examine the different paths that the precocious young schoolboy... might have taken later in life and... create alter-ego characters whose song-section identities illustrate the

hugely varied potential twists and turns of fate and opportunity'
— Anderson adds that it will also 'echo how our own lives
develop, change direction and ultimately conclude' — The
story unfolds as Gerald reflects on his life, and brings up some
"what ifs" concerning the different paths he could've taken.
There are subtle references to Anderson's path over the last
forty years woven into the story as well. So that's the tale of
Gerald, but what of the music within? Long-time Tull fans will
be happy, as this new *Brick* has vintage Tull written all over it.
Though credited to "Jethro Tull's Ian Anderson", it's more like
Tull than much of Anderson's solo work over the years. Some
familiar themes and melodies creep in periodically to subtly tie
it to the original album, but while it by no means sounds like
a 1972 release, it does have that certain something that allows
past and present to walk hand in hand. You'll hear spoken word
narration, and of course Anderson's flute is still front and centre
when called upon. As you'd expect, prog-esque bravado and top
shelf musicianship are also in full flight. Dynamically produced
by all around renaissance man, Steven Wilson (Porcupine
Tree, No Man and many more), he captures a very full sound,
sonically merging the warmth of the old with the attack of the
new. He's also intimately familiar with Tull's music — last
year he did the remix/remaster thing with *Aqualung* and has
recently done the same for the original *Thick*, which is due out
later this year. Ultimately, *Thick As a Brick 2* is an album sure
to please long-time Tull and Anderson fans, and possibly one
of the best examples of an elder statesman artist finding his way
back from whence he came without cliché. It's doubtful non-
believers will be converted by it, but that's okay — the disc is a
nice journey from present to past to future for those who want
to ride along. Stay tuned as Anderson takes both *Bricks* on the
road this fall."

Thick As A Brick was performed in its entirety, as on the
original album, live on tour in 2012. It was the first complete

performance since the original tour. In August 2014, *Thick As A Brick — Live In Iceland* was released on DVD. The concert was recorded in Reykjavík on 22nd June 2012 and featured complete *Thick As A Brick* and *Thick As A Brick 2* performances by the Ian Anderson Touring Band. Some of the humour and stage antics were maintained. For instance, where there was originally a telephone ringing in the middle of a song, it was replaced by a cell phone and a Skype call.

Whilst *Thick As A Brick 2* was a follow up about Gerald Bostock, the 2014 Ian Anderson solo album, *Homo Erraticus*, was presented as a follow up work by Gerald Bostock. In the back story Anderson created for the album, the now middle-aged Bostock came across an unpublished manuscript by one Ernest T. Parritt (1873–1928), entitled *Homo Britanicus Erraticus*. Parritt was convinced that he had lived past lives as historical characters. He wrote detailed accounts of the lives in his work and he also wrote of fantasy imaginings of lives yet to come. Bostock then created lyrics based on Parritt's writings, while Anderson set them to music. As with *Thick As A Brick*, authorship of each song on this album is explicitly credited to both Anderson and Bostock.

Prior to performing *Thick As A Brick* in its entirety in 2012 sections from the album have been a staple of Jethro Tull's and Ian Anderson's concert repertoire to this day. An amount of *Thick As A Brick* was still played by Jethro Tull during their 1973 tour for *A Passion Play*. Since it came out in 1972, *Thick As A Brick* is very much regarded as a classic by the band and fans alike.

Thick As A Brick
A Comprehensive Discography

Album Personnel

Jethro Tull

Ian Anderson - vocals, acoustic guitar, flute, violin, trumpet, saxophone, production

Martin Barre - electric guitar, lute

John Evan - piano, organ, harpsichord

Jeffrey Hammond (credited as Jeffrey Hammond-Hammond) - bass guitar, spoken word

Barriemore Barlow - drums, percussion, timpani

David Palmer -orchestral arrangements

Terry Ellis - executive producer

Robin Black - engineer

Track Listing

(Please note that this isn't an official listing of how *Thick As A Brick* is structured but that it does go some way to accounting for all of the individual sections within it)

Side One

0:00-3:01 "Really don't mind..."

3:01-3:36 "See there! A son is born..."

3:36-6:09 (Instrumental)

6:09-7:16 "The Poet and the painter..."

7:16-9:21 (Instrumental)

9:21-10:30 "The cattle quietly grazing..."

10:30-11:20 (Instrumental)

11:20-11:52 "What do you do..."

11:52-13:16 (Instrumental)

13:16-14:13 "I've come down…"
14:13-15:26 (Instrumental)
15:26-15:54 "Your bread and water's…"
15:54-16:35 (Instrumental)
16:35-17:06 "You curl your toes in fun…"
17:06-17:41 (Instrumental)
17:41-18:08 "I see you shuffle…"
18:08-18:39 (Instrumental)
18:39-19:05 "So! come on ye childhood…"
19:05-19:29 "You put your bet on…"
19:29-19:59 (Instrumental)
19:59-20:25 "So! Where the hell was…"
20:25-22:39 (Instrumental)

Side Two
0:00-0:48 (Instrumental)
0:48-1:24 "See there! A man is born…"
1:24-2:58 (Instrumental)
2:58-4:05 "We will be geared toward…"
4:05-5:13 "In the clear white circles…"
5:13-6:00 (Instrumental)
6:00-6:30 "The legends worded…"
6:30-11:00 "The poet and the wise man…"
11:00-13:15 (Instrumental)
13:15-13:52 "Let me tell you the tales…"
13:52-14:55 (Instrumental)
14:55-15:10 "So come all ye…"
15:10-16:14 (Instrumental)
16:14-16:50 "Let me help you…"
16:50-17:21 (Instrumental)
17:21-17:51 "So! come all ye…"
17:51-18:16 (Instrumental)
18:16-18:38 "So! come on ye…"
18:38-19:01 (Instrumental)
19:01-19:30 "So! Where the hell…"
19:30-20:36 (Instrumental)
20:36-21:05 "So you ride yourselves…"

Country By Country

This list includes all releases for the main territories of UK, USA, Japan and Germany. Canadian releases by and large mirrored US ones and other European countries generally mirrored Germany.

A few oddball releases with different cover designs from USA, Portugal, Italy and Germany exist but these are all unofficial pirate releases and outside the scope of this discography.

UK
Original 10th March 1972 releases:
Chrysalis CHR 1003, LP
Chrysalis ZCHR 1003, cassette
Chrysalis Y8HR 1003, 8-track cartridge*
Chrysalis RST 2072-B, reel-to-reel
*This version necessitated the recording being split into four parts to accommodate the format.

Original 1985 CD release:
Chrysalis ACCD 1003, CD

Reissues:
There have been numerous vinyl re-pressings and reissues, both with the newspaper sleeve, and later versions in a single sleeve without the newspaper, but they all have the same catalogue number.

Chrysalis CDP 32 1003 2, 1987, CD
Mobile Fidelity Sound Lab 48UD510, 1988, CD

Chrysalis 7243 8 57705 2 4, 1997, CD
This is the 25th Anniversary Special Edition that coincided with the 100th Anniversary of EMI who now had control of the Chrysalis back catalogue. It came with a 6-page booklet; 12-page newspaper and a 28-page Biography: "EMI 100 - 1997 - The First Centenary".
It also included extra tracks: Thick As A Brick (Live At Madison Square Garden 1978) and Interview With Jethro Tull's Ian Anderson, Martin Barre And Jeffrey Hammond.

Chrysalis 7243 4 95400 2 6, 1998, CD

Chrysalis 5099970461923, 6th November 2012, CD/DVD
Steven Wilson remixes including DVD audio with 5.1 mixes and the original 1972 mix.

Chrysalis 0825646146468, 2015, CD
Chrysalis 0825646139507, 2015, LP
Stereo Steve Wilson mix.

USA
Original May 1972 releases:
Reprise RST 2072MS 2072, LP
Reprise MS 2072, LP (club edition)
Reprise M 52072, cassette
Reprise M 82072, 8-track cartridge
Reprise RST 2072-B, reel-to-reel

Original 1985 CD release:
Chrysalis VK 41003, 1985

Reissues:
Chrysalis CHR 1003, 1973, LP
Chrysalis M5C 1003, cassette
Chrysalis FVT 41003, cassette
Chrysalis F4 21003, cassette
Chrysalis M8C 1003, 8-track cartridge
Chrysalis 8CH 1003, 8-track cartridge
Chrysalis F1 21003, 1982, LP
Chrysalis FV 41003, 1985, LP
Mobile Fidelity Sound Lab MFSL 1-187, 1985 LP
Original Master Recording, record pressed in Japan. Comes in gatefold sleeve with thick MFSL cardboard inner sleeve and antistatic sleeve.

Chrysalis PV 41003, LP

Chrysalis F2 21003, CD
Chrysalis VK 41003, CD
Mobile Fidelity Sound Lab UDCD 510, August 1988, CD
Mobile Fidelity Sound Lab MFSL C-187, 1988, cassette

Chrysalis 7243 8 57705 2 4, 21st October 1997, CD
25th Anniversary Special Edition. It came with a 4-page booklet; 3 panel fold out of
Tull catalogue and a 12-page newspaper.
It also included extra tracks: Thick As A Brick (Live At Madison Square Garden
1978) and Interview With Jethro Tull's Ian Anderson, Martin Barre And Jeffrey
Hammond.

Chrysalis CDP 595400 2 6, 1998, CD
With extra tracks: Thick As A Brick (Live At Madison Square Garden 1978) and
Interview With Jethro Tull's Ian Anderson, Martin Barre And Jeffrey Hammond.

Chrysalis 5099970461923, 2012, CD/DVD
Steven Wilson remixes including DVD audio with 5.1 mixes and the original 1972
mix.

Chrysalis RP2 139507, 2015, CD
Stereo Steve Wilson mix.

Japan
Original May 1972 release:
Reprise P-8233R, LP

Reissues:
Chrysalis CHR 1013, 1974, LP
Chrysalis WWS-80939, 1977, LP

CD releases:
Chrysalis TOCP-7815, 1993
Chrysalis TOCP-65883, 2001
Chrysalis TOCP-67665, 2005
Chrysalis WPCR-80069, 2014
Chrysalis WPCR-16473, 2015

Germany
Original 10th March 1972 releases:
Chrysalis 6307 502, LP
Chrysalis 7107 501, cassette

Reissues:
Chrysalis 02 654-320, 1980, LP
Chrysalis 202 654, 1981, LP
Chrysalis 1C 038-3 21003 1, LP

Chrysalis 252 654, 1986, CD

Chrysalis 7243 8 57705 2 4, 1997, CD
This is the 25th Anniversary Special Edition that coincided with the 100th Anniversary of EMI who now had control of the Chrysalis back catalogue. It came with a 6-page booklet; 12-page newspaper and a 28-page Biography: "EMI 100 - 1997 - The First Centenary".
It also included extra tracks: Thick As A Brick (Live At Madison Square Garden 1978) and Interview With Jethro Tull's Ian Anderson, Martin Barre And Jeffrey Hammond.

Chrysalis 7243 4 95400 2 6, 1998, CD

Chrysalis 5099970461923, 6th November 2012, CD/DVD
Steven Wilson remixes including DVD audio with 5.1 mixes and the original 1972 mix.

Chrysalis 0825646146468, 2015, CD
Chrysalis 0825646139507, 2015, LP
Stereo Steve Wilson mix.

Thick As A Brick 2

In 2012 Ian Anderson released a sequel to Tull's 1972 album.

Album Personnel

Ian Anderson - vocals, flutes, acoustic guitars, production
Florian Opahle - electric guitar
John O'Hara - accordion, Hammond organ, piano, keyboards
Pete Judge - trumpet, flugelhorn, tenor horn, E-flat tuba
Ryan O'Donnell - additional vocals
David Goodier - bass guitar, glockenspiel
Scott Hammond - drums, percussion

Steven Wilson - mixing engineer
Mike Downs - recording engineer
Ian Anderson - liner notes
Peter Mew - mastering engineer

Thick As A Brick 2 was released as both a CD and as a CD / DVD format.

Divergence: Interventions, Parallel Possibilities - Pebbles Thrown
1   From A Pebble Thrown 3:06
2   Pebbles Instrumental 3:30
3   Might-Have-Beens 0:50
Gerald The Banker
4   Upper Sixth Loan Shark   1:13
5   Banker Bets, Banker Wins 4:28
Gerald Goes Homeless
6   Swing It Far 3:28
7   Adrift And Dumfounded 4:25
Gerald The Military Man
8   Old School Song 3:07

9 Wootton Bassett Town 3:44
Gerald The Chorister
10 Power And Spirit 1:59
11 Give Till It Hurts 1:12
Gerald: A Most Ordinary Man
12 Cosy Corner 1:25
13 Shunt And Shuffle 2:12
Convergence: Destiny, Fate, Karma, Kismet - A Change Of Horses
14 A Change Of Horses 8:04
22 Mulberry Walk
15 Confessional 3:09
16 Kismet In Suburbia 4:17
What-Ifs, Maybes, Might-Have-Beens
17 What-Ifs, Maybes, Might-Have-Beens 3:36

DVD contents:
1 5.1 Surround Mix 53:42
2 Super Quality 24-bit Stereo Mix 53:42
3 TAAB2 "The Making Of..." Video 14:35
4 Studio Recording, Interviews And More 15:40
5 The Lyric Reading Video 20:25
6 Multilingual Lyric Translations PDF Files

Thick As A Brick Live In Iceland
Filmed at the Harpa Concert Hall, Reykjavik, Iceland, 2012, Anderson performed both the original Thick As A Brick and Thick As A Brick 2.
It was released in 2014 in multiple formats: CD, DVD, Blu-ray and vinyl.

Tour Dates

I have included tour dates from 1971 through to 1973. '71 was so busy and it informed the writing of *Thick As A Brick*. Also '73 dates tell a story because *A Passion Play* was panned so much.

1971
By January 1971, Jethro Tull were Ian Anderson, Martin Barre, Clive Bunker, John Evan and Jeffrey Hammond-Hammond. The band continued with this line-up until May.

Thursday 7th January	Rep Fyns Forum, Odense, Denmark
Friday 8th January	Marselisborg Hallen, Arhaus, Denmark
Saturday 9th January	K.B. Hallen, Copehagen, Denmark
Sunday 10th January	Konserthuset, Gothenburg, Sweden
Monday 11th January	Njardhallen, Oslo, Norway
Tuesday 12th January	Konserthuset, Bergen, Norway
Thursday 14th January	Konserthus Stockholm, Sweden
Friday 15th January	Tivoli Konsertsal, Copenhagen, Denmark
Saturday 16th January	Holstebro, Holsted, Denmark
Sunday 17th January	Musichalle, Hamberg, Germany
Monday 18th January	Rheinhalle, Düsseldorf, Germany
Tuesday 19th January	Sporthalle Boblingen, Stuttgart, Germany
Wednesday 20th January	Meistersinger Halle, Nurnberg, Germany
Thursday 21st January	Konzerthaus, Vienna, Austria
Friday 22nd January	Deutsches Museum, Munich, Germany (two shows)

Saturday 23rd January	Kongresshalle, Frankfurt, Germany
Sunday 24th January	Deutschlandhalle, Berlin, Germany
Monday 25th January	Stadthalle, Wolfsburg, Germany
Tuesday 26th January	Munsterlandhalle, Munster, Germany
Wednesday 27th January	Westfalenhalle, Dortmund, Germany
Thursday 28th January	Stadthalle, Heidelberg, Germany
Friday 29th January	Stadthalle, Freiburg, Germany
Saturday 30th January	Altes Casino, Montreux, Switzerland
Monday 1st February	Teatro Smeraldo, Milan, Italy
Tuesday 2nd February	Teatro Brangaccio, Rome, Italy (two shows)
Friday 26th February	Gaumont State Theatre, London, UK (two shows)
Sunday 28th February	Gaumont State Theatre, London, UK (two shows)
Wednesday 3rd March	Dome, Brighton, UK
Friday 5th March	Winter Gardens, Bournemouth, UK
Sunday 7th March	Guildhall, Plymouth, UK (two shows)
Thursday 11th March	Town Hall, Leeds, UK
Friday 12th March	Victoria Guildhall, Stoke on Trent, UK
Saturday 13th March	Mountford Hall, Liverpool, UK (two shows)
Sunday 14th March	Opera House, Blackpool, UK
Friday 19th March	Empire Theatre, Edinburgh, UK
Saturday 20th March	Empire Theatre, Sunderland, UK (two shows)
Thursday 1st April	Tyrone Guthrie Theatre, Minneapolis, USA (two shows)
Friday 2nd April	Civic Opera House, Chicago, USA
Saturday 3rd April	Kiel Convention Hall, St Louis, USA
Sunday 4th April	Civic Centre, Baltimore, USA

Monday 5th April	Filmore East, New York, USA (two shows)
Tuesday 6th April	Filmore East, New York, USA (two shows)
Saturday 10th April	Cincinnati Gardens, Cincinnati, USA
Tuesday 13th April	Municipal Auditorium, Atlanta, USA
Wednesday 14th April	Uhlein, Milwaukee, USA (two shows)
Friday 16th April	Pirates World Park, Dania, USA
Saturday 17th April	Pirates World Park, Dania, USA
Sunday 18th April	Civic Centre, Roanoke, USA
Tuesday 20th April	State Fairground Coliseum, Detroit, USA
Thursday 22nd April	Robertson Memorial Field House, Peoria, USA
Saturday 24th April	Monmouth College, West Long Beach, USA
Sunday 25th April	New York State University, Stony Brook, USA
Monday 26th April	C.W. Post College Dome, Greenville, USA
Tuesday 27th April	Capitol Theatre, Port Chester, USA (two shows)
Thursday 29th April	New York State University, Delhi, USA
Saturday 1st May	Spectrum, Philadelphia, USA
Sunday 2nd May	Kutztown University Hall, Kutztown, USA
Tuesday 4th May	Filmore East, New York, USA (two shows)
Wednesday 5th May	Filmore East, New York, USA (two shows)

From May '71, Jethro Tull were Ian Anderson, Martin Barre, John Evan, Jeffrey Hammond-Hammond and Barriemore Barlow. The band continued with this line-up until December 1975.

Wednesday 9th June	Salt Palace, Salt Lake City, USA
Thursday 10th June	Red Rocks Amphitheatre, Morrison, USA
Friday 11th June	Civic Auditorium, Albuquerque, USA
Saturday 12th June	Hic Arena, Albuquerque, USA
Wednesday 16th June	San Diego Convention Centre, San Diego, USA
Thursday 17th June	San Diego Convention Centre, San Diego, USA
Friday 18th June	Los Angeles Forum, Los Angeles, USA
Saturday 19th June	Anaheim Convention Centre, Anaheim, USA
Sunday 20th June	Berkeley Community Theatre, Berkeley, USA
Thursday 24th June	Gardens, Edmonton, Canada
Friday 25th June	Pacific Coliseum, Vancouver, Canada
Saturday 26th June	Seattle Coliseum, Seattle, USA
Sunday 27th June	Memorial Auditorium, Sacramento, USA
Tuesday 29th June	Kansas City Auditorium, Kansas City, USA
Wednesday 30th June	Oklahoma City State Fairgrounds, Oklahoma City, USA
Thursday 1st July	Municipal Auditorium, San Anton Dallas Memorial Auditorium, Dallas, USA
Saturday 3rd July	Sam Houston Coliseum, Houston, USA
Sunday 4th July	Warehouse, New Orleans, USA
Monday 5th July	National Guard Armoury, Indianapolis, USA
Wednesday 7th July	Sports Stadium, Orlando, USA

Thursday 8th July	Casino Ballroom, Hampton Beach, USA
Friday 9th July	Wildwood Convention Centre, Wildwood, USA
Saturday 10th July	Ashbury Park Convention Centre, Ashbury Park, USA
Sunday 11th July	Alexandria Roller Rink, Alexandria, USA
Wednesday 14th July	Fox Theatre, Hackensack, USA
Thursday 15th July	Bayfront Centre, St Petersburg, USA
Friday 16th July	Civic Centre, Jacksonville, USA
Saturday 17th July	Coliseum, Charlotte, USA
Sunday 18th July	Madison Square Garden, New York, USA
Monday 19th July	Civic Centre, Springfield, USA
Wednesday 21st July	Civic Arena, Pittsburgh, USA
Thursday 22nd July	Jenison Field House University, East Lansing, USA
Friday 23rd July	St John Veterans Arena, Columbus, USA
Saturday 24th July	Hara Arena, Dayton, USA
Sunday 25th July	Sports Arena, Ohio, USA
Monday 26th July	Chicago Amphitheatre, Chicago, USA
Tuesday 27th July	University Assembly Hall, Champaign, USA
Wednesday 28th July	New Haven Arena, New Haven, USA
Thursday 29th July	Exposition Centre, Portland, USA
Saturday 30th October	Rochester War Memorial, Rochester, USA
Sunday 31st October	Harper College, Binghamton, USA
Monday 1st November	Memorial Auditorium, Buffalo, USA

Wednesday 3rd November	Lowell Technical College, Lowell, USA
Friday 5th November	W & M College Field House, Williamsburg, USA
Saturday 6th November	Carmichael Auditorium, North Carolina University, Chapel Hill, USA
Sunday 7th November	East Carolina University Coliseum, Greenville, USA
Monday 8th November	Coliseum, Greensboro, USA
Tuesday 9th November	Bradley University Field House, Peoria, USA
Wednesday 10th November	Ima Sports Arena, Flint, USA
Thursday 11th November	Mid South Coliseum, Memphis, USA
Friday 12th November	Louisville Convention Centre, Louisville, USA
Saturday 13th November	Cleveland Public Hall, Cleveland, USA
Sunday 14th November	Civic Centre, Baltimore, USA
Monday 15th November	Boston Tea Gardens, Boston, USA
Tuesday 16th November	Palace Theatre, Albany, USA
Thursday 18th November USA	Madison Square Garden, New York,

1972

Thursday 6th January	Holstelbrohallen, Holstelbro, Denmark
Friday 7th January	Fyns Forum, Odense, Denmark
Saturday 8th January	KB Hallen, Copenhagen, Denmark (two shows)
Sunday 9th January	Konserthuset, Gothenburg, Sweden
Monday 10th January	Konserthuset, Oslo, Norway
Tuesday 11th January	Konserthus, Stockholm, Sweden
Friday 14th January	Lund University Akademiska Foreningen, Lund, Sweden
Saturday 15th January	Tivoli Konsertsal, Copenhagen, Denmark

Sunday 16th January	Tivoli Konsertsal, Copenhagen, Denmark
Monday 17th January	Munsterlandhalle, Munster, Germany
Tuesday 18th January	Deutchlandhalle, Berlin, Germany
Wednesday 19th January	Musikhalle Grosser Saal, Hamburg, Germany
Thursday 20th January	Hansahalle, Lubeck, Germany
Friday 21st January	Grugahalle, Essen, Germany
Saturday 22nd January	Stadthalle, Offenbach, Germany
Sunday 23rd January	Meistersingerhalle, Nurnburg, Germany
Monday 24th January	Konserthaus, Vienna, Austria
Tuesday 25th January	Meistersingerhalle, Nurnburg, Germany (cancelled)
Wednesday 26th January	Frederich-Ebert Halle, Ludwigshafen, Germany
Thursday 27th January	Niedersachsenhalle, Hannover, Germany
Friday 28th January	Oberheinhalle, Offenburg, Germany
Saturday 29th January	Hallenstadion, Zurich, Switzerland
Sunday 30th January	Festhalle, Berne, Switzerland
Monday 31st January	?, Milan, Italy
Tuesday 1st February	Palasport, Rome, Italy
Wednesday 2nd February	Palazzo Dello Sport, Bologna, Italy (two shows)
Thursday 3rd February	Bocciodromo Ovest, Treviso, Italy
Friday 4th February	Palazzo Dello Sport, Varese, Italy
Saturday 5th February	Palasport, Novaro, Italy
Sunday 6th February	Palasport, Novaro, Italy
Friday 11th February	De Doelen, Rotterdam, Holland
Saturday 12th February	Concertgebouw, Amsterdam, Holland
Thursday 2nd March	Guildhall, Portsmouth, UK
Friday 3rd March	ABC Cinema, Exeter, UK
Saturday 4th March	Guildhall, Plymouth, UK
Sunday 5th March	Colston Hall, Bristol, UK
Monday 6th March	Town Hall, Birmingham, UK
Tuesday 7th March	City Hall, Newcastle, UK
Wednesday 8th March	University Central Hall, York, UK
Friday 10th March	Winter Gardens, Bournemouth, UK
Saturday 11th March	City Hall, Sheffield, UK
Monday 13th March	St Andrews Hall, Norwich, UK

Tuesday 14th March	De Montfort Hall, Leicester, UK
Wednesday 15th March	St Georges Hall, Bradford, UK
Thursday 16th March	Victoria Hall, Stoke on Trent, UK
Friday 17th March	ABC Cinema, Stockton, UK
Sunday 19th March	Civic Hall, Wolverhampton, UK
Monday 20th March	Town Hall, Oxford, UK
Tuesday 21st March	Royal Albert Hall, London, UK
Wednesday 22nd March	Royal Albert Hall, London, UK
Friday 24th March	Empire Theatre, Edinburgh, Scotland
Saturday 25th March	Caird Hall, Dundee, Scotland
Sunday 26th March	Playhouse Cinema, Glasgow, Scotland
Monday 27th March	Liverpool Stadium, Liverpool, UK
Tuesday 28th March	Free Trade Hall, Manchester, UK
Wednesday 29th March	Royal Albert Hall, London, UK
Friday 14th April	Forum, Montreal, Canada
Saturday 15th April	Varden Hall, Cornell University, Ithaca, USA
Sunday 16th April	War Memorial Auditorium, Syracuse, USA
Monday 17th April	Capitol Plaza Convention Centre, Frankfort, USA
Tuesday 18th April	High School Hall, Lorain, USA
Wednesday 19th April	Cumberland County Auditorium, Fayetteville, USA
Thursday 20th April	Dorton Arena, Raleigh, USA
Friday 21st April	University of Alabama, Tuscaloosa, USA
Saturday 22nd April	Norfolk Scope, Norfolk, USA
Sunday 23rd April	Salem Valley Civic Centre, Salem, USA
Monday 24th April	Memorial Hall Bowling Green State University, Bowling Green, USA
Tuesday 25th April	West Virginia University Hall, Morgantown, USA
Wednesday 26th April	Tech University Hall, Blacksburg, USA
Thursday 27th April	Municipal Auditorium, Atlanta, USA
Friday 28th April	University of Georgia Coliseum, Athens, USA
Saturday 29th April	Auditorium, West Palm Beach, USA
Sunday 30th April	Marine Stadium, Miami Beach, USA

Monday 1st May	Municipal Auditorium, New Orleans, USA
Tuesday 2nd May	Coliseum, Indianapolis, USA
Wednesday 3rd May	Dane County Coliseum, Madison, USA
Thursday 4th May	Southern Illinois University, Carbondale, USA
Friday 5th May	Keil Convention Hall, St Louis, USA
Saturday 6th May	Stokely Athletic Centre, Knoxville, USA
Sunday 7th May	Stadium Amphitheatre, Chicago, USA
Monday 8th May	Cobo Hall, Detroit, USA
Tuesday 9th May	Gardens, Cincinnati, USA
Wednesday 10th May	Sports Centre, Hershey, USA
Thursday 11th May	Spectrum, Philadelphia, USA
Friday 12th May	Tea Gardens, Boston, USA
Saturday 13th May	Nassau Veterans Coliseum, Uniondale, USA
Sunday 14th May	Nassau Veterans Coliseum, Uniondale, USA
Friday 2nd June	Quebec Coliseum, Quebec, Canada
Saturday 3rd June	Civic Centre, Ottawa, Canada
Sunday 4th June	Maple Leaf Gardens, Toronto, Canada
Tuesday 6th June	Milwaukee Arena, Milwaukee, USA
Wednesday 7th June	Entertainment Convention Centre (unconfirmed), Duluth, USA
Thursday 8th June	Gardens, Edmonton, Canada
Friday 9th June	Stampede Corral, Calgary, Canada
Saturday 10th June	Pacific Coliseum, Vancouver, Canada
Sunday 11th June	Seattle Centre Coliseum, Seattle, USA
Monday 12th June	Memorial Coliseum, Portland, USA
Wednesday 14th June	Oklahoma City State Fairgrounds, Oklahoma City, USA
Thursday 15th June	Municipal Auditorium, Kansas City, USA
Friday 16th June	Coliseum, Oakland, USA
Saturday 17th June	Convention Centre, Las Vegas, USA
Sunday 18th June	Dallas Memorial Coliseum, Dallas, USA
Monday 19th June	Sam Houston Coliseum, Houston, USA

Tuesday 20th June	Convention Centre Arena, San Antonio, USA
Wednesday 21st June	Civic Centre, El Paso, USA
Thursday 22nd June	University of New Mexico, Albuquerque, USA
Friday 23rd June	Forum, Los Angeles, USA
Saturday 24th June	Forum, Los Angeles, USA
Sunday 25th June	San Diego Sports Arena, San Diego, USA
Monday 26th June	Community Centre Arena, Tucson, USA
Tuesday 27th June	Veterans Coliseum, Phoenix, USA
Wednesday 28th June	Salt Palace, Salt Lake City, USA
Thursday 29th June	Denver Coliseum, Denver, USA
Friday 30th June	Denver Coliseum, Denver, USA
Saturday 1st July	Hic Arena, Honolulu, USA
Wednesday 5th July	Town Hall, Auckland, New Zealand
Friday 7th July	Festival Hall, Melbourne, Australia
Saturday 8th July	Apollo Stadium, Adelaide, Australia
Sunday 9th July	Festival Hall, Melbourne, Australia
Tuesday 11th July	Horden Pavilion, Sydney, Australia
Wednesday 12th July	Horden Pavilion, Sydney, Australia
Thursday 13th July	Horden Pavilion, Sydney, Australia
Friday 14th July	Festival Hall, Brisbane, Australia
Saturday 15th July	Koseinenkin Kaikan, Tokyo, Japan
Sunday 16th July	Budokan, Tokyo, Japan
Monday 17th July	Koseinenkin Kaikan Dai Hall, Osaka, Japan
Friday 13th October	Buffalo Memorial Auditorium, Buffalo, USA
Saturday 14th October	Rochester War Memorial, Rochester USA
Sunday 15th October	Bangor Auditorium, Bangor, USA
Monday 16th October	Springfield Civic Centre, Springfield, USA
Tuesday 17th October	Civic Arena, Pittsburgh, USA
Wednesday 18th October	Civic Centre, Charleston, USA
Thursday 19th October	South Carolina Coliseum, Columbia, USA
Saturday 21st October	Cleveland Public Hall, Cleveland, USA

Sunday 22nd October	Mid-South Coliseum, Memphis, USA
Monday 23rd October	Barton Coliseum, Little Rock USA
Tuesday 24th October	Municipal Auditorium, Nashville, USA
Wednesday 25th October	Louisville Convention Centre, Louisville, USA
Thursday 26th October	West Kentucky University, Diddle Arena, Bowling Green, USA
Friday 27th October	Mississippi Coliseum, Jackson, USA
Saturday 28th October	Louisiana State University, Baton Rouge, USA
Sunday 29th October	Macon Coliseum, Macon, USA
Monday 30th October	Spectrum, Philadelphia, USA
Tuesday 31st October	Spectrum, Philadelphia, USA
Wednesday 1st November	Boston Gardens, Boston, USA
Thursday 2nd November	Boston Gardens, Boston, USA
Friday 3rd November	Bayfront Centre, St Petersburg, USA
Saturday 4th November	Convention Hall, Miami Beach, USA
Sunday 5th November	Jacksonville Coliseum, Jacksonville, USA
Monday 6th November	Civic Centre Arena, Savannah, USA
Tuesday 7th November	Allen County Memorial Coliseum, Fort Wayne, USA
Wednesday 8th November	Detroit Cobo Hall, Detroit, USA
Thursday 9th November	Detroit Cobo Hall, Detroit, USA
Friday 10th November	Chicago Stadium, Chicago, USA
Saturday 11th November	Chicago Stadium, Chicago, USA
Sunday 12th November	Baltimore Civic Centre, Baltimore, USA
Monday 13th November	Madison Square Garden, New York, USA
Thursday 7th December	Convocation Centre, Athens, USA
Friday 8th December	Madison Square Garden, New York, USA

1973

Monday 29th January	Stadthalle, Vienna, Austria
Friday 2nd February	Festhalle, Frankfurt, Germany
Sunday 4th February	Hallenstadion, Zurich, Switzerland
Friday 2nd March	Scandinavium, Gothenburg, Sweden
Sunday 4th March	Brondby Hallen, Copenhagen, Denmark
Tuesday 6th March	Congress Centrum Halle, Hamburg Germany
Wednesday 7th March	Congress Centrum Halle, Hamburg, Germany
Thursday 8th March	Munsterlandhalle, Munster, Germany
Friday 9th March	Philipshalle, Düsseldorf, Germany
Sunday 11th March	Deutschlandhalle, Berlin, Germany
Tuesday 13th March	Olympiahalle, Munich, Germany
Thursday 15th March	Palasport, Vicenza, Italy
Friday 16th March	Palazzo Dello Sport, Rome, Italy
Sunday 18th March	PaPalasport, Bologna, Italy
Tuesday 20th March	?, Milan, Italy
Monday 26th March	Phillipshalle, Düsseldorf, Germany
Wednesday 28th March	Empire Pool Wembley, London, UK
Thursday 29th March	Empire Pool Wembley, London, UK
Friday 4th May	Roberts Stadium, Evansville, USA
Saturday 5th May	Clemson University Coliseum, Clemson, USA
Monday 7th May	War Memorial, Johnstown, USA
Wednesday 9th May	Millet Hall, Miami University, Oxford, USA
Friday 11th May	Scope, Norfolk, USA
Sunday 13th May	Civic Coliseum, Knoxville, USA
Monday 14th May	Louisville Convention Centre, Louisville, USA

Tuesday 15th May	Mid-South Coliseum, Memphis, USA
Wednesday 16th May	Hershey Park Arena, Hershey, USA
Thursday 17th May	Hofstra University, Hempstead, USA
Friday 18th May	Richmond Coliseum, Richmond, USA
Saturday 19th May	Coliseum, Greensboro, USA
Sunday 20th May	Omni, Atlanta, USA
Monday 21st May	Municipal Auditorium, Nashville, USA
Tuesday 22nd May	Indiana Convention Expo Centre, Indianapolis, USA
Wednesday 23rd May	Keil Convention Hall, St Louis, USA
Thursday 24th May	Keil Convention Hall, St Louis, USA
Thursday 24th May	Assembly Centre, Tulsa, USA
Tuesday 29th May	Memorial Auditorium, Kitchener, Canada
Wednesday 30th May	Maple Leaf Gardens, Toronto, Canada
Thursday 31st May	Civic Centre Lansdowne Arena, Ottawa, Canada
Friday 1st June	Coliseum, Quebec City, Canada
Saturday 2nd June	Forum, Montreal, Canada
Friday 22nd June	Empire Pool Wembley, London, UK
Saturday 23rd June	Empire Pool Wembley, London, UK
Saturday 30th June	War Memorial Auditorium, Syracuse, USA
Sunday 1st July	Memorial Auditorium, Buffalo, USA
Tuesday 3rd July	Metropolitan Sports Centre Arena, Minneapolis, USA
Wednesday 4th July	Municipal Auditorium, Kansas City, USA
Saturday 7th July	Berkeley Community Theatre, Berkeley, USA
Sunday 8th July	University of New Mexico, Albuquerque, USA
Monday 9th July	Denver Coliseum, Denver, USA
Tuesday 10th July	State Fair Arena, Oklahoma City, USA
Thursday 12th July	Convention Centre Auditorium, Dallas, USA
Friday 13th July	Convention Centre Arena, San Antonio, USA
Saturday 14th July	Sam Houston Coliseum, Houston, USA

Sunday 15th July	Sam Houston Coliseum, Houston, USA
Monday 16th July	Tarrant County Convention Centre, Fort Worth, USA
Wednesday 18th July	LA Forum, Inglewood, USA
Thursday 19th July	San Diego Sports Arena, San Diego, USA
Friday 20th July	LA Forum, Inglewood, USA
Saturday 21st July	LA Forum, Inglewood, USA
Sunday 22nd July	LA Forum, Inglewood, USA
Monday 23rd July	Oakland Coliseum, Oakland, USA
Tuesday 24th July	Pacific Coliseum, Vancouver, Canada
Wednesday 25th July	Seattle Coliseum, Seattle, USA
Thursday 26th July	Seattle Coliseum, Seattle, USA
Friday 27th July	Seattle Coliseum, Seattle, USA
Saturday 28th July	Memorial Coliseum, Portland, USA
Monday 30th July	Salt Palace, Salt Lake City, USA
Wednesday 1st August	Sam Houston Coliseum, Houston, USA
Sunday 26th August	Civic Centre, Baltimore, USA
Monday 27th August	Civic Centre, Baltimore, USA
Tuesday 28th August	Madison Square Gardens, New York, USA
Wednesday 29th August	Madison Square Gardens, New York, USA
Thursday 30th August	Providence Civic Centre, Providence, USA
Friday 31st August	Nassau Coliseum, Uniondale, USA
Saturday 1st September	Nassau Coliseum, Uniondale, USA
Monday 3rd September	Dane County Coliseum, Madison, USA
Tuesday 4th September	Chicago Stadium, Chicago, USA
Wednesday 5th September	Chicago Stadium, Chicago, USA
Thursday 6th September	Detroit Cobo Hall, Detroit, USA
Saturday 8th September	Cleveland Public Hall, Cleveland, USA
Sunday 9th September	Cleveland Public Hall, Cleveland, USA
Monday 10th September	War Memorial Auditorium, Rochester, USA
Tuesday 11th September	Pittsburgh Civic Arena, Pittsburgh, USA

Wednesday 12th September	Pittsburgh Civic Arena, Pittsburgh, USA
Thursday 13th September	Detroit Cobo Hall, Detroit, USA
Friday 14th September	Detroit Cobo Hall, Detroit, USA
Saturday 15th September	Milwaukee Arena, Milwaukee, USA
Monday 17th September	Hirsch Coliseum, Shreveport, USA
Tuesday 18th September	Municipal Auditorium, New Orleans, USA
Wednesday 19th September	Municipal Auditorium, New Orleans, USA
Thursday 20th September	Municipal Auditorium, Mobile, USA
Friday 21st September	Coliseum, Jacksonville, USA
Saturday 22nd September	Bayfront Centre, St Petersburg, USA
Sunday 23rd September	Jai Alai Fronton, Miami, USA
Monday 24th September	Jai Alai Fronton, Miami, USA
Wednesday 26th September	Civic Centre Coliseum, Roanoke, USA
Thursday 27th September	Springfield Civic Centre, Springfield, USA
Friday 28th September	Boston Tea Gardens, Boston, USA
Saturday 29th September	Boston Tea Gardens, Boston, USA

In-depth Series

The In-depth series was launched in March 2021 with four titles. Each book takes an in-depth look at an album; the history behind it; the story about its creation; the songs, as well as detailed discographies listing release variations around the world. The series will tackle albums that are considered to be classics amongst the fan bases, as well as some albums deemed to be "difficult" or controversial; shining new light on them, following reappraisal by the authors.

The first four titles published were:

Jethro Tull - Thick As A Brick	*978-1-912782-57-4*
Tears For Fears - The Hurting	*978-1-912782-58-1*
Kate Bush - The Kick Inside	*978-1-912782-59-8*
Deep Purple - Stormbringer	*978-1-912782-60-4*

Other titles in the series:

Deep Purple - Slaves And Masters
Emerson Lake & Palmer - Pictures At An Exhibition
Korn - Follow The Leader
Jethro Tull - Minstrel In The Gallery
Kate Bush - The Dreaming
Elvis Costello - This Year's Model
Deep Purple - Fireball
Talking Heads - Remain In Light
Jethro Tull - Heavy Horses
Rainbow Straight Between - The Eyes
The Stranglers - La Folie